AF535074

# Dollmaking for Everyone

*Also by* Helen Young:

*Here Is Your Hobby: Ceramics*
*Here Is Your Hobby: Doll Collecting*
*The Complete Book of Doll Collecting*
*Dolls, New and Old, You Can Make*

# Dollmaking for Everyone

*Helen Young*

*South Brunswick and New York: A. S. Barnes and Company*
*London: Thomas Yoseloff Ltd*

A. S. Barnes and Co., Inc.
Cranbury, New Jersey 08512

Thomas Yoseloff Ltd
Magdalen House
136–148 Tooley Street
London SE1 2TT, England

Library of Congress Cataloging in Publication Data

Young, Helen.
Dollmaking for everyone.

Includes index.
1. Dollmaking. I. Title.
TT175.Y68 1976 745.59'22 75-38447
ISBN 0-498-01867-9

PRINTED IN THE UNITED STATES OF AMERICA

# Contents

# *Introduction*

Dolls are for everyone.

Children play with them, often more than half believing that the toys are alive; women, who perhaps in their childhood never cared for dolls, now that their children are grown often become fanatics about dolls and organize clubs where doll collecting is a serious hobby; men also collect dolls—there are many of them, not to mention those who call their tin soldiers military miniatures. A man's traditional role has been that of a dollmaker, rather than one who plays with dolls, and in the following chapters it is planned to give him ideas for making new types and mention where he can share in the making of a particular doll.

So it is that dolls are for everyone, and "everyone" means not only every North American, European, African, Asian, South American, and Australian, but also those who live near the North Pole, the coral islands of the Pacific, and even the Easter Islanders, far from all the others.

"Everyone" also means that even beyond the humans for whom we have records, fragments have been found of what were either dolls or idols—and the line between them is often hard to determine. Sometimes unwritten folktales passed down from faraway ancestors give clues about these antiquities, but the safest conclusion is probably for us to say that they are either toys or ritual objects. There is therefore neither a known beginning nor a foreseeable end to the history and variety of the dolls of the world, and so, in spite of the uncountable number of words written about them, there is always more to say.

Best of all, there are always more dolls to make, and one of the most exciting things about dolls is that you can take someone else's patterns and directions, follow them exactly, and still come up with a doll that is touched with your own individuality. In addition, when you take the patterns and instructions given in this book, I repeat again and again that you can use them as a starting place for dolls of your own unique design. This is not as impossible as you may believe, if you are a person who claims that he isn't an artist. You can let Nature do the shaping of a face and make an apple-head doll. Anyone who can hold a paring knife can do that, and there is no secret formula to use to preserve the apple, contrary to what you may have been told. There are no mysteries about apple dolls except the reason that there are never two apples that dry exactly the same.

In the past twenty years, since doll collectors have been battling over early factory-made dolls, to the point of absurdly high prices, what are now called collectors' dolls are coming to include all dolls. The rag doll your grandmother made is now "a collector's item." The Bye-lo baby and Shirley Temple dolls of the 1930s are priced beyond reason. Take care of everything you have, the saying goes, and in a few years it will be an antique. That is what can happen to the dolls you make, and many dollmakers are realizing it. Best of all, by making your dolls you can have the future value of them added to the fun of seeing them come to life in your hands.

Added to these other incentives, dollmaking is an inexpensive craft. It involves the use of small pieces of material, odds and ends of trimming, and no elaborate equipment, since even a sewing machine can be dispensed with if necessary. The use of scraps and throwaways encourages a dollmaker to be inventive and find uses for the materials he has saved or salvaged. As an example, taking a shortcut down an alley, watch the ground. Often you will find a bit of red taillight glass that glows like a ruby you need for a queen's crown, or a short piece of wood that is just the right length for wrapping in cotton and burying in the stuffing of a doll to keep its neck from flopping.

Even when you must buy all the materials for a doll, the amounts are so small that the cost is hardly worth mentioning. In some of the hobby magazines there are sometimes ads for rolls of remnants or short lengths for quilt-making. These are ordinarily small patterns that are suitable for doll clothes.

Researching doll costumes is an enriching pastime, for as you search through books and pictures, visit museums for ideas, and study photographs in family albums, you will soon discover that dolls and their clothing reflect the history of mankind, geography, ethnology, as well as the legends and superstitions of all continents. Knowledge of this kind will add interest to travel in foreign countries, where you can see how dollmakers there make and dress their dolls. Although good ethnic dolls are not as easy to find as they once were, there are still many. Even in Zulu villages and Mexican markets dolls are being increasingly made of plastic, replacing the early ones that had more real meaning. Several of the dolls shown here had ancient counterparts well worth perpetuating for yourself.

If you live in the section of America where lobstering is a means of livelihood, you can follow the instructions here and make your own Maine lobsterman. Or if the legend of Paul Bunyan, the stories of Sleepy Hollow or Hiawatha linger from your childhood, turn those characters into dolls. You can keep them, sell them, donate them to charities, or use them as gifts, with the assurance that they will not be duplicated, since no commercial doll manufacturer is able to put the personality into his products that you will give yours.

In line with this idea, and in addition to the chapter I devote to selling dolls, if you live near a famous landmark, you might find a good market for your dolls right at hand, since tourists are buyers, and not all of them care for mass-produced souvenirs.

All through this book I have insisted that dolls are not always just playthings for children, and that with a little courage and a dab of patience that dolls are not only for everyone, but that dollmaking is for you.

# Dollmaking for Everyone

Note on illustrations:

In pattern grids throughout the book each box=1 inch.

# 1

# *General Directions*

The earliest efforts at dollmaking have left no examples for us to study, but if we look at the dolls that have survived the ages, we can make positive statements. Ancient dolls were as primitive and uncomplicated as the dolls small children make: a stick or two, perhaps, roughly tied with the tendrils of a vine; hair made by adding bits of moss; body colored by daubing on clay or red ochre from a streambank. As children, we ourselves probably turned a hollyhock blossom into a dancer with flounced skirts, or a fuchsia bloom into a doll by running a short piece of stem into the calyx. Nobody ever has to tell a child these things, because nothing has ever been done to blunt his imagination and the wish to make expressions of his creativity. It is this childlike confidence and imagination that make children's art so fascinating to study, and that we should not dismiss in ourselves with the statement: "I'm not an artist."

A creative child will think, "I'm going to make a dress for my doll," and cut a hole in a square of cloth large enough to admit a doll's head. "My doll has a beautiful dress with a long cape on top, just like mine."

It is this imagination and secret meaning that make a favorite doll irreplaceable, even though it may appear to others to be battered and ragged. It must always be the ambition of dollmakers to keep something of these childhood emotions alive, so that the dolls they make will be unlike any others. They will be their own, and never exact duplicates of the ones someone else has planned. They will never be perfect, per-

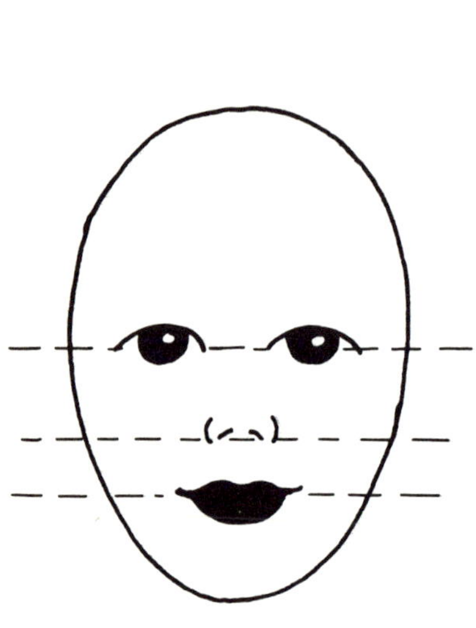
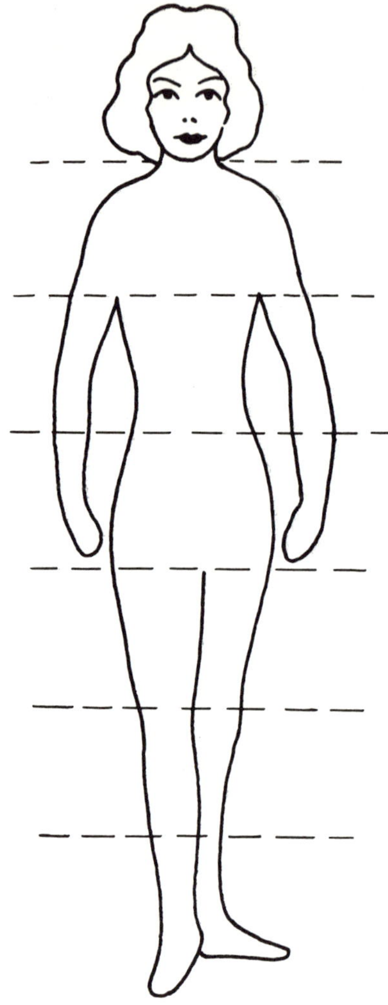

*Artist's formulas place features at the points indicated at broken lines, and body proportions based on total head units.*

haps, but they will have the individual spirit never found in the millionth doll shipped out of a factory.

However, even though dolls should have personality and be individual, there are certain basic rules to follow in making them. The pictures and diagrams given in this book are planned to be used in just that way—as the beginning.

So it is appropriate to repeat here the artist's basic formula for drawing the human figure. Use the length of the head, from crown to tip of the chin, as the measuring unit for the entire body. These proportions change with the age of the person: an infant's body may be only one or two head lengths high at birth, five or six before adolescence, and then seven or eight at maturity.

The second rule of the artist is necessary in placing the features. Place the eyes an eye's length apart, halfway between the top of the head and the tip of the chin. The mouth should be as long as the space between the eyes and halfway between the nose and the chin. The nose is halfway between the eyes and the mouth. Ears are set halfway between the center-back of the head and the tip of the nose, and extend in length from the bridge of the nose to the nostrils.

Caricature, which may also have a place in dollmaking, relies upon an exaggeration of these placements and proportions, in whole or in part. As an example, a cartoonist takes his subject's most noticeable features and draws attention to them, almost ignoring the others. But unless you are making a Pinocchio make the nose of your doll of normal length. Big, floppy ears would look all wrong on a dainty little fashion doll, just as a rosebud mouth would be grotesque on an Indian chief.

Another dollmaking rule is to always use suitable material: soft, fine cloth, small designs, narrow ribbons, fine, narrow lace, and tiny buttons. By thus keeping the doll and its clothes all in scale the air of reality is given and the doll will look more professional. Mention must be made here that again, if caricature is used, this rule may be ignored.

It is hard to find new material, particularly the drip-dries and permanent finishes, that are pliable enough for clothes for extremely small dolls. If you are lucky you may have a scrap bag that antedates such materials. Or perhaps a salvage shop will yield a roll of remnants, or even old garments that can be turned into doll clothes. Soft leather is sometimes to be found, also, and should be bought. Old kid gloves are particularly good for making doll shoes. On several of the dolls shown in this book, the black wig purchased in a thrift shop reappears as a doll wig, and the straggly hairpiece costs much less than a dollar.

### *Patterns*

The method of transferring the patterns shown here to a working pattern is simple, and the book will not be damaged. Take a sheet of white tissue paper or tracing paper the size of the page, and draw around the printed lines carefully with a soft lead pencil. Now either pin the tracing to the material being used, or cut out the pattern and draw around it on the material. If merely pinned to the material, particularly if it is lace or chiffon, baste the pattern to the material on the pencil line and seam the two together when called for. Then pull the paper away.

The patterns in this book may all be enlarged or reduced in size by copying them on a sheet of paper ruled into either smaller or larger squares. This is a method commonly used by instruction books and magazines and is accurate if done with care.

When patterns shown here are longer than page length, they are shown in two parts, to be joined at the darts indicated to make a complete pattern. Seam allowances, unless otherwise noted, are not included. It is the best plan to adapt the seam width to the material being used; on an easily frayed open fabric, it may even be best to make French seams, while with a close weave like felt, use extremely narrow seams. Ordinarily, a seam of about 1/4-inch is best.

### *Sewing and Stuffing*

In making cloth doll bodies, always use firm, soft material such as muslin, sateen, or percale. The modern permanent-finish broadcloth is excellent for our purpose, since it is opaque, but pliable. This material will not pucker when wet, and may therefore be cleaned by wiping with a slightly damp cloth. It is a matter of choice whether to use white or pink material for the doll, but whichever you decide on, do the sewing with matching thread. Another choice to be made is whether to stitch the seams by hand or on the sewing machine. Small dolls really demand the hand sewing, but a large doll is probably best stitched on the machine, since the pressure of stuffing puts a certain amount of strain on the seams and they tend to spread more than is desirable when sewed by hand.

No matter which way you select, do not cut the piece out until the stitching is done, then trim away to the seam allowance outside the pencil lines. In this way there will be no pulling out of shape, and it is easier to see what you're doing.

Be sure to leave a place on each piece for turning it rightside out. This is generally best done by leaving open the top of the head, arms, or legs, depending on the pattern.

After the doll is sewed together and then cut out, reinforce all sharp angles, such as underarms, crotch, and curves of the neck by trimming away most of the seam allowance and then overcasting closely at the points of strain. The turns will be much neater, as well as stronger, if this is done. Don't eat into the space beyond the seam allowance or these stitches will show on the right side.

Turn the body rightside out, using small, sharp-pointed scissors or a wooden skewer to help. This is a tiresome thing to do on a small doll, and sometimes it is necessary to also use a big needle, such as a darning needle, to help. Don't punch holes in the cloth.

Begin stuffing with the feet, pushing small wads of the stuffing material down firmly as you go, so there will be no lumps. Old-time dolls were stuffed with cotton, cotton waste, or sawdust, as well as wool and even hay, but for us the artificial fibers seem the least expensive and the easiest to use. Nylon hose have been used for some kinds of dolls, and so has foam rubber. If you wish, you can still use them for heavy, rough materials.

After filling the feet and legs, bend the feet up into a natural position and tack securely to the legs to keep them in position. Do this with invisible stitches.

Continue stuffing the doll. If there are to be unstuffed spaces at knees, elbows, or shoulders, as indicated by dotted lines, make small running stitches at the lines before continuing the stuffing.

Stuff attached arms before doing the body section, following the particular pattern you are using.

In all but very small dolls it is best to reinforce the neck to prevent the head from being limp. Do this by wrapping either a wooden skewer or wooden match stick with cotton or a piece of the stuffing material and burying it halfway between the back and the head, then packing more of the stuffing around it. Take particular care with the stuffing of the head, and be sure to pack it in firmly with a blunt stick while at the same time squeezing and shaping with your fingers to make the head as round and natural looking as possible.

When the head is as fully packed as possible, close the top by sewing the raw edges flat. This joining will be covered by the hair so it is not necessary to turn in the edge.

### *Face*

It is best to not even transfer or draw the features on the doll's face until it is stuffed. At that time, trace them lightly with pencil, not carbon paper.

On rag dolls it is possible to use a fabric paint or to embroider the features. Two strands of six-strand embroidery cotton will mark the eyebrows, nose, and mouth. Then fill in the outline of the mouth with satin stitch. Do the same with the eyes. Never use French knots to represent the nostrils, but only a short line, or on large dolls, two short lines.

Painted features as used on the dolls in this book are described more fully in their respective chapters. The acrylic paint that is recommended is inexpensive, may be mixed with water, is waterproof, and dries quickly. Brushes may be washed only in water. This paint is packaged either in tubes or ready mixed with water in jars. Buy the smallest tubes or jars you can find, because the amounts needed are small. Pale yellow, red, ultramarine blue, brown, and black, with a large tube of white for blending will paint many, many dolls.

As for brushes, a watercolor brush and a fine sable liner, 00 or 000, will take care of the work planned. Wash the brushes well after each use, reshape to a point with the fingers, then stand upright until dry. When brushes are treated with care they will last for years.

Skin color is not just a mixture of red and white. It also needs a bit of yellow and a touch of brown. Test the color against the back of your wrist until it matches. A child's skin will of course be a trifle different, needing perhaps a little more red or white. Dolls representing dark-skinned people should not be painted with colors made by adding varying amounts of brown and white, but should also have enough red and yellow to give warmth.

Another flat rule: never paint a fringe of eyelashes on a doll or you will get an effect reminiscent of the boudoir dolls of the twenties. Instead, as soon as the brows are painted, make a thin arching line for the eyes and a thinner faint line of pale gray to indicate the lower lid.

The lips will look more natural if the lower lip is painted a trifle fuller than the upper, and the mouth is not too red. A tiny touch of blue added to the lip color will tone down the red. Also, blur the edges of the lips slightly with a dry brush before they are entirely dry.

Paint the eyes last, beginning with the whites. When they are dry, apply the circle of color. Dry again, then touch the center with a dot of black.

The method of coloring a doll's cheeks is similar to applying rouge to a person's face. Rub a drop of paint into a wisp of cotton and dab it on the cheeks, blending it so there will be no sharp line of color. Even old-people dolls should have a little color on their cheeks.

### *Hair*

Wigs for dolls need not be made of human hair, though for some small dolls that may be practiral to use. Some dollmakers even collect combings and barber-shop snippings for doll wigs. Certain dolls in this book have hair made of yarn—either knitting worsted or rug yarn—and you can also use six-strand embroidery cotton, darning cotton, natural wool, or bits of absorbent cotton.

Ideas for hair and wigs are shown with the individual dolls that follow.

# 2

# *Materials for Dollmaking*

Commercially made dolls have their place, but as appreciation for natural materials grows, I feel that the craft of making dolls by hand should be encouraged and the old ways remembered, even though the substitution of modern balsa wood from a hobby shop may seem a far cry from a chunk of wood from the woodpile; or the use of old nylon hose instead of straw or raw wool for stuffing a rag doll may appear to be a contradiction.

Aside from the well-known ways of making dolls from cloth, paper, and wood, all described in the following chapters, there are a few easy-to-come-by mixtures that may include newer materials and that have an extensive range of uses. One of these is a modern version of papier-mâché.

### *Papier-máché*

Papier-mâché means "chewed paper." This is one of the oldest man-made preparations to be used in making dolls and in a modern version may be purchased in hobby shops as a dry powder, to be mixed with water. It is easier, however, to make papier-mâché at home in your electric blender, and considerably cheaper. Use unglazed paper, such as paper toweling or newspaper, and tear it into pieces about one-half inch square. Pack these bits into a cup, tightly, to measure, then place in an electric blender with two or three cups of water. Run the blender at medium speed for two or three minutes. Pour into a kitchen sieve and press out as much water as possible. To this pulp add about two tablespoonfuls of white glue and knead the mass with your hands until it is smooth and doughlike.

This dough may be used immediately or stored in a plastic bag in the refrigerator. It will keep for several days.

After shaping, allow the object you make with it to dry for several days, speeding up the process by placing in a pilot-lighted oven or in a warm place. Sand the surface lightly to make it as smooth as possible. Tear—do not cut— white tissue paper into half-inch strips an inch or so long. Dip each strip into diluted white glue, and cover, overlapping the edges, the papier-mâché surface. This may require two or three layers of tissue paper strips to make a smooth surface. Dry again, very, very thoroughly. Otherwise your object might mildew or the paint on it might peel.

### *Paste*

If you wish to make your own paste, instead of using white glue, make your own just as your grandmother did by combining smoothly four tablespoons flour and one-half cup water. Boil until clear, stirring constantly, and cover until cold so a skin will not form on top. Add enough of this paste to damp paper pulp to turn it into a stiff dough. Then proceed as with white glue.

### *Bread Dough*

An especially useful material for dollmakers is an Americanized version of bread dough used by South American natives for making their quaint, brilliantly colored little glazed figures. It dries to a soft ivory color with a matt surface and may be painted, then glazed with clear lacquer or colorless nailpolish. It will be hard, waterproof, and permanent.

To make the dough, trim the crusts from one slice of white bread and crumble it as fine as possible in your fingers. To this add one tablespoonful of white glue. Mix it well with a spoon, then knead it in the palm of your hand. It will be sticky at first, but quickly becomes smooth and doughy in quite a miraculous way. Tiny rose petals, for example, may be shaped from it and other delicate and finely detailed things. It may also be stored in a plastic bag in the refrigerator. Allow the shapes to dry completely, which will take several days, depending on the thickness of the piece.

When dry, it will be ivory-colored with a mat surface. It may be painted and/or glazed with clear lacquer or nail polish. It will be waterproof and permanent.

The proportions of bread crumbs and glue given here will make enough dough for modeling hands and feet for a small doll but may be increased as needed. Unused amounts will remain workable for a week or more if placed in a plastic bag and returned to the refrigerator.

As described in later chapters, this mixture may be used in making jewelry, parts of costumes, or accessories, as well as hands and feet.

## *Acrylic Paints*

Repeating and also adding to the painting remarks and suggestions made in chapter 1, you will have no difficulty in finding acrylic colors in hobby shops, most hardware stores, and often in dime stores, and while they are packaged in various sizes and forms, the thrifty dollmaker will be wise to buy only the smallest size tubes, and restrict himself to the three primary colors of red, blue, and yellow, and black, white, and brown. Correctly, the name of this material is acrylic polymer plastic color and it is made by numerous manufacturers. It is permanent, waterproof, quick-drying, flexible, and may be applied even without thinning. In most instances it is better to thin with water for a smooth surface. For our purpose, apply with a watercolor brush.

To mix acrylic color squeeze out a tiny amount onto a shallow saucer or dish and add water by the drop to thin it. Tints or secondary colors are easy to get by making combinations. Flesh color, for example, is made by first thinning a bit of white color, adding a dab of red, a tiny amount of yellow, and for an Indian or other brown-skinned doll, a mere touch of brown. Realistically, flesh color isn't just pale pink. Check the color against the color of your own hand or wrist for accuracy. As we all learned in first grade, green is a mixture of yellow and blue, orange of red and yellow, and purple of red and blue. A faint touch of brown is better to use for dulling a shade than is black.

As soon as the day's painting is finished wash your brushes thoroughly with water. If you have unfortunately allowed acrylic paint to dry, soak it off with alcohol.

## *Brushes*

As said before, watercolor brushes are generally the best to use with acrylic color on dolls, but for tiny lines, such as around the eyes, buy a sable liner—00 or 000. A brush should be cared for with great respect and should last for years. After washing, and while still damp, gently shape it to its original point.

## *Stuffing*

There was little choice in the old days of materials for stuffing dolls. Cotton or cotton batting predominated, but because it tends to be lumpy and is heavy, it is good to know that there are better and more modern materials now.

Shredded polyester fiber is a good choice for large dolls, and is washable and lightweight. Beware of the foam scraps that are inexpensive but are lumpy and will eventually become powdery. They are not permanent.

Kapok is preferable for small dolls for it is smooth-packing and lightweight. Personally, I never plan to wash any doll except with a quick sponging of the outer surface.

Certain dolls may be stuffed with sawdust—the least expensive of any material. Take a large paper sack to the nearest lumber yard and ask the way to the sawdust pile. No cost. When you get home, sift it through a colander to remove chips and splinters. Use only the sawdust from pine or fir, not a dark wood.

Nylon hose are often used for stuffing material, and do nicely, since they are also lightweight and smooth-packing. Kind friends will be happy to save their castoffs for you.

Natural wool is an old and still good stuffing material, available if you have a sheep-grower or hand-spinner in your circle, for when a sheep is sheared there are often short cuts of wool too short for spinning, and when washed and carefully dried, they may be pulled into a fluffy mass that makes beautiful stuffing. Great-grandmother often used wool.

I once acquired a Mexican-made doll whose cloth body was filled with dried grass that had survived long years of use. In our nature-conscious day, there are those who would prefer to use these primitive materials rather than plastics in any form.

## *Cloth*

That there is no one material for making dolls is too obvious to dwell on, for dolls have been made of almost everything from cloth to rocks.

Rag dolls used to be made of muslin, white or pink or unbleached, but now the magic of permanent finish cottons broadens the range. We can buy it in all colors and in plain weave or satin-finish yardage and be assured that dust and grime may be washed off with a damp cloth.

Burlap is usable for some of the craft-type dolls and in addition is one material with which a coarse plastic stuffing could be used, in spite of its lumpiness.

Felt is another good material, especially for miniature dolls and for clothing, since raw edges may simply be whipped together without turning, in an invisible joining. It is particularly good for making trousers for men or boy dolls. I use it in the making of the Indian men shown in chapter 9.

### *Closings*

Play dolls should always be made with removable clothes, for even small children like to pull off the carefully made lacy tucked dress and carry the doll around by an arm or leg. Therefore, use buttons or snap fasteners and let the child learn how to make them work. Ties and ribbons aren't too practical.

Collectors' dolls are another matter, however, since with them it is the general effect you are striving for rather than play qualities. Even if collectors' dolls sometimes need grooming, tack their clothes in place instead of bothering to make buttonholes. You can then resew the garments on the doll, or simply pin them.

### *Find and Save*

Dollmakers never throw anything away—that is, anything as insignificant as an inch-long piece of elastic, ribbon, or lace; a few beads; a scrap of braid; a single small button; a bird's feather found on the grass; a minute shell on the beach. If your sense of organization demands it, file these oddments away in plastic envelopes or boxes, also salvaged.

When your savings fail you, browse around in a dime store, letting your imagination range freely, seeing a new use for something quite different. Try to shun plastic, for it is yet an untested substance and may not be as enduring as we think. Time and care involved in making a doll warrant considering this.

### *Marking*

Modesty should not keep you from putting your name or initials on the handwork you make, particularly something that embodies your own original ideas. Add the date, also, for your own benefit and that of whoever acquires it later. The sole of a doll's foot or the back of its neck are good spots to place your mark.

To fully personalize your doll, give it a name. Add that, too.

# 3

# *Adventure with the Pippins*

When you introduce these dolls as Grandfather Jonathan or Navaho Rosy nobody will believe that their heads were made of dried apples and that you carved them yourself with a paring knife—you, who can't draw a straight line.

One of the charms of apple dolls is that there can never be two exactly alike, even though several of the same variety may have been carved at the same time. There is something about the chemistry of apples that does this.

The cliché expression, "As American as apple pie," should be reworded to, "As American as corn on the cob," or, "As American as an apple doll," for it was probably the American Indians who were responsible for both.

To turn an apple into a doll head, select a large, symmetrically shaped apple that is free from bruises and blemishes, and is firm, not mushy. Color and variety are not important, but a slightly oval shape will make a more effective head than will a round or squatty one. Remove the stem, then peel the apple as smoothly as possible, leaving a small unpeeled disk at both ends. Do not core.

Next, with a small paring knife follow the same general procedure as when carving a Jack o' lantern, except that the cuts are not more than one-quarter inch deep. The drawing shows how to place them. This carving is to give little more than a rough indication of the features, so is easy to do. Undercut the blossom end slightly for the neck. Press the dull edge of the knife down gently to make wrinkles on

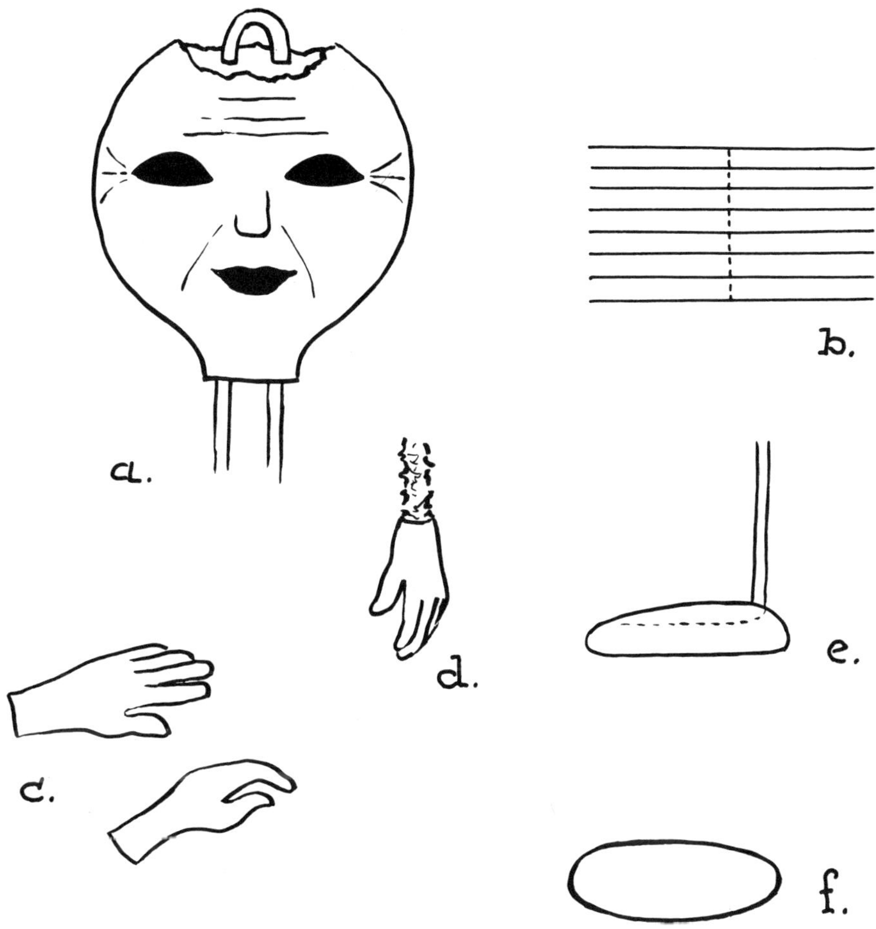


*a—Apple, peeled, has an eleven-inch loop of wire pushed through it and ready to be dried.*

*b—Lay strands of human hair, yarn, or embroidery floss on a strip of tissue paper, then stitch down the center with flesh-colored thread to make a part, then glue to head.*

*c—Hands are made of bread dough, then painted to match dried face.*

*d—Hands are modeled on the pipe cleaners, which form a base for the arms.*

*e—Bread dough foot is modeled over wire loops of feet.*

*f—Sole of foot should be flat on bottom so that doll may stand without support.*

*a—Apple doll is ready for feet, to be modeled around wire loops. A cloth body section is stuffed lightly and sewed to body to make dressing doll easier.*

*b—Wind narrow strips of cloth over entire body before gluing wig on head.*

the forehead, along the sides of the nose, and at the outer corners of the eyes. These lines will deepen as the apple dries.

At this point some people dip or soak the apple in lemon juice, but I've never found it necessary, since the color remains the same, either way.

Bend a long hairpin of coathanger wire, making it about ten or eleven inches long when bent, and force it gently through the apple from the stem end and out through the blossom end. Pull the loop down so it is even with the top of the apple. As the apple dries it will tend to slide down the wire, so hold it in place by winding a few twists of string on the wire just below the head.

Rub a faint blush of rouge on the cheeks.

The head is now ready to dry—a most important step that requires gentle, even heat, such as the warm, dry air of the average living room. If left in a place that is too cool or damp the apple will probably mold or rot. It is also important that nothing touch the apple during the drying period, so hang the apple on a line, or stand in something like a pop bottle where nothing will touch it.

Depending on the weather, temperature, and the apple itself, the drying period will take two or three weeks. Pinch the features occasionally to shape them. As soon as the apple is pithy and will not respond to pinching it is ready for the next step.

With pliers, bend the ends of the wire hairpin into loops an inch long. These will be the feet. Lash two pipe cleaners to the wire just below the neck. Bend the ends of the wires to form bases for the hands. Bend slightly at the shoulders.

Cut two rounded pieces of muslin to form the upper torso, having it extend to below the doll's waist. Stuff this firmly with cotton and secure it firmly to the wires of the legs. This padded section will make it easier to dress the doll and will be entirely covered by the clothing.

Mix a batch of the dough mixture described in chapter 2, and press a lump of it into the depression where the loop of wire enters the apple, smoothing it with a knife blade. Shape hands and feet of the dough directly onto the wire loops of the feet and the pipe cleaner loops of the hands.

Allow the doll to stand undisturbed until the dough is hard, then tint it with acrylic paint colored to match the color of the apple. Brush the head with three or four coats of clear lacquer, clear nail polish, or the "dope" sold in hobby shops. Brush this all over the apple head and well down into the stem and blossom ends.

Glue beads, either blue or brown, in the eye spaces. Wait until the doll is dressed before attaching a wig.

Cover the body wires and the cotton torso section with narrow strips of cloth the color of the applehead, winding it smoothly and fastening invisibly. This gives a good solid base for the clothing, better than the strips of nylon hose sometimes suggested. As these are not play dolls, the clothes are sewed on them directly and not made to be taken off.

Dressing apple dolls is fun, even if you don't sew very well. Make a pattern by first fitting and cutting facial tissue or paper toweling, then using the pattern on fine, soft material, adding a small seam allowance. Felt is one of the easiest materials to use because the seams do not need to be turned. For men's clothes it is particularly good, whipping the edges together with fine stitches and self-color thread.

Finally, make the shoes, of either felt or soft leather. Before using the pattern given here, first check the measurements with those of your doll. The flatter the soles the easier it will be to make the doll stand alone.

Apple-head dolls are most appropriately old people, so the hair is either gray or white. It may be made of fine, soft yarn, unspun wool, or snippings of real hair. Glue the material directly on the head, or make a wig by cutting strands of yarn about eight inches long, spreading them out on paper and stitching through the center with a line of outline stitches to indicate a part. Glue this to the head, holding the sides down with tiny stitches of the same material.

Grandpa's beard or chin whiskers are made of wisps of cotton glued in place. A fringe of hair circling his bald spot is made the same way, as are bits of cotton glued above his eyes to form bushy eyebrows.

Apple dolls may be dressed in many ways: a St. Francis feeding his little birds (made of the dough and painted), a folk dancing couple of senior citizens, a grandmother knitting a sock or peeling apples, an elderly cowboy—bow legs and all—ready to rope a steer, a Maine lobsterman with his trap, or a Colonial Dame.

By combining an apple head with a cornhusk body you have a truly American doll, for this is the way the Iroquois Indians of eastern Canada and New York state first made dolls used in their medicine rites. At first these were made without clothing, but after contact with white men, they often dressed their dolls in skin or fabrics. They were from six to ten inches tall.

The Navaho woman shown here is eleven inches tall, because the cob used for her body was a large one. The making of a cornhusk-apple-head doll begins with a well-dried corncob and the dried husks from an ear of corn. Soak the husks for an hour or so in water, then tear one or two into strips about one-quarter inch wide. These will be used for tying.

*Maine lobsterman is carrying home a trap containing a lobster. His head is a dried apple, hair and beard are made of cotton. His hat and sou'wester are made from a plastic shower cap.*

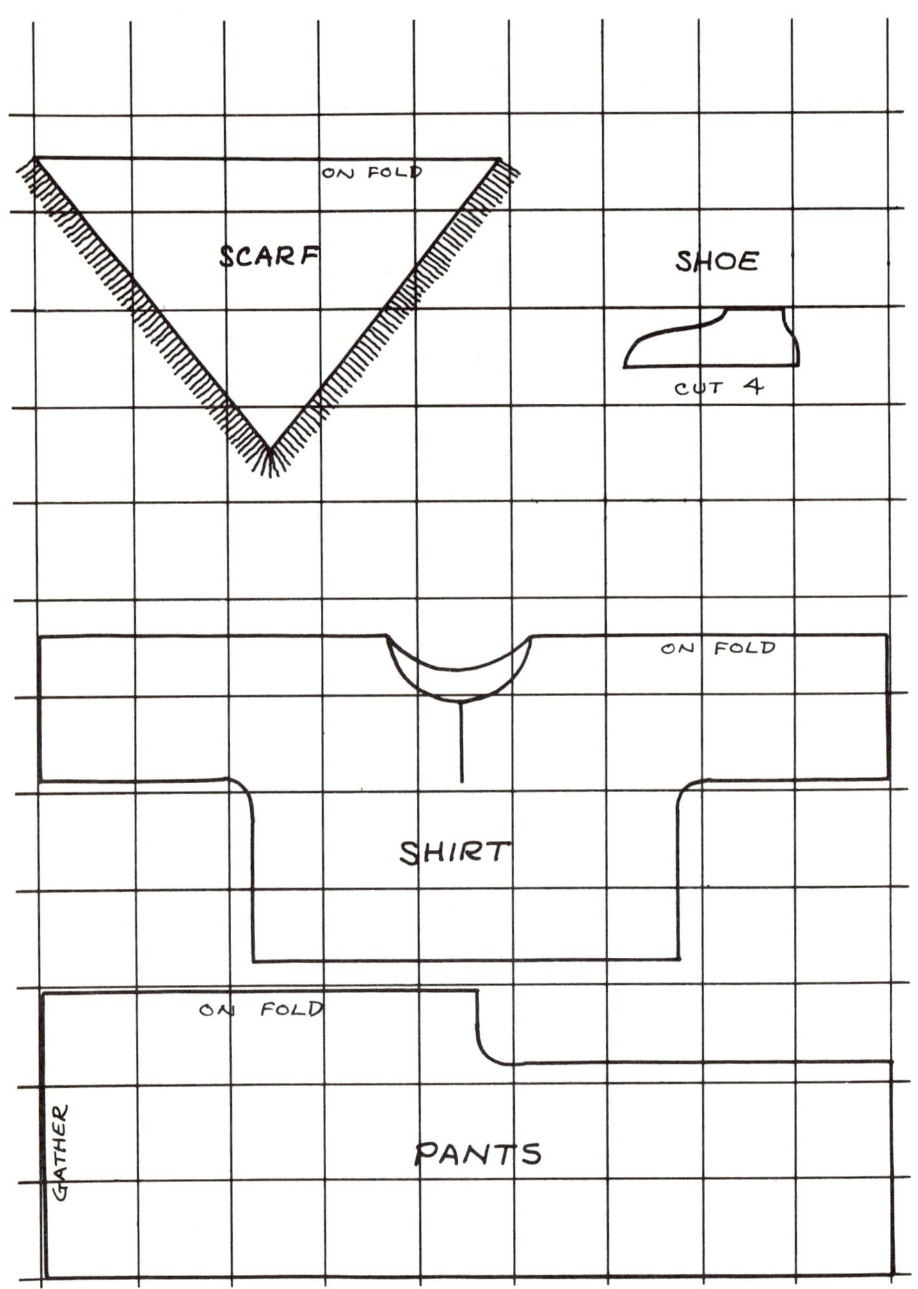


*Patterns for clothes for Maine lobsterman.*

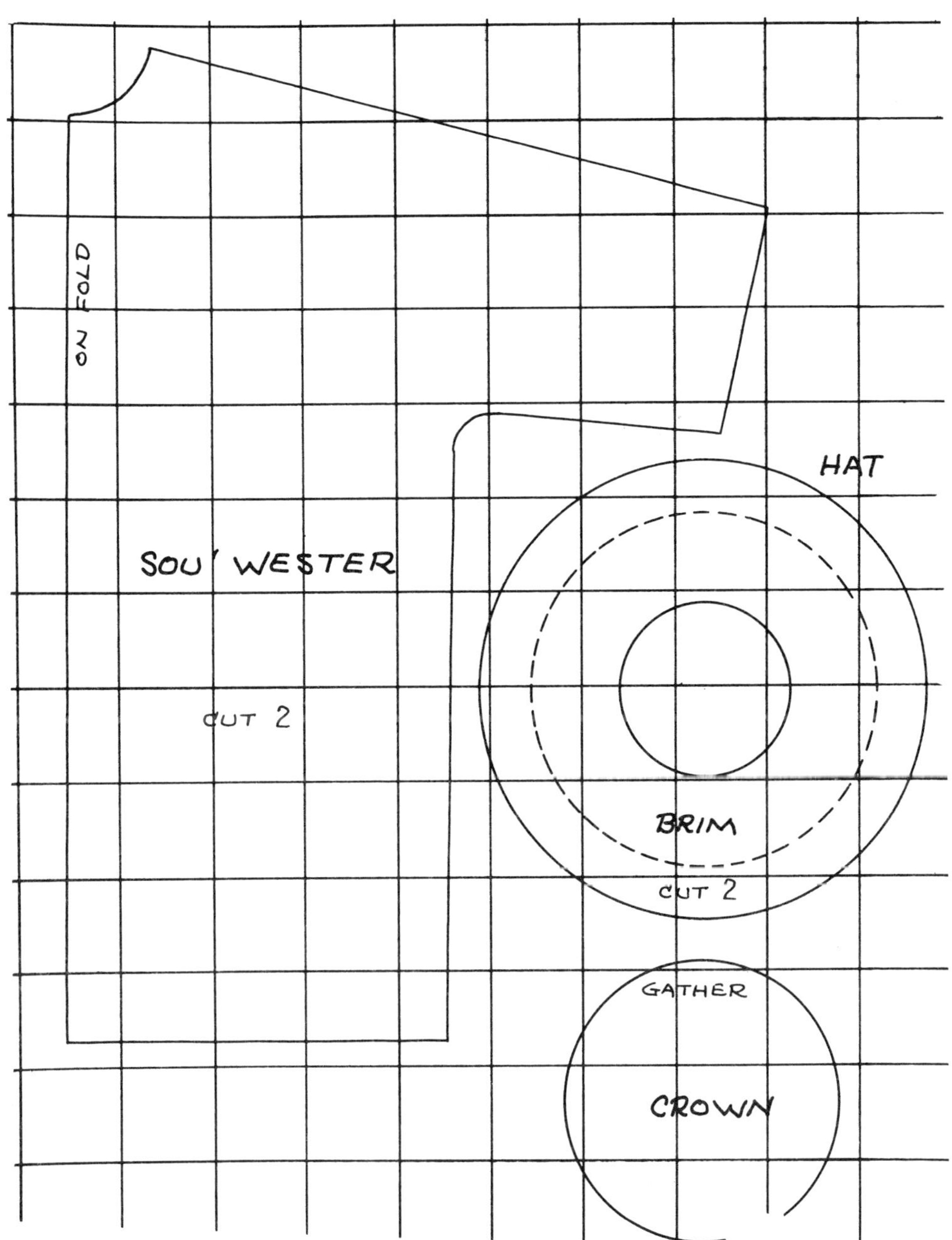


*Patterns for Maine lobsterman's outdoor clothes.*

*St. Francis of Assisi wears the grey wool, simple cowled habit of his order, with a knotted white cord about his waist. The halo is made of gilded cardboard, fastened on the back of his tonsured head. Hair is made of a few short bits of gray wool yarn. The bird is made of the bread-dough material used for his hands, top of head, and bare feet. It is painted yellow with acrylic paint. Other birds may be made to be placed at his feet.*

Take the previously dried apple head and cut the wires to about two inches. Push the wires into the top of the piece of corncob, which has been cut to about a four-inch length.

Make the arms next by rolling together strips of the husk and tie them at the wrist and elbow with the fine strips of husk. No effort is made to simulate real hands or arms, but the ties are made quite frankly in double knots, trimmed close.

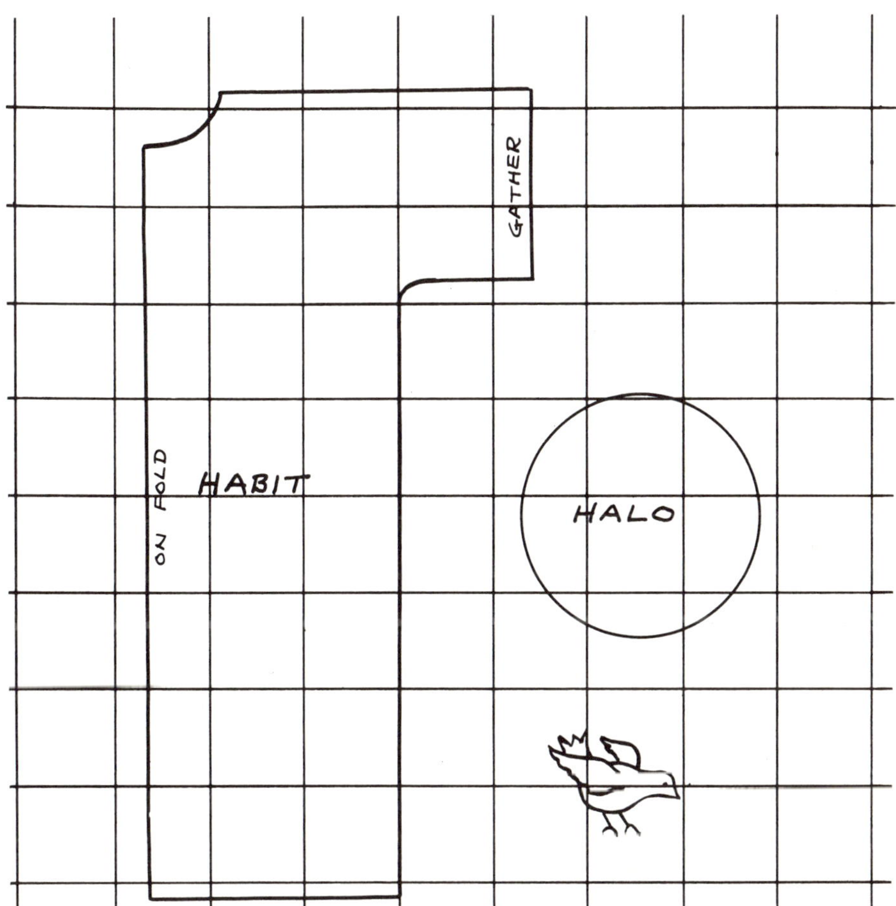


*Habit, halo, and little bird, are patterns used in dressing and displaying a St. Francis figure made with an apple head.*

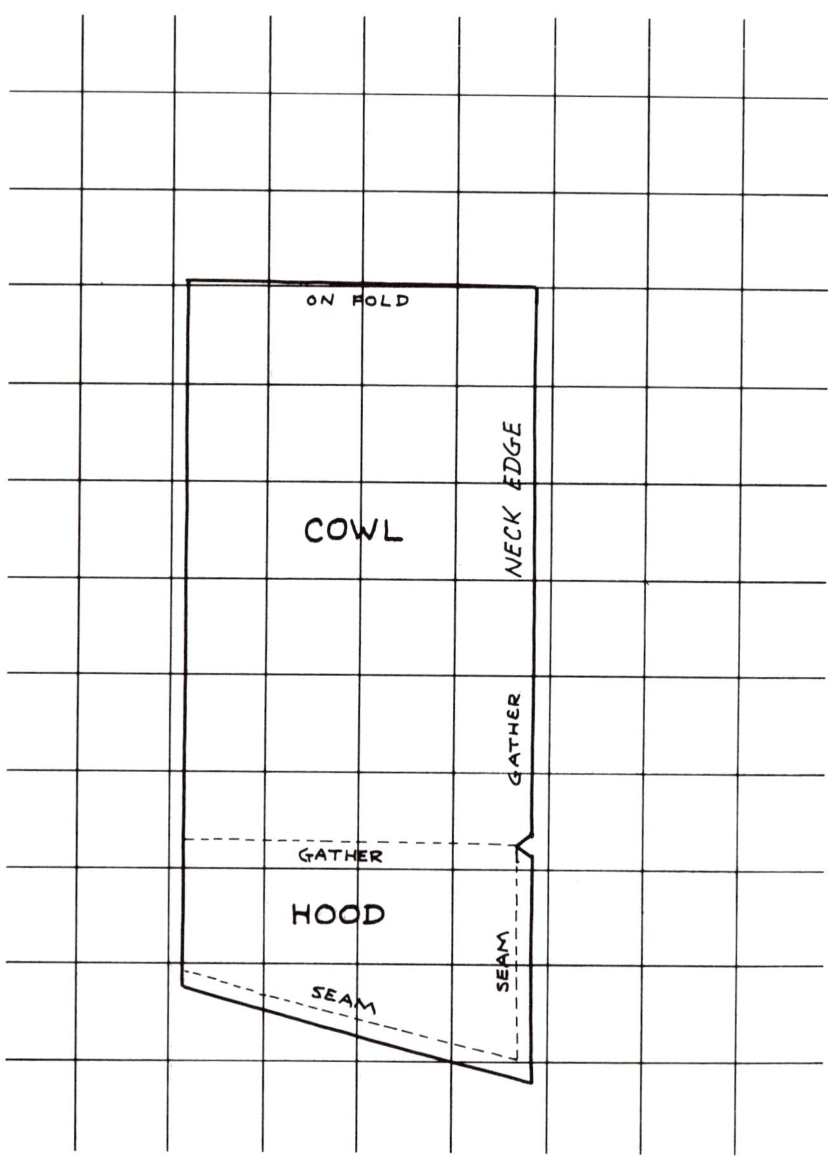


*Pattern for cowl and hood to complete the St. Francis costume.*

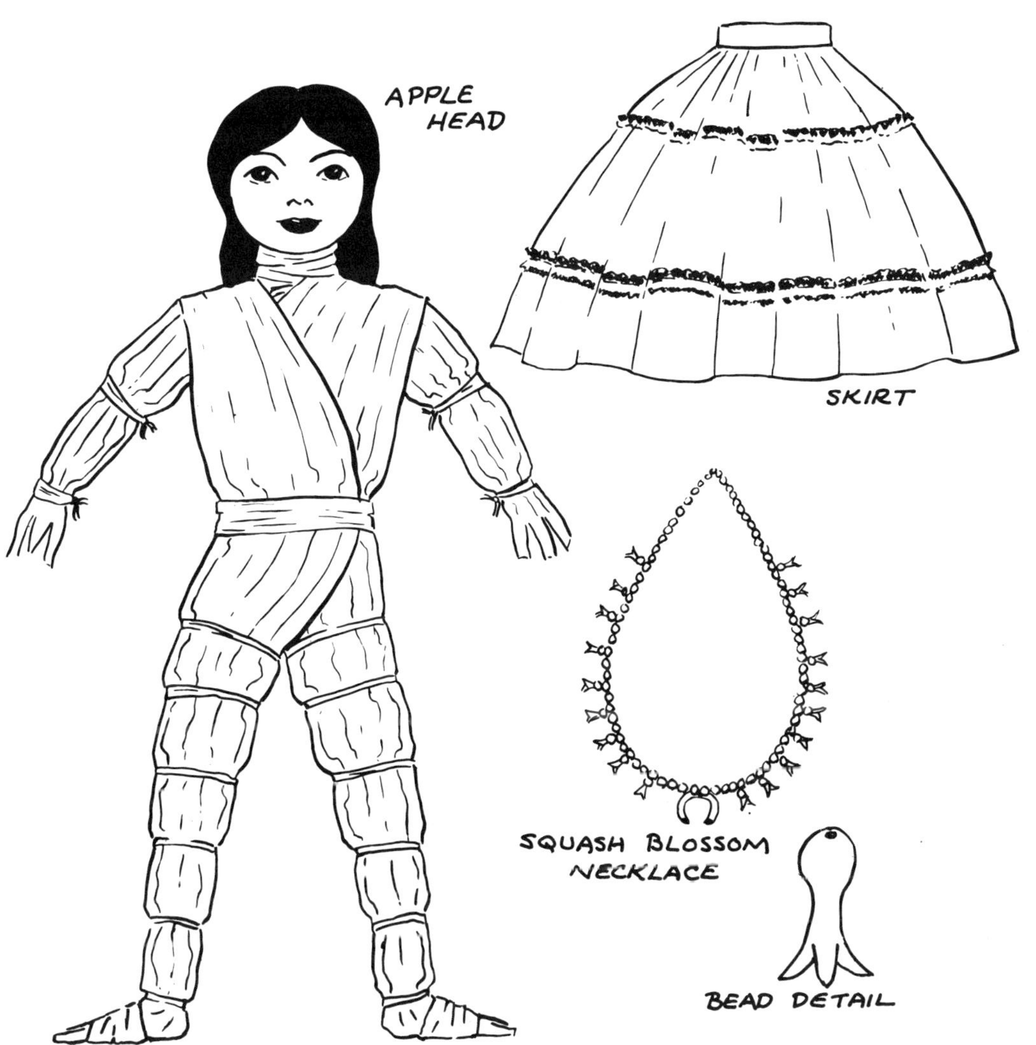


*Cornhusk body is made with apple head for the Navaho doll. The broomstick skirt and squashblossom necklace are shown here in detail.*

*Navaho woman is dressed authentically in velvet blouse and full yellow skirt trimmed in colored braid. Her squashblossom necklace is made of the bread-dough mixture, then painted silver. Tiny turquoise beads form her earrings.*

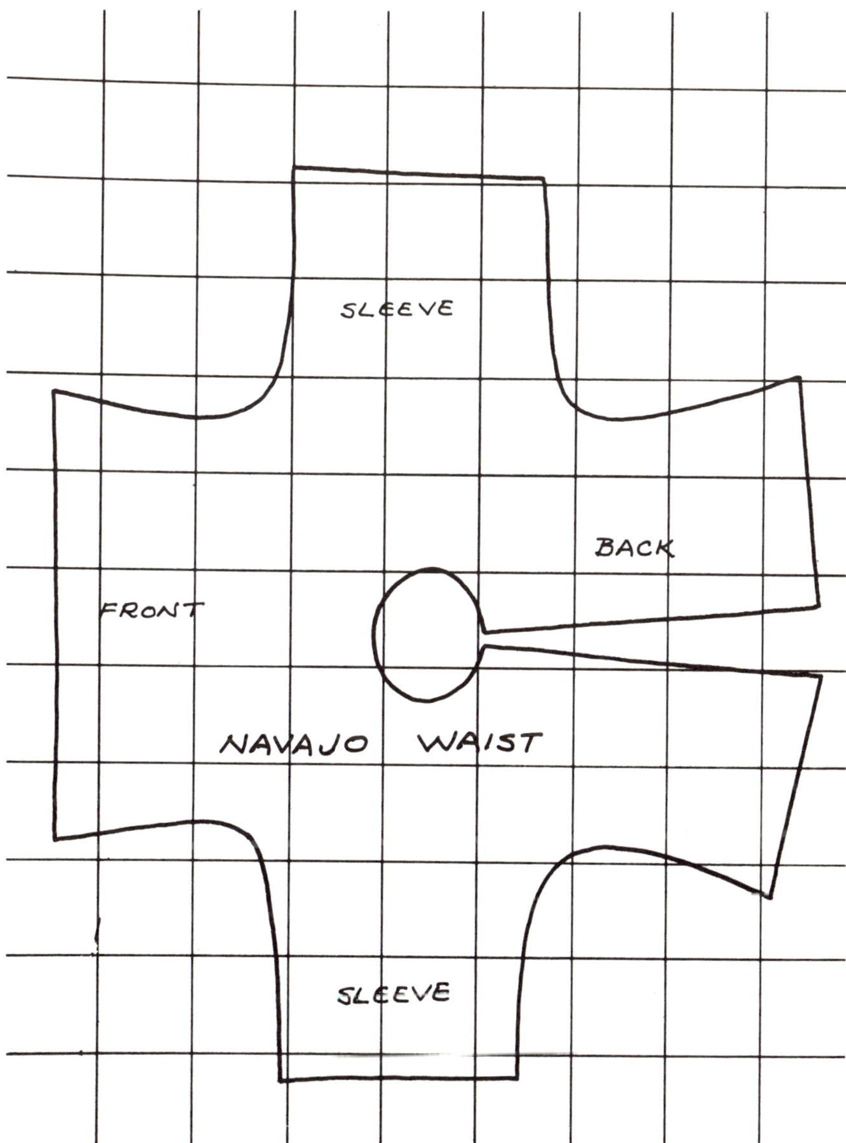


*Waist pattern for the apple-head Navaho doll is made in one piece.*

This arm strip is about twelve inches long.

Make another, larger strip for the legs, about the same length. Tie at several places on the legs, again at the ankles, and then around the feet, bending them up at right angles to hold in place.

Tie the arm strip at the back of the cob and the leg strip under the lower end of the cob. Now wrap strips of husk diagonally around the

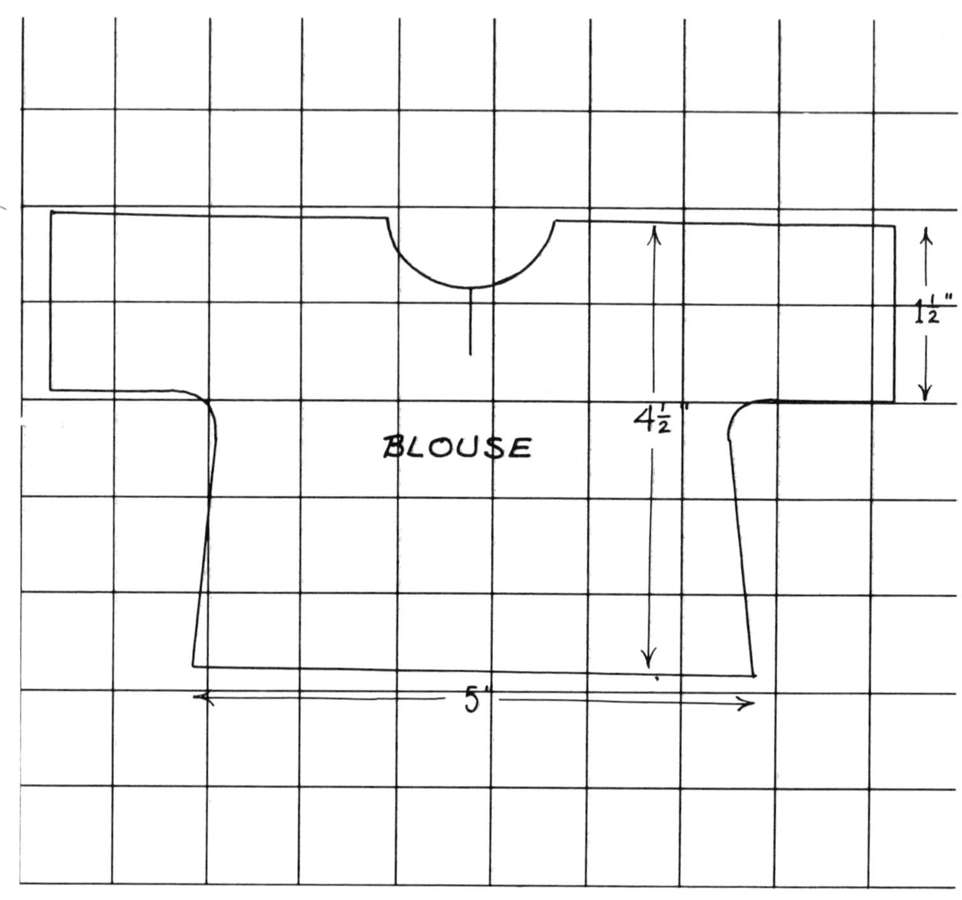


*Navaho Indian woman.*

body to completely cover the cob and hold the arms and legs in place. Hold them in place at the waistline with narrow strips of husk. Tie at the back of doll.

Our Navaho woman wears the traditional velvet waist and the "broomstick" skirt so familiar to visitors at Navaho reservations in Arizona, New Mexico, and Utah. The skirt was made of a seven by twenty-four-inch strip of cotton cloth, given a narrow rolled hem, and gathered to a waistband. It was then dipped in water and tied tightly to a piece of broomstick to dry.

Her squash-blossom necklace was made of small beads and bits of the bread dough mixture. They were painted with aluminum paint and touched with turquoise-blue paint, to simulate silver and turquoise. Dangling earrings and the silver buttons on her waist were made the same way.

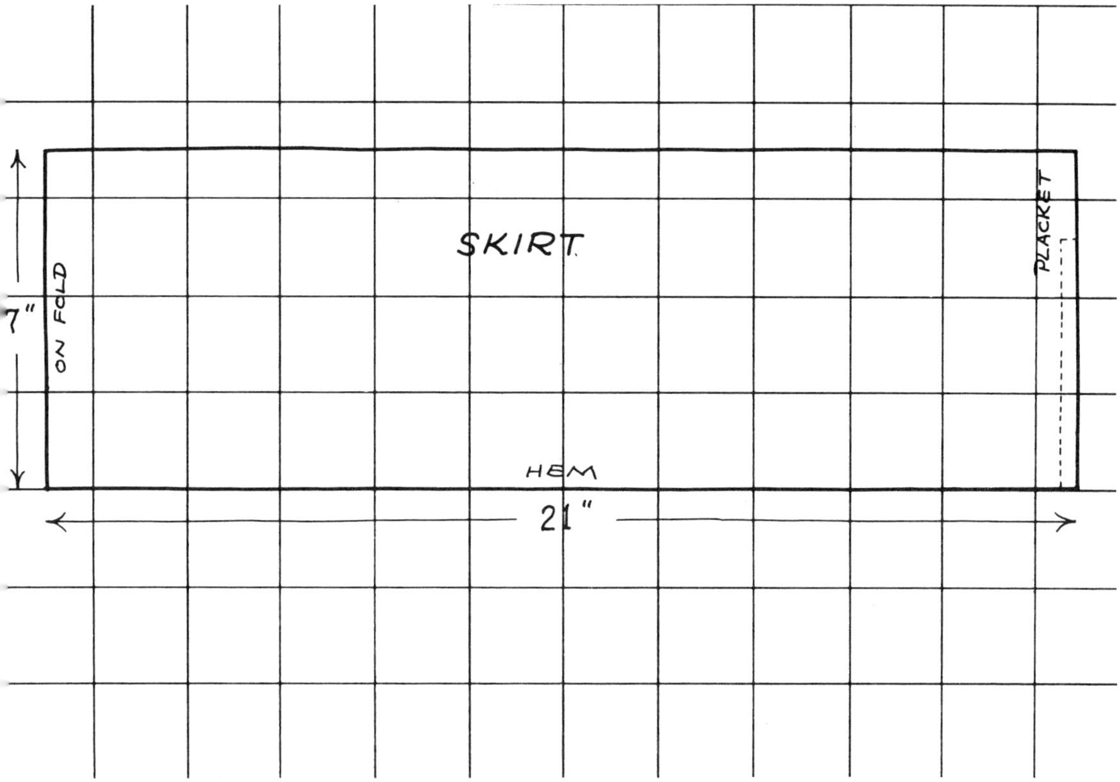

SKIRT
ON FOLD
7"
PLACKET
HEM
21"

*Navaho Indian woman.*

Her wig, cut from hair from a black, thrift-shop wig, is held at the back of her head with a ribbon in the way Indian women often wear theirs.

One such doll was made for an Indian trader who placed it in front of a miniature Navaho rug loom in which a rug had been started.

SHOE
SOLE
UPPER

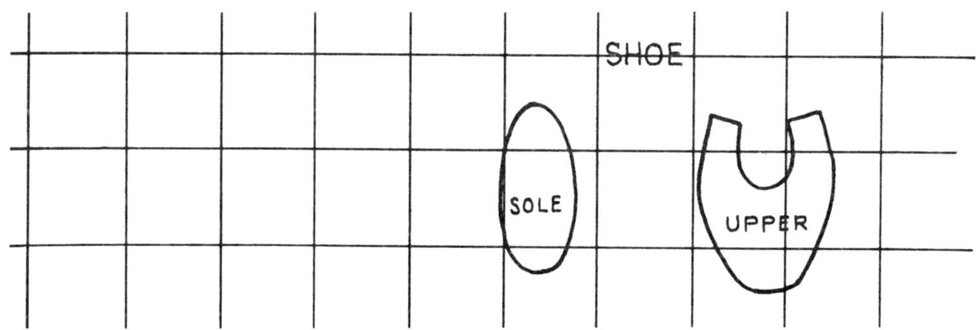

*Navaho Indian woman.*

He sat the doll down on a sheepskin rug in front of the loom, as the women do when they weave rugs.

These are a few of the ways apple-head dolls may be dressed and arranged, but they are only a beginning, for there are few other dolls that challenge attention the way they do. And there is no way to predict how long an apple doll will survive, provided it is protected from mice and robins. Its life should be a long one.

# 4

# *Ridiklis and Peter Piper*

Although wooden dolls seem to be forgotten by manufacturers during this plastic age, their virtues and durability have been tested by many generations, on all continents. Sometimes the difference between a doll and an idol is illusive, and the farther back we go into history the more the two seem to merge. It may be that in the beginning children's toys—dolls—were religious objects—idols. Or vice versa. Or it is possible that their origins were in some way derived from the same motivation as were the kachina dolls of the American Indians, described in a later chapter—education. Wood, being an enduring material, has survived, so that wooden figures of antiquity may be battered and scarred, but they are still to be found in various churches and cathedrals of Europe. These figures of saints and martyrs, carved, gilded, and painted, were in a way remotely related to dolls, for they often had chests of clothes and vestments made for them, to be worn on special days and seasons.

The material for these figures came from the forests of Europe for centuries, and it was also there that many of the world's toys were made until World War I. Sometimes the dolls were made partly of bisqued china and partly of a composition made from glue and sawdust; sometimes they were carved entirely from wood.

The most simple of these all-wooden dolls came at first from what is now Germany, and were therefore called *Deutsch* dolls, which later became mistranslated to Dutch dolls. These dolls were given a great many other names: peg dolls, peggitys, penny woodens, woodentops,

*Ridiklis and Peter Piper completed, ready for dressing. The hands are shaped in the old-time way without fingers, simply scooped out on the side next to the body.*

wooden Bettys, Flanders babies, penny Gretchens, and woodentops, demonstrating that the dolls were plentiful and inexpensive.

The children's story favorite, *The Adventure of Two Dutch Dolls and a Golliwog*, by Florence and Bertha Upton has preserved the name of Dutch dolls as well as introducing the beloved black doll, the Golliwog.

*Ridiklis is fluffy in nylon net and much lace. Her pantalets reach just to slipper straps. Bonnet is tied under her chin with a strand of silver cord. She can be dressed in more simple clothing just as easily.*

There is very little change in the way wooden dolls of the Dutch type and later ones made by American pioneers were made, and that we can also make. It is perhaps the simplicity and honesty of these primitive dolls that accounts for their popularity, and that appeals to our age, which is looking for those qualities in both crafts and living.

Perhaps the most famous Dutch dolls are those dressed in the early nineteenth century by the little Princess Victoria who became Queen Victoria. She and her governess, Baroness Lehzen, dressed the 132 wooden dolls now on display in London's Kensington Palace. They are far from beautiful, with their sharp little noses, cheeks dabbed with circle of red paint, and tight little painted mouths. They were dressed

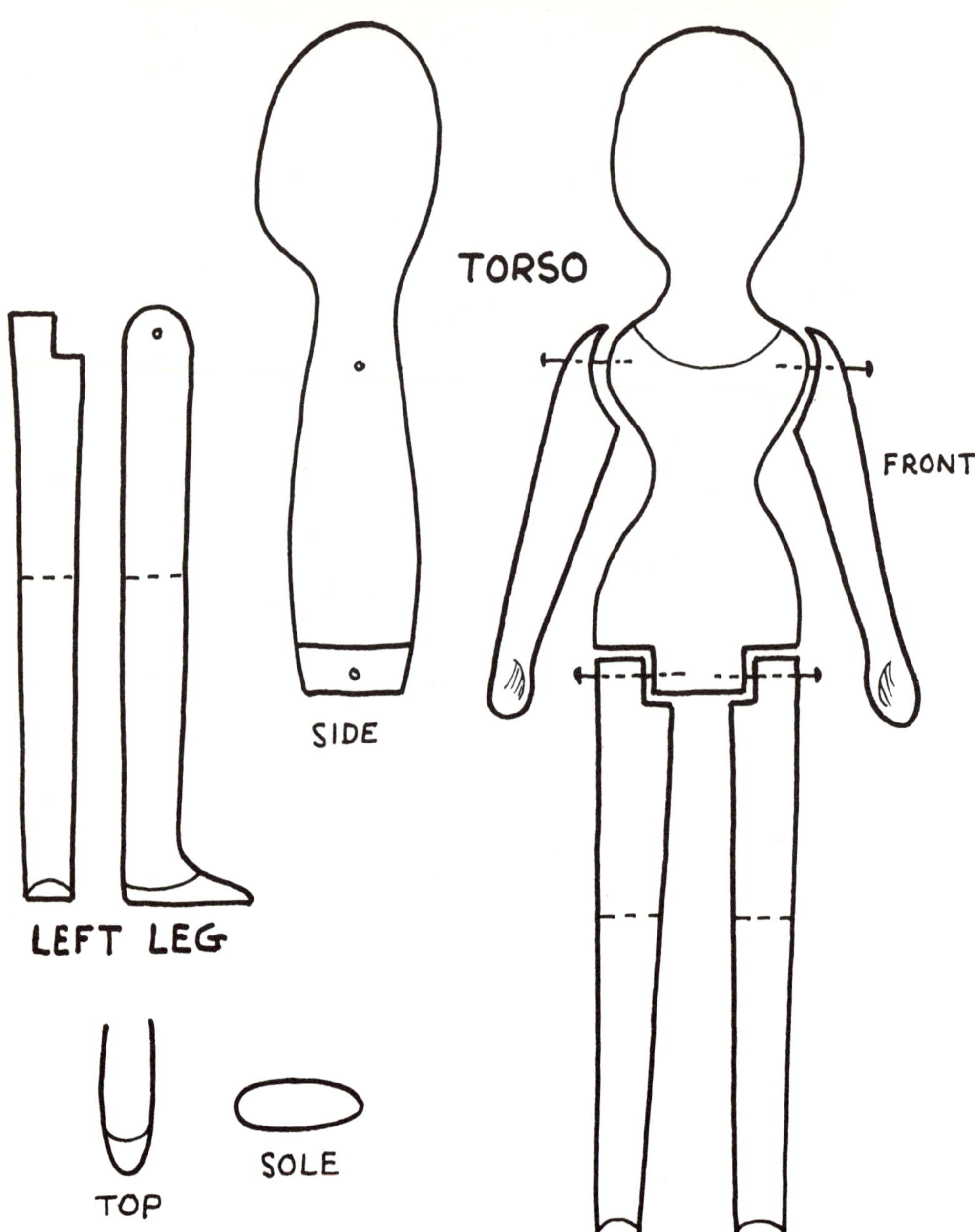


*Construction of these wooden dolls is simple when using soft wood. Paint the lower arms and legs to dotted lines and the neck as shown to the shoulders, then paint the features and if wished, give a final coat of clear gloss.*

as ladies of the court and theatrical personages, and today fascinate us with the styles of their century.

It was no doubt these dolls that inspired Frances Hodgson Burnett to write her story, *Racketty Packetty House* in the early 1900s, in which a family of wooden dolls lived. They were gaily led by Ridiklis and her comical brother Peter Piper. Forgotten by their owner, they were broken and ragged, but brave and gay. They were rescued just in time by the little Princess, and restored to their former perfection. The illustrations in Mrs. Burnett's book, which was reprinted in later years, inspired the making and dressing of the two wooden dolls pictured here, and gave the name to this chapter.

Obviously, wooden dolls are not always dressed in Victorian frills, but as mentioned, American pioneers made and dressed theirs in prints and calicoes, as they were dressed. In fact, wooden dolls of this kind are still found in New England and the Appalachians, almost identical with those of past centuries. Fathers carve the dolls, and mothers dress them. More than a few wooden dolls crossed the plains in the arms of small girls, and today look stolidly out from museum cases at a plastic world so unlike their own.

Any person old enough to be trusted with a jackknife can in a few hours shape a wooden doll, using no other tool. The patterns and diagrams here are for a doll eight or nine inches tall, but may be made larger or smaller if desired. Soft white pine is the preferred material to use, but balsa wood is easier to carve.

### *Materials Needed*

One-inch thick piece of balsa wood, five inches long and two inches wide for head and torso
Two-foot length of balsa wood one-half-inch square for arms and legs
Box of one-inch-long wire brads
Small tubes of acrylic paint in white, red, blue, and black
One watercolor brush
One 00 liner
Fine sandpaper
White glue
An inexpensive coping saw may be used to block out the figure but is not essential.

### *Method*

Trace the pattern for the head and body section to a sheet of tracing paper, then onto a wide piece of the wood.

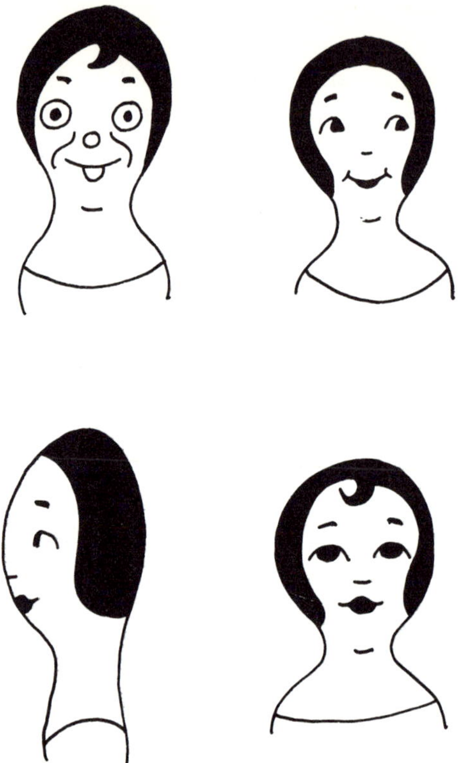

*A few of the faces that can be used on wooden dolls. Create your own.* Courtesy Charles Scribner's Sons.

Cut the pieces for arms and legs from the one-half-inch square piece of wood, and also cut pieces for the feet.

Shape all pieces according to the diagram and rub smooth with sandpaper.

Glue the feet to the legs with white glue and reinforce this joint by pushing a wire brad up through the soles of the feet and into the legs.

Also, push brads into the tops of the arms and through into the body. Leave enough clearance so that both arms and legs can be moved slightly.

Paint the head and neck down to the curved line, using white paint. After it is thoroughly dry, paint on the features, using the finest brush and the acrylic paint. Allow to dry over night.

Rub a bit of red paint into a small cotton ball and touch it lightly on the cheeks, blending the edges well. Old dolls often had extremely pink cheeks, and some even definite round red spots of color, but the shaded edges are more attractive. Paint slippers on the feet.

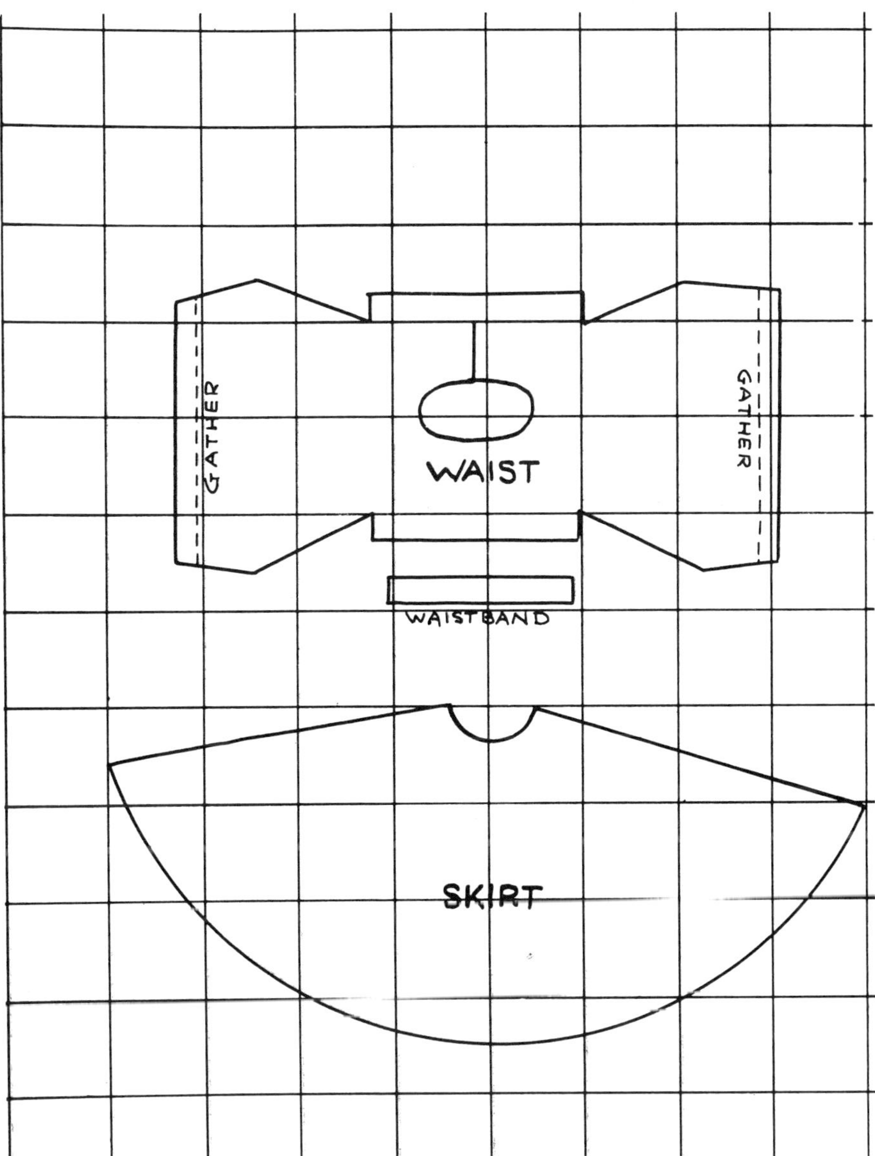


*Patterns for Ridiklis's dress can be easily lengthened or shortened, made with a straight skirt, tight sleeves. Add a narrow seam allowance to each piece.*

You may now apply two or three coats of clear plastic, colorless nail polish, or the "dope" sold in hobby shops for model-making. This will protect the paint and make it easier to keep clean. The doll is now ready to dress.

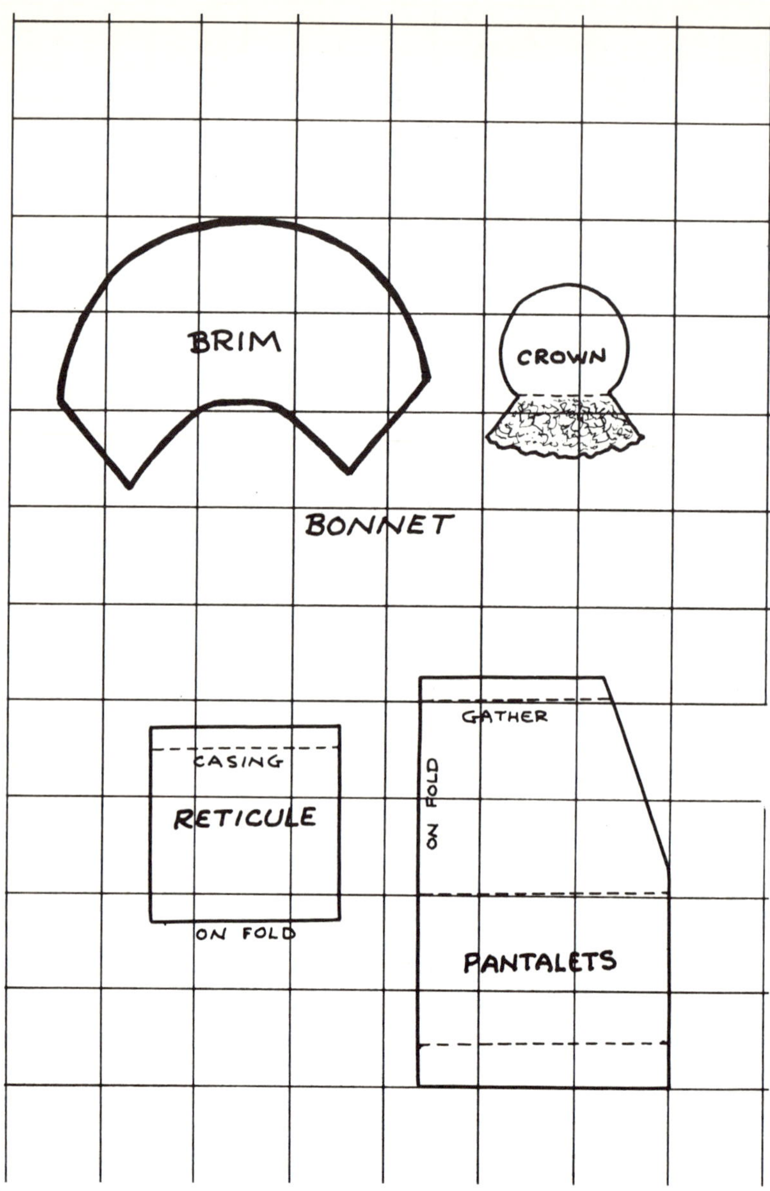


*Bonnet brim is made of stiff interlining or heavy paper, lined and faced with a contrasting color. The crown is made separately, then sewed to brim. The reticule (bag), to hang on doll's arm, may be made of fine silk with a drawstring of matching embroidery cotton. Pantalets are made of batiste or strips of lace, and ruffles of lace sewn on dotted lines. Gather the top and sew in place, since these dolls are not intended to be play dolls.*

*Peter Piper's costume is made of light felt, the top in red, the pants tan. His hat was purchased in a toy shop but could have been crocheted of raffia or straw-fiber.*

The patterns shown here for clothes do not include seam allowances, so add about one-quarter inch for seams. Sew the clothes by hand.

As has been said, clothes for men and boy dolls are easier to dress if felt is used, whipping the seams together on the right side so that they will not have to be turned.

Wooden dolls like these may easily be turned into marionettes by fastening one end of a piece of nylon fish-line to the top of the doll's head, another piece to each hand, and another to each foot. The other

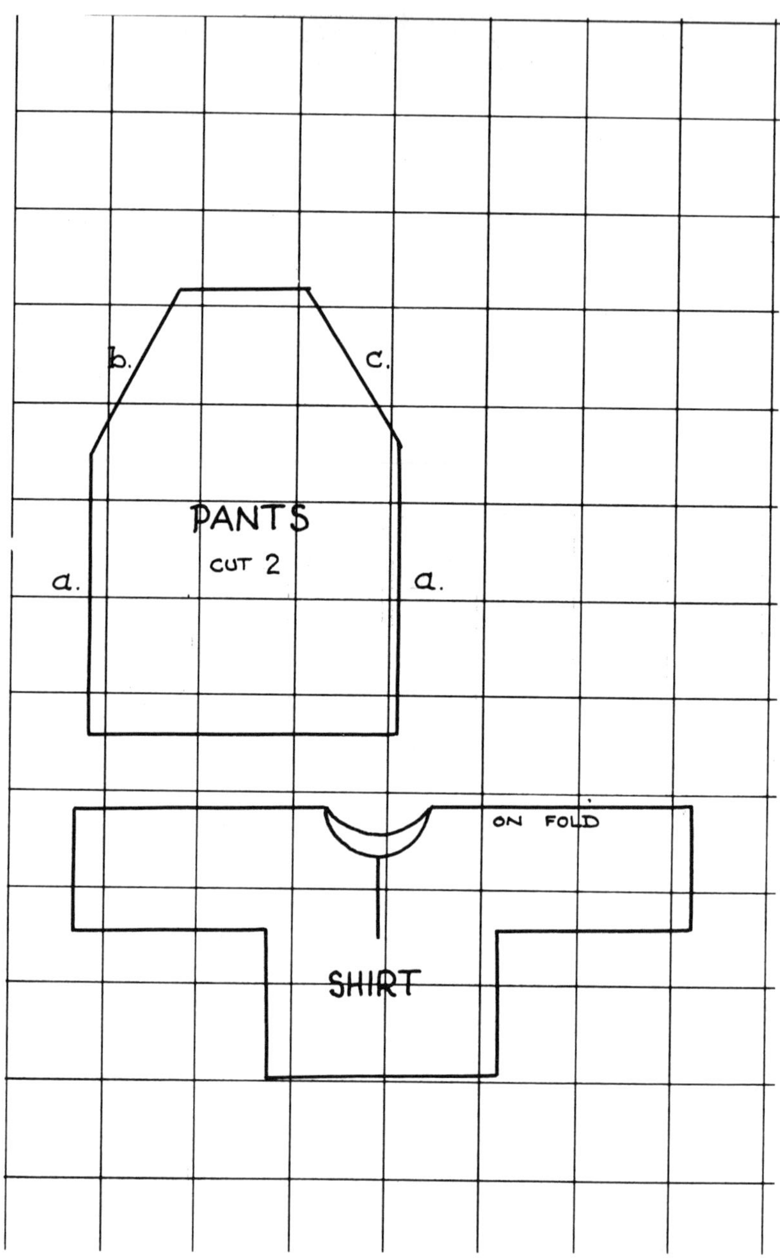


*Patterns for Peter's simple costume require little material. In making the pants, sew each leg separately as far as the crotch, then join the two top sections. Gather top to fit his waist and fasten securely. Slash front of top as shown before slipping it over his head. Tack the neck of top and add buttons.*

ends are fastened to a small strip of wood. The marionette is made to move by jiggling and turning this strip of wood, manipulating the strings.

An amateur show using wooden marionettes could be produced in a homemade version of a puppet theater, using a table for the stage, and two opaque curtains, one above the other, and coming to the floor, to hide the operators and the reader.

There are many puppet plays in print, and others may be adapted from children's stories. This is a project a group of children would enjoy, and if the stage scenery and props are also made, just that many more members of a class would share the fun.

The only thing to compare with a marionette theater is a dollhouse, and while not many pieces of furniture need be made for it, it still needs tiny dishes, cardboard or wooden furniture, rugs, pictures, and perhaps miniatures, plus the wings and backdrop. As a side-project, it is a chance to do a little research on stage productions.

The many angles of such a theater would give every person in a class something to do, both boys and girls, and projects of that type are not too easy to find.

Best of all, everything used in the making and producing of a marionette show could be restricted to scrap materials of various kinds, and the salvage of discards—a point that should be emphasized to the children.

# 5

# *The Lost and Found Doll*

There are many mysterious things about dolls—ask any doll lover. Do dolls move when people aren't around? Do they talk and laugh, as fanciful writers have told us? Nobody can prove that they don't, but I know that Dilly, the rag doll in this chapter, once went away, and because she was exactly the one we needed, we looked for her lost pattern everywhere. She couldn't have fallen into the trash because the wastebaskets were all empty. There was nobody around to take her. The worst part of her loss was that she was wrapped in patterns a friend had lent me. Someone said, "Maybe she doesn't want to be put in a book"; someone else, "Maybe if you stop looking she'll come back." I said, "As soon as I finish this chapter I'll make a new pattern."

Then one morning she was lying in her envelope in the yellow straw wastepaper basket, every piece of her. The borrowed pattern was there, too, and was quickly returned to its owner. The pattern for Dilly can never be lost again, for here she is. But, first, having gone this far with personal reference, I am reminded that most people have a lifelong unfulfilled wish. For years mine was to own a big rag doll. A neighbor child owned one, but she never let any of us hold it, and I never happened to receive one of my own. When Dilly came, and my wish came true, I *had* to make her.

The name *rag doll* should perhaps be changed to *cloth doll,* for the word *rags* somehow seems to imply tattered throwaways. In the past cloth dolls have been made of muslin, felt, silk, burlap, rubberized cloth, stockinette, and stockings. They have been filled with straw, grass, cotton, unspun wool, cotton waste, and now the modern synthetics.

Rag dolls have been made life-size, as the Martha Chase dolls were made to be used in hospitals and clinics for training nurses how to handle patients. Chase dolls were made also as play dolls, but the hospital dolls were manufactured almost to the beginning of the second World War.

During this same period and a little earlier, dolls were printed in color on cloth and given as premiums with breakfast cereals. There were Rastus, with Cream of Wheat; Aunt Jemima, with pancake flour; Sunny Jim, with Force; to say nothing of the rag dolls given with soups, washing powder, and clothing. The Adams Print Works in North Adams, Massachusetts, printed many of these cloth dolls in color, ready to be cut out, sewn together, and stuffed. Some of the original plates have

*Dilly is a modern doll made in old-time style.*

*Dilly, the rag doll has red hair and blue eyes and wears a wistful look.*

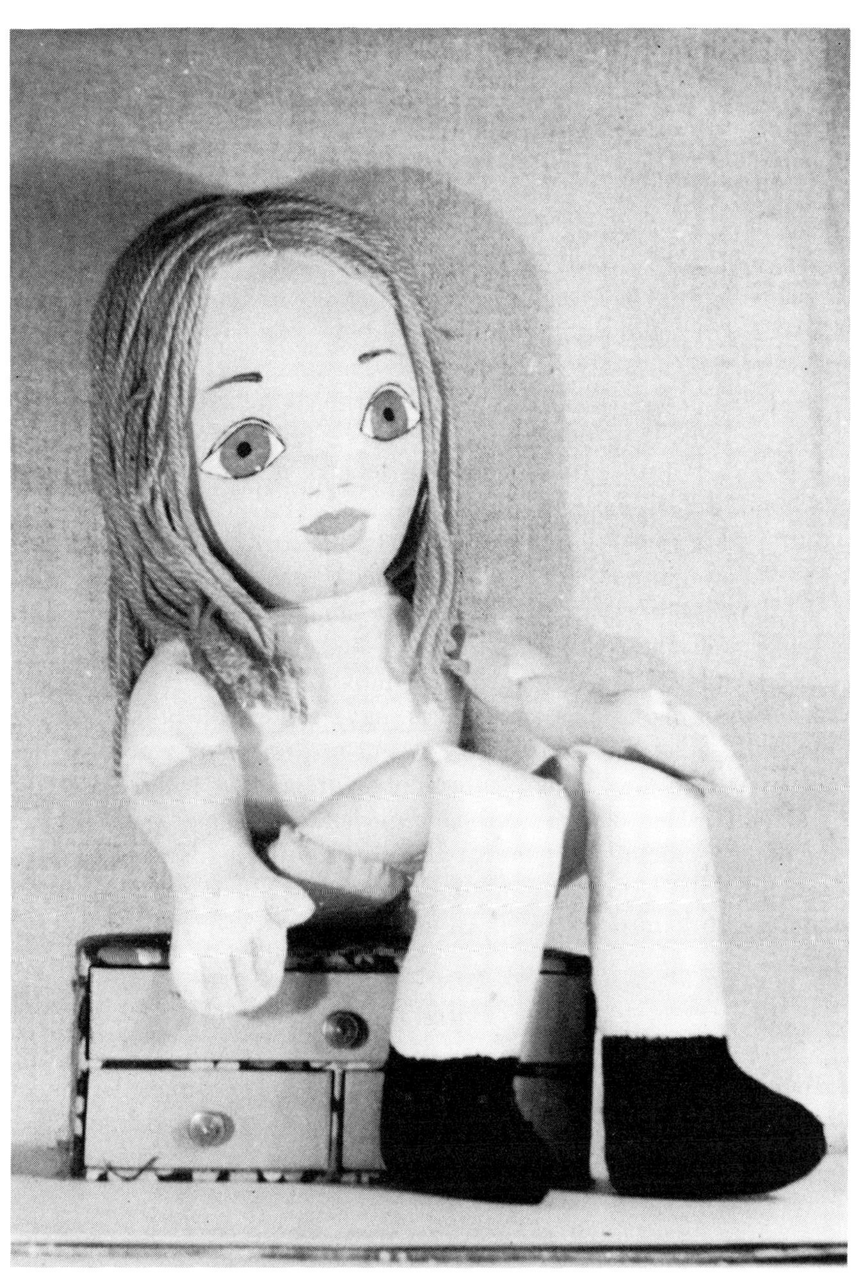

*Dilly's arms and legs bend nicely so she can sit down or stand up.*

been reprinted for modern doll collectors, and some day they will have the charm of the mellowed originals.

Later types of rag dolls were the long-legged, floppy ones called "boudoir dolls," popular with ladies in the 1920s, and often placed on the guest-room bed, made into telephone covers or lamp shades. Some day they will be considered antiques, and collectors will pay fantastic prices for them.

In the more than fifty years since Johnny Gruelle wrote the Raggedy Ann stories, the Raggedy Ann and Andy dolls have never lost their appeal. They are true rag dolls, and as sentimental as can be imagined, with the red heart sewed to their bodies bearing the words, "I Love You." These dolls have changed very little during their long lives, and the holders of their copyright also hold the copyright for the paper patterns and transfers sold to home dollmakers.

Browsing today through a toy department, one is struck by the scarcity of dolls that look like dolls, not caricatures, pretty, soft, and huggable; to be played with, not just looked at. Dilly is just a doll, a modernized version of the lost and found doll.

Little girls go through a period of taking a doll friend with them wherever they go, and such a soft doll is Dilly, neither too large nor too small, one to dress and undress, one a mother, aunt, or grandmother can make, and one that can even be washed.

Instead of the old-fashioned rag dolls with printed features and heavy, cotton-filled bodies, our doll is made of permanent-finish cotton stuffed with today's delightfully light and resilient polyester fiber that is also washable, and either embroidered or painted with waterproof acrylic paint. Her clothes can be removed or changed, as children enjoy doing, and unlike some of the other dolls in this book she is a play doll. She is about twenty-five inches tall. Please read chapters 1 and 2 again before you begin to make her.

### *Pattern*

To use the pattern, trace the sections shown on a sheet of paper and cut out. The head and body back are to be considered one piece, and should be joined at the neck edge, matching the letters as shown on each.

### *Materials Needed*

One-half yard pale pink permanent finish broadcloth for body

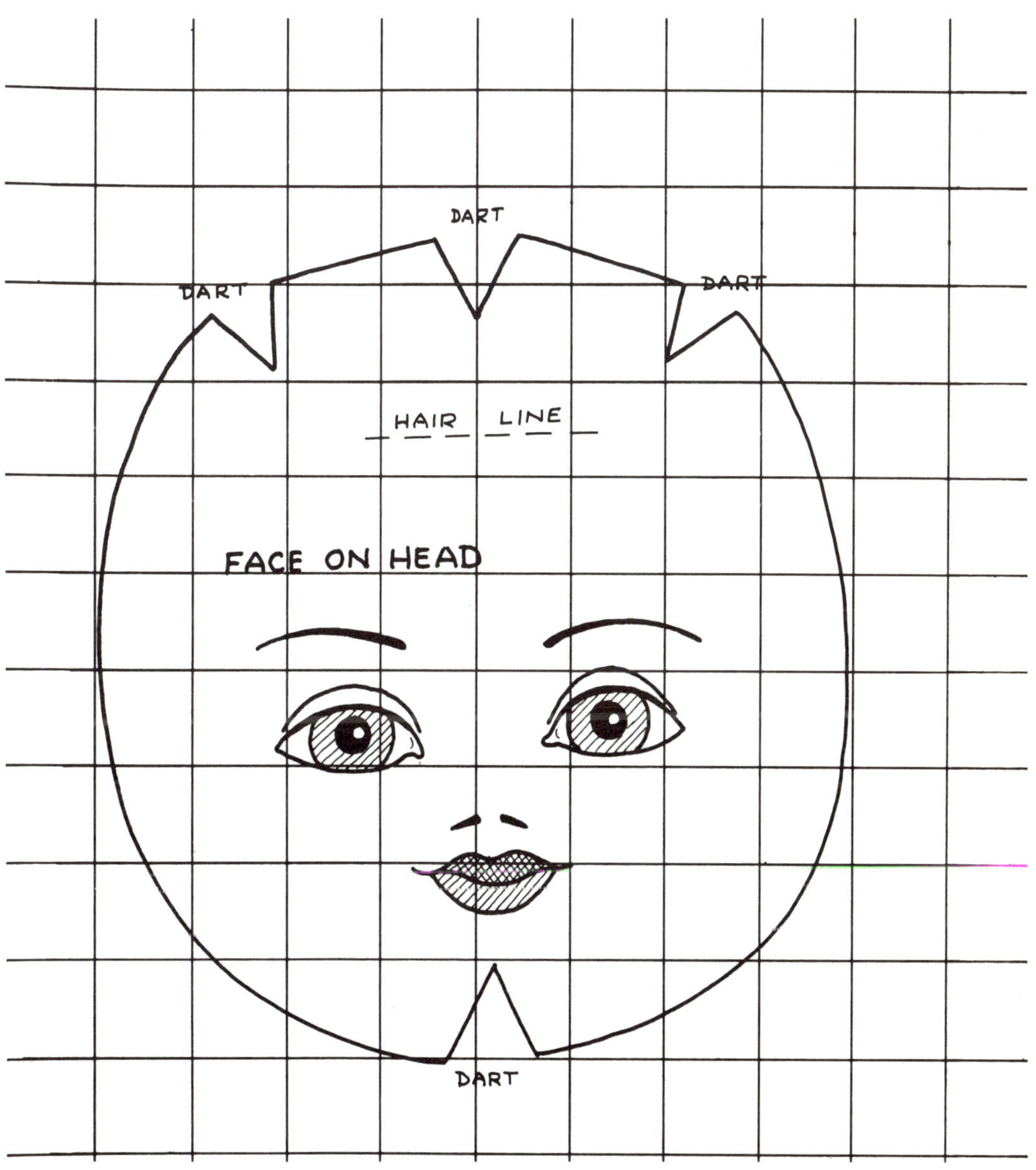


*Face and head pattern for rag doll.*

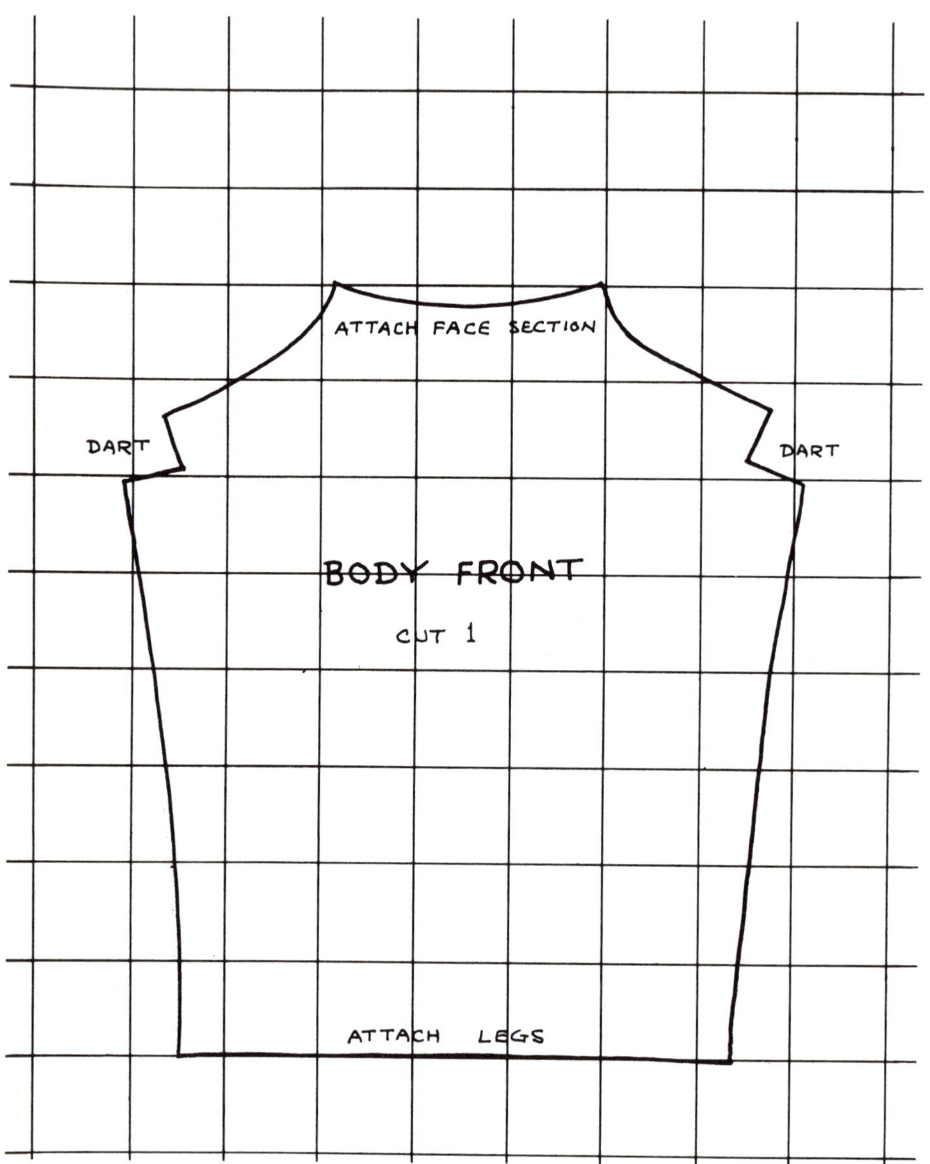


*Body front pattern for rag doll.*

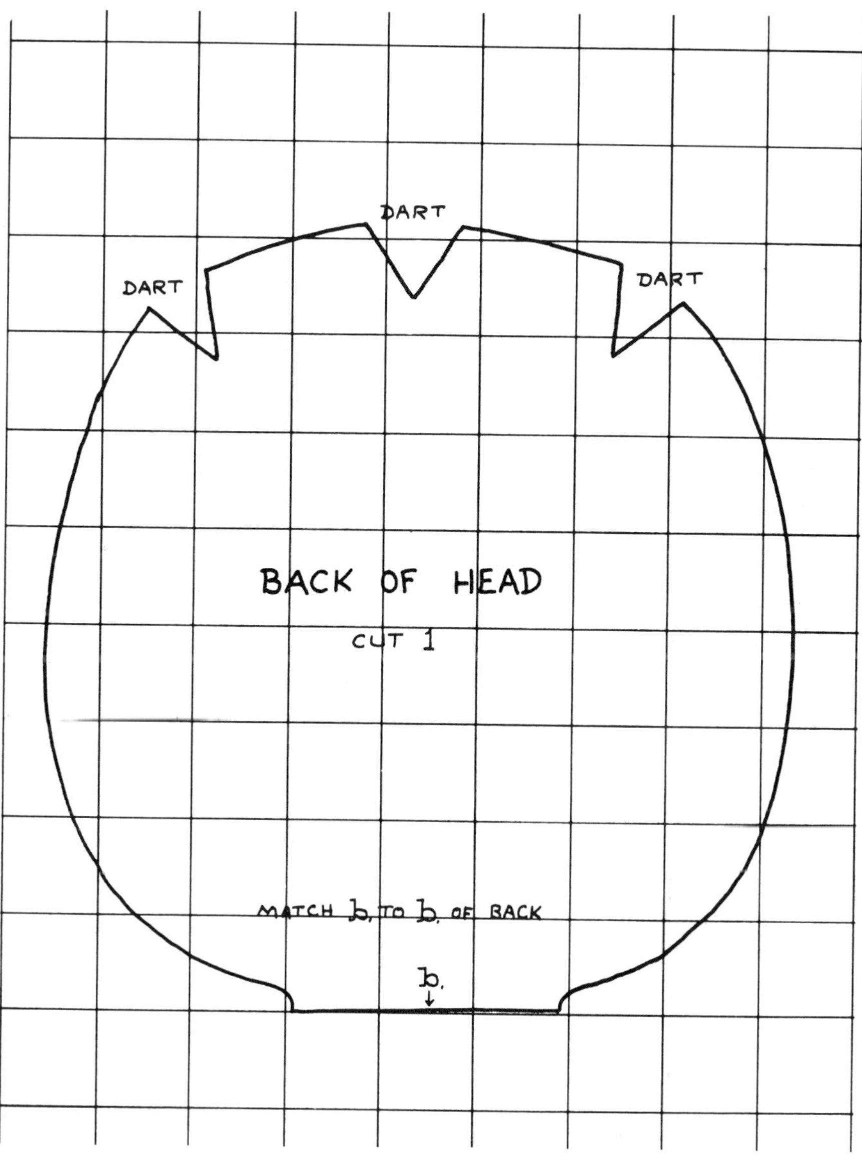


*Back of head is cut with pattern for back of body, matching patterns for the two at the neck, before cutting.*

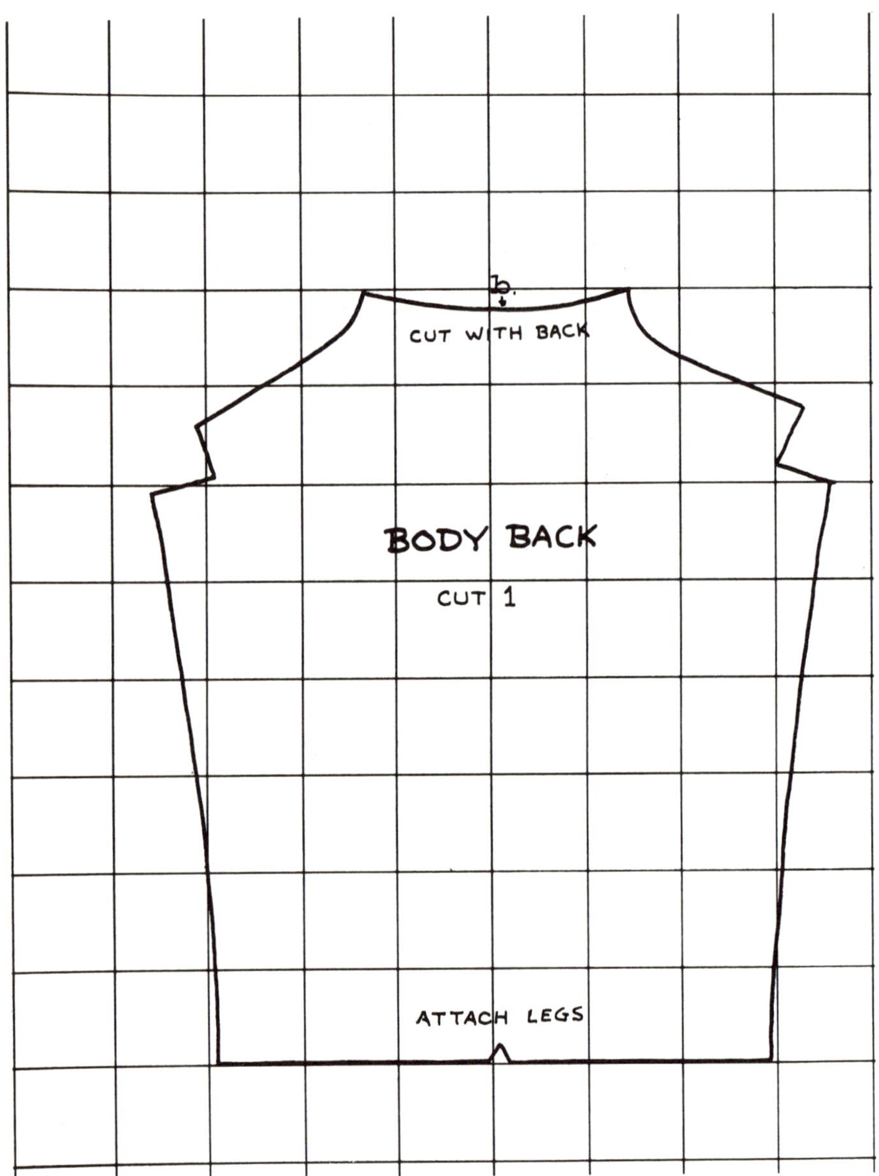


*Back of body.*

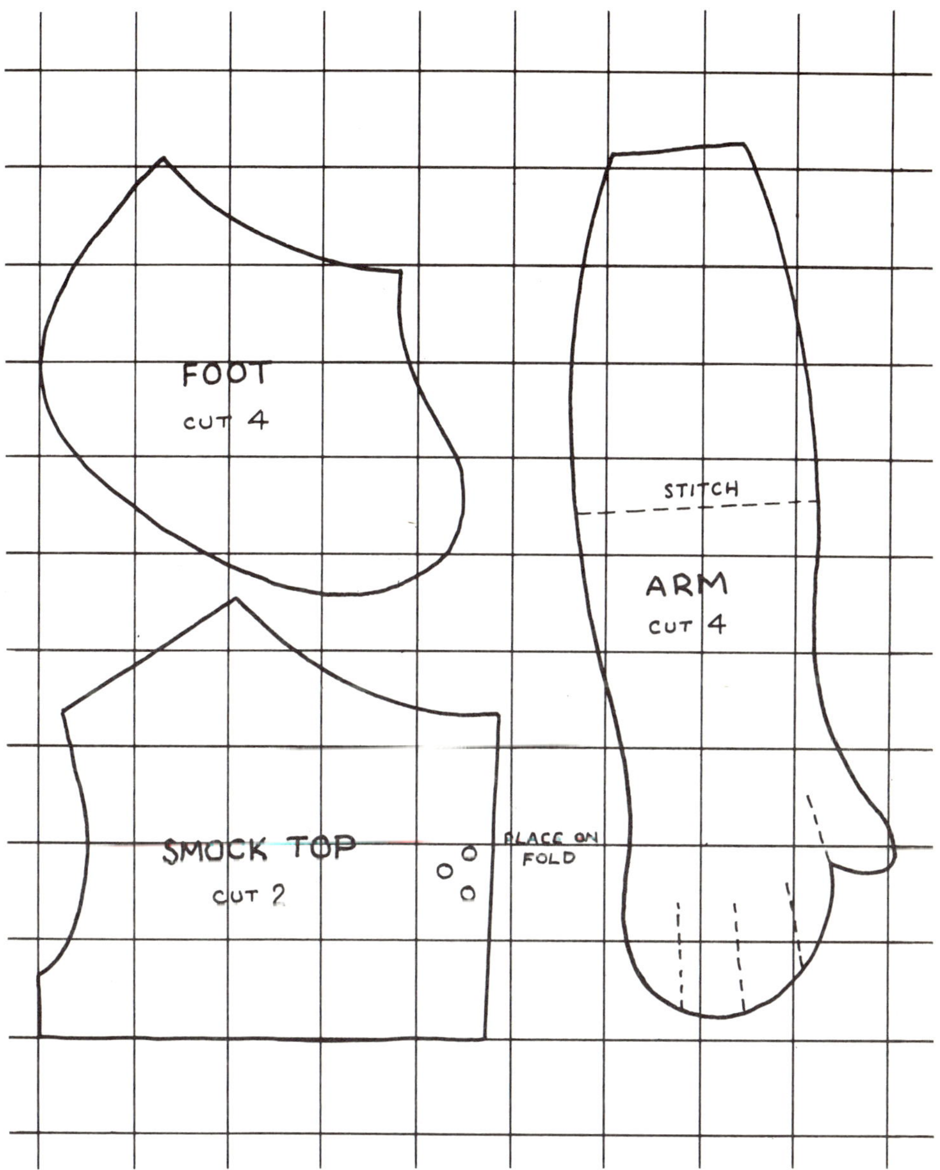


*Arm and leg patterns.*

One hank nylon and cotton rug yarn for the hair—black, brown, or yellow
Small scrap of black or brown felt for the feet
One-quarter yard small-flowered cotton cloth for smock
One-quarter yard plain colored cotton material for pants
Blue, red, white, and black acrylic paint
Watercolor brush

### *Method*

Spread out the body material and place the pattern pieces on it. Then draw lightly with pencil around each piece. Join seams on marks.

Cut out one-quarter inch from the pencil marks.

Sew the darts as shown on the pattern, making one-quarter-inch seams.

Trace the face on the front head section and paint as indicated on the diagram. Let dry thoroughly.

Whip edges of foot pieces together and sew to edge of leg section.

Stuff feet and legs firmly to the dotted line. Then stitch along dotted line across the legs. Leave one-half-inch and stitch again across legs at the next dotted lines. Stuff top part of legs. Turn in top edges and baste together.

Sew the arms seams on the pencil line, but leave the tops open for stuffing. Begin stuffing at hand, stitching the fingers as indicated on diagram. Stitch across arm at dotted line. Finish stuffing the arm very lightly. Close top edge and whip edges together.

Sew the face section to the top body section at neck. Baste, and then stitch the front to the back, leaving the space between notches at top of head open for stuffing later.

Turn rightside out and stuff the body and head as far as the neck.

Take a Popsickle stick or a tongue depressor and wrap it tightly in cloth and then some of the stuffing to pad it. Place this inside the body halfway between the shoulder and the top of the head. This will keep the head from flopping and is very important. Continue stuffing firmly. Turn in top edges previously left open at the top of head and whip them together. This joining will be covered by the wig.

Sew upper leg section to the bottom of the body section firmly, with double thread, since the greatest strain will take place here when the doll is played with. Fasten thread securely. Now sew the arms to the body, at the dart, in the same way as the legs were sewed.

Make a wig by spreading out the hank of rug yarn and indicating the part with a row of basting stitches run through a strip of cellophane tape. This will keep the yarn in place while the part is being marked by a row of backstitches made with thread the color of the body. Attach the wig to the head at the part line. With half-strands of the yarn, tack the wig to the sides of the head, invisibly, at several places. Trim to the desired length for braids or a shoulder-length cut, or make curls instead of the straight hair, as shown in sketch. The hair line is shown on the pattern, and is two inches above the eyes.

### *Dressing*

The patterns for smock and pants may be easily changed, with slight variations, to underwear and knee-length or long dress. Allow one-quarter-inch seams when cutting out the garments. Instead of making a waistband on the pants run elastic through the casing at the top. Fasten the smock with snap fasteners at neck and waist, or with hooks and eyes rather than buttons, because they are easier for a small child to use.

Don't forget to put your name and the date someplace on the doll.

As for washing a doll like this, do not place in a washing machine, but make a stiff suds and wipe it lightly over the surface, then rinse the same way.

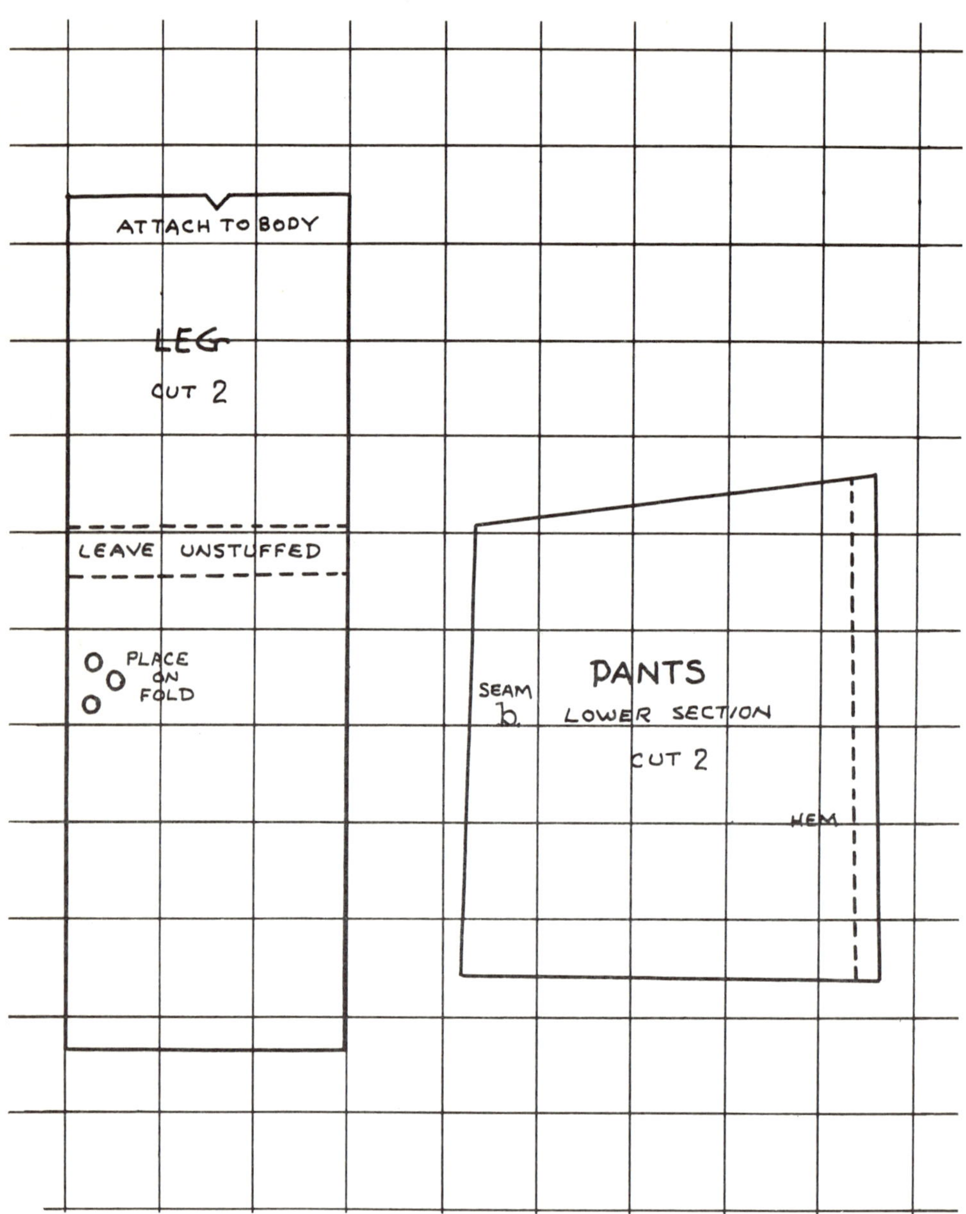


*Lower section of pants pattern is cut in one with the upper section.*

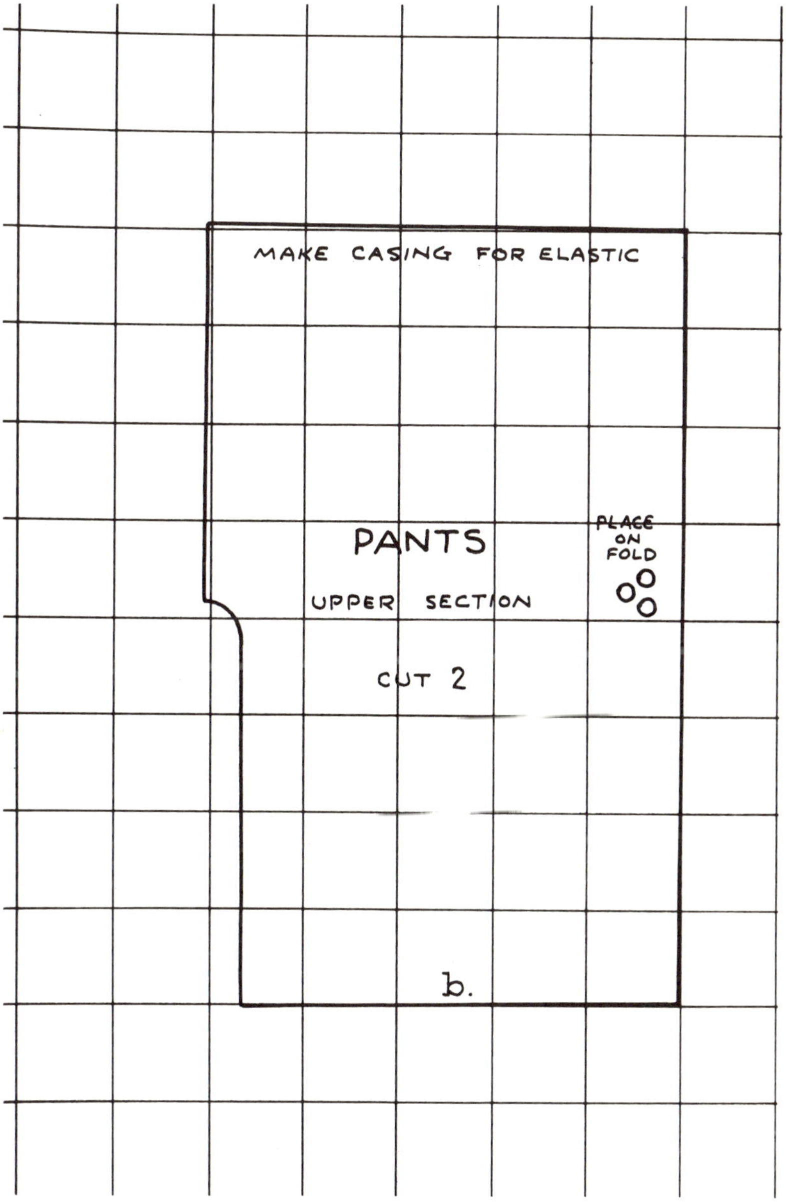

MAKE CASING FOR ELASTIC

PANTS

UPPER SECTION

CUT 2

PLACE ON FOLD

b.

*Upper section of pants pattern is cut in one with the lower section.*

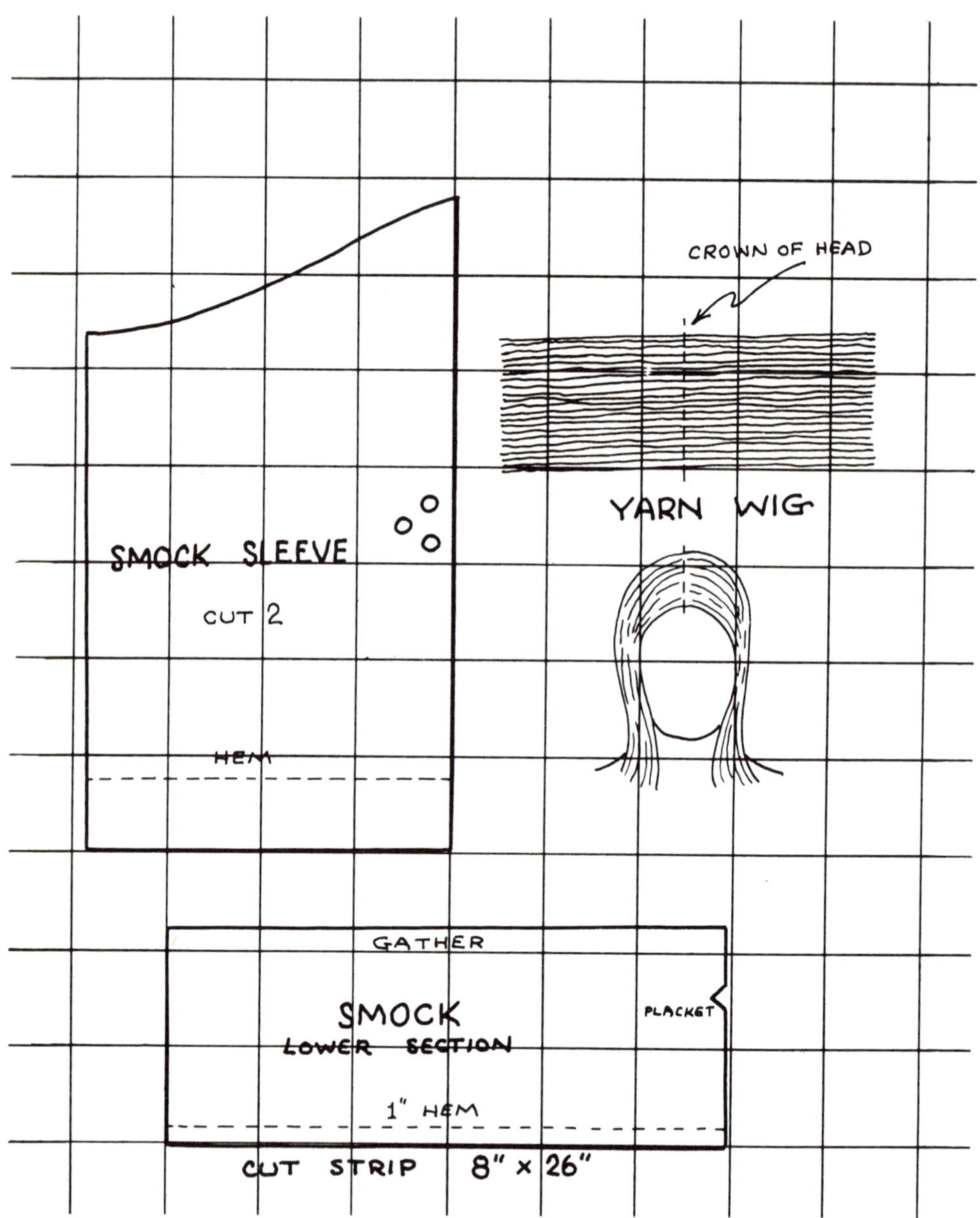


*Pattern for the doll's smock and the shoe or foot section. The foot is to be joined to the leg section.*

# 6

# *Black and Beautiful Baby*

Call it revolution, or the beginning of a resolution of old, old problems, the late 1900s are making changes in social attitudes that are being absorbed by our culture in various and subtle ways. Attitudes toward racial differences, changing so much in one brief lifetime, are perhaps among the most drastic. Dolls have always told a great many things about the people who made them, for dolls are extensions of their tastes, appearance, fashions, and occupations.

In the Middle Ages, the Church was the inspiration for the elaborate crêche figures of France and Italy, and these were in reality dolls. In later Europe, fashion and entertainment were often the preoccupations of moneyed people who could afford luxuries and their interests were recorded in the fragile and lovely fashion dolls and their fabulous wardrobes.

A collection of American dolls would systematically illustrate the history of the continent, beginning with the Indian primitives, the dolls contrived by pioneer mothers, the doll trade with Europe, the scarcity of domestically produced dolls, the effects of World War I, ending the domination of the toy industry by Germany, and the eventual entry of other countries into the importation and manufacture of dolls. Increase in travel, all forms of communication, and the unheard of prices being paid for rare dolls, all affected what was being made as well as what was being sold. The development of plastics had both good and evil results, while the popularity of children's television programs shifted part of the interest in dolls from children to adults. Along with all of these changes there were others being made, socially and racially.

In the early part of the nineteenth century, France, England, Spain, and Holland were building empires, and many of their colonies were in parts of the world where the natives were dark-skinned. France, particularly, with its eye on markets for its doll factories, made brown bisque dolls for its colonies in the West Indies. They were usually different from the pink bisques only in skin color, the identical molds being used for both. These were lovely dolls, but hardly ethnic.

The American minstrel shows that toured the country created the image of the black as a comedy character, and the Rastus and Sambo and Aunt Jemima dolls perpetuated the idea. Again, dolls reflected the customs and ideas of the people.

After the race riots of the 1960s, and particularly the Watts, California, riots, where large sections of a city were burned, a movement was begun by the black residents themselves, and they called it Operation Bootstrap. The idea of it was to do just what the name implied, pull the people up by their own bootstraps, creating industries and businesses, rebuilding "charcoal alley," and most of all, training and hiring the horde of unemployed black people living in Watts.

Shindana—a Swahili word which means *to compete*—was organized as a part of Operation Bootstrap. It was formed in November 1968, and as a nonprofit organization, became the first one of its kind in the United States devoted only to the making and selling of black dolls, designed by black designers and under black management.

Their honorary manager, Louis Smith, is quoted as saying, "By getting black dolls into the hands of Negro girls, it hopes to upgrade their self-image. It has always disturbed us that dolls were not representative of black kids; imagine black kids playing with blonde, blue-eyed dolls." Smith also believes that by playing with black dolls, "white kids will have less chance of growing up with racist attitudes."

The Shindana dolls are therefore not brown-skinned dolls made in the same mold as white-skinned dolls, and neither are they the comedy toys once entirely made by white manufacturers, but expressions of changing attitudes toward various parts of society, both white and black.

It seems appropriate to have Baby be a play doll, one a small child can hold and take to bed, with no danger of its eyes being pulled off and swallowed, or its body being broken when thrown on the floor. The simple clothes are easy to take off and put back on, with no bothersome ties or buttons to struggle with. Another doll mystery, of course, is why children promptly remove a doll's clothes the first thing. With Baby it doesn't matter.

Baby is also one of the simplest dolls to make, and one not too

*Baby is a lovable armful for even a small child.*

hard for a young dollmaker to achieve alone. As with Dilly, this stuffed toy is made of cloth, in this instance entirely of felt, which is easy to work with and comes in many colors. Babies love bright red and yellow, and Baby's clothes would be fun to make in their gayest shades.

The hair is made of black yarn sewed directly on the head, so there is no wig to bother with, and the features are either embroidered on in simple stitches or are bits of felt, appliquéd.

If you prefer making and dressing Baby in some other material than felt, brown broadcloth is suggested for the body, and almost any kind of woven material could be used for the clothes. If that is done, the pieces should be cut with a narrow seam allowance.

### *Materials*

One-half yard dark brown felt for the doll's body
Two twelve-inch squares white felt for shirt
Scraps of black felt for eyes
Small scrap red felt for mouth
Two twelve-inch squares turquoise-blue felt for overalls
Three ounce hank black rug yarn or knitting worsted
Sewing thread to match the colored felts
Polyester fiber for stuffing

### *Pattern*

No seam allowance need be made, since the edges of the felt are whipped together.

### *Method*

Cut out all pieces as shown on the drawings.

Trace the features onto the face section, using white chalk or white pencil.

Overcast the edge of the nose piece and pull up the stitches to fit the pattern. Stuff lightly with the fiber stuffing and tack the nose securely onto the face with no stitches showing.

Cut circles of black felt for the eyes and appliqué on the face with black thread. At the corners of the eyes, make short stitches of white thread to represent the whites of the eyes.

Indicate the eyebrows with two or three outline stitches of black thread.

Appliqué the mouth on the face section and make a short line of outline stitches through the center, of dark red. Make one short couching stitch over the center of this line. If the center line and couching stitch are kept short, the lips will seem to be fuller, which is desirable.

Cut out the dart under the chin and overcast the edges together with short, fine stitches.

Match the notch on the head section with the notch on the head insert section, overcasting the two together.

Whip together the arms and legs sections, leaving open at the top edge to insert the stuffing. When stuffed, close these openings.

Place the two body sections together and overcast closely, leaving an opening at the back of the head for stuffing the doll.

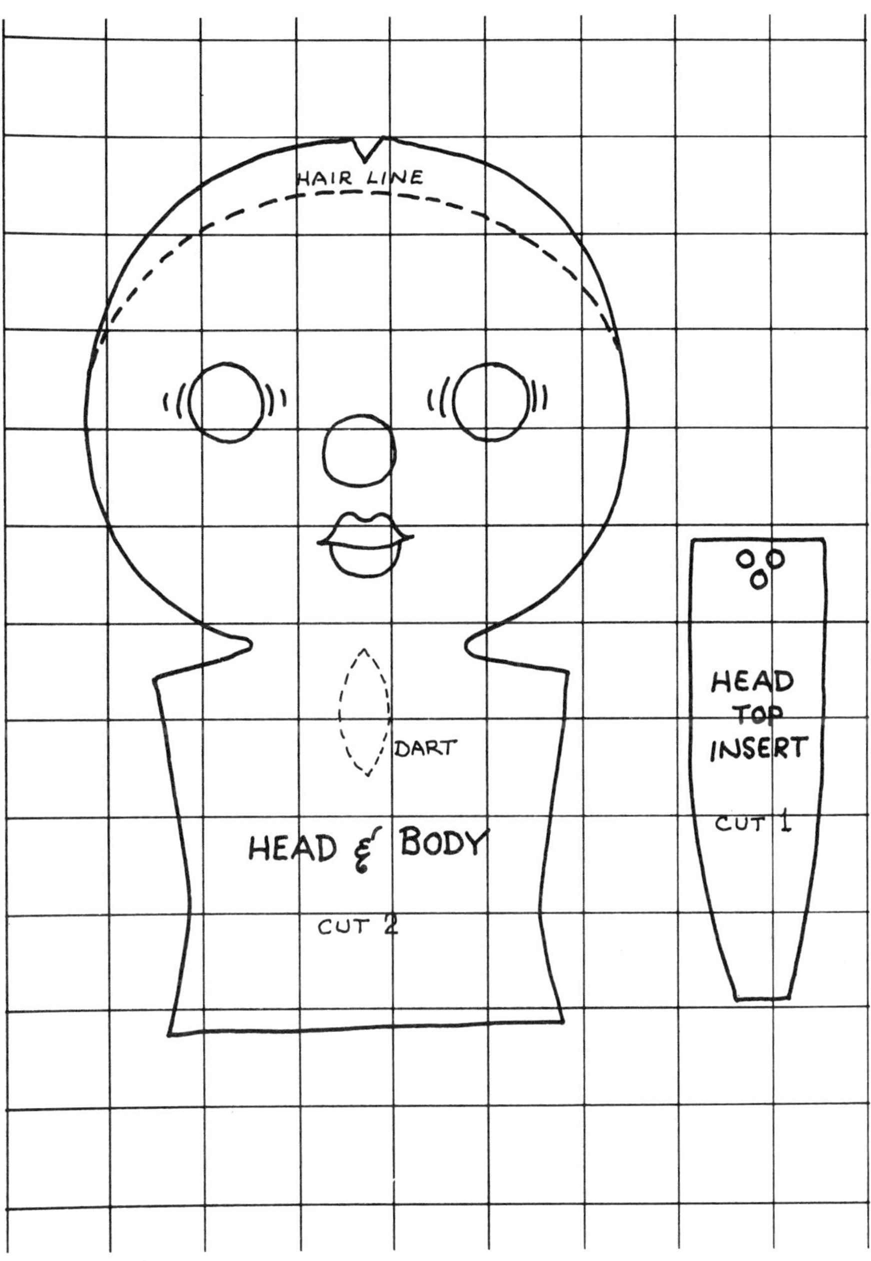


*Head and body for Baby are cut double, with a section inserted at top of head to make it round.*

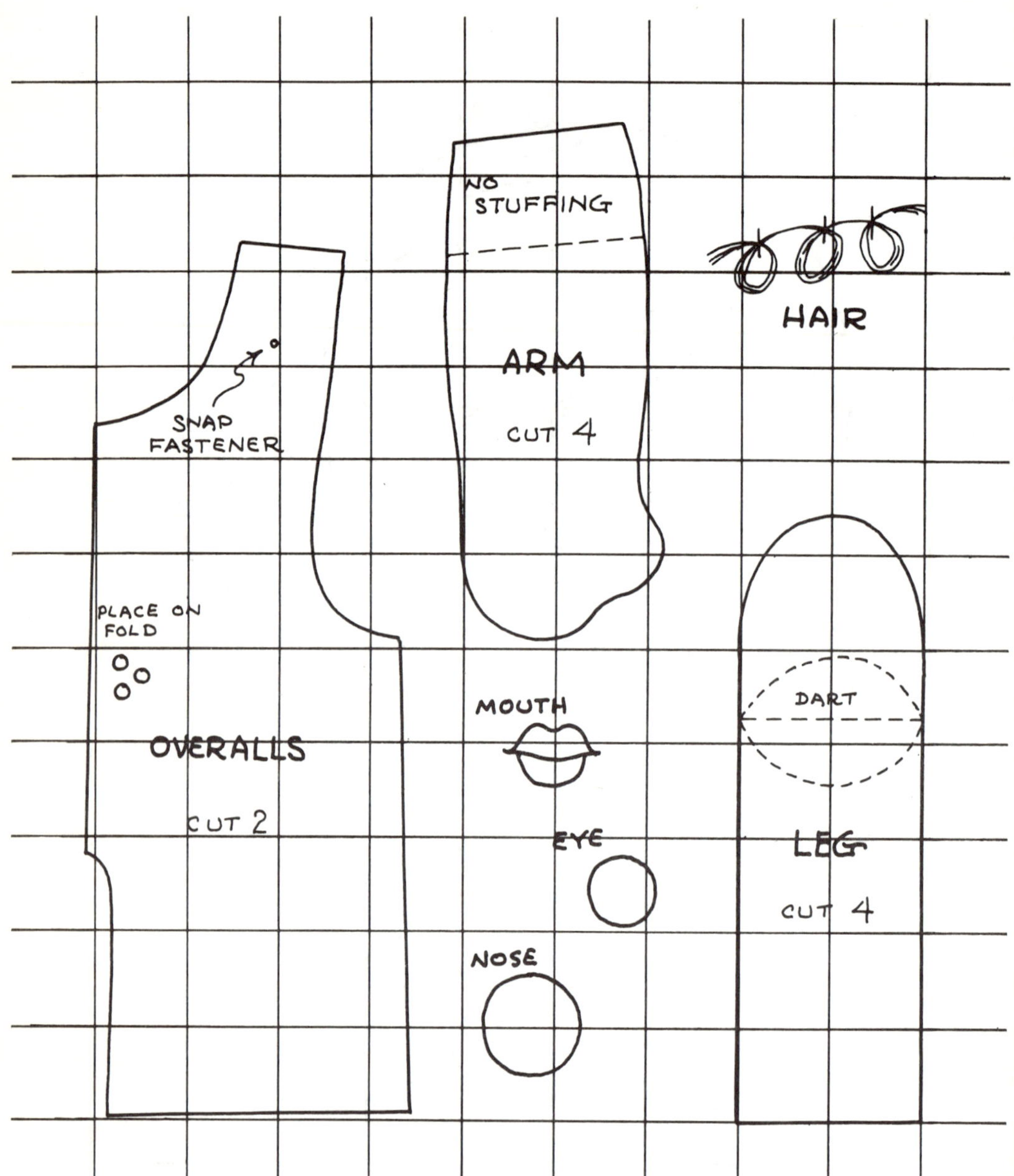


*Patterns for arms and legs and the doll's overalls.*

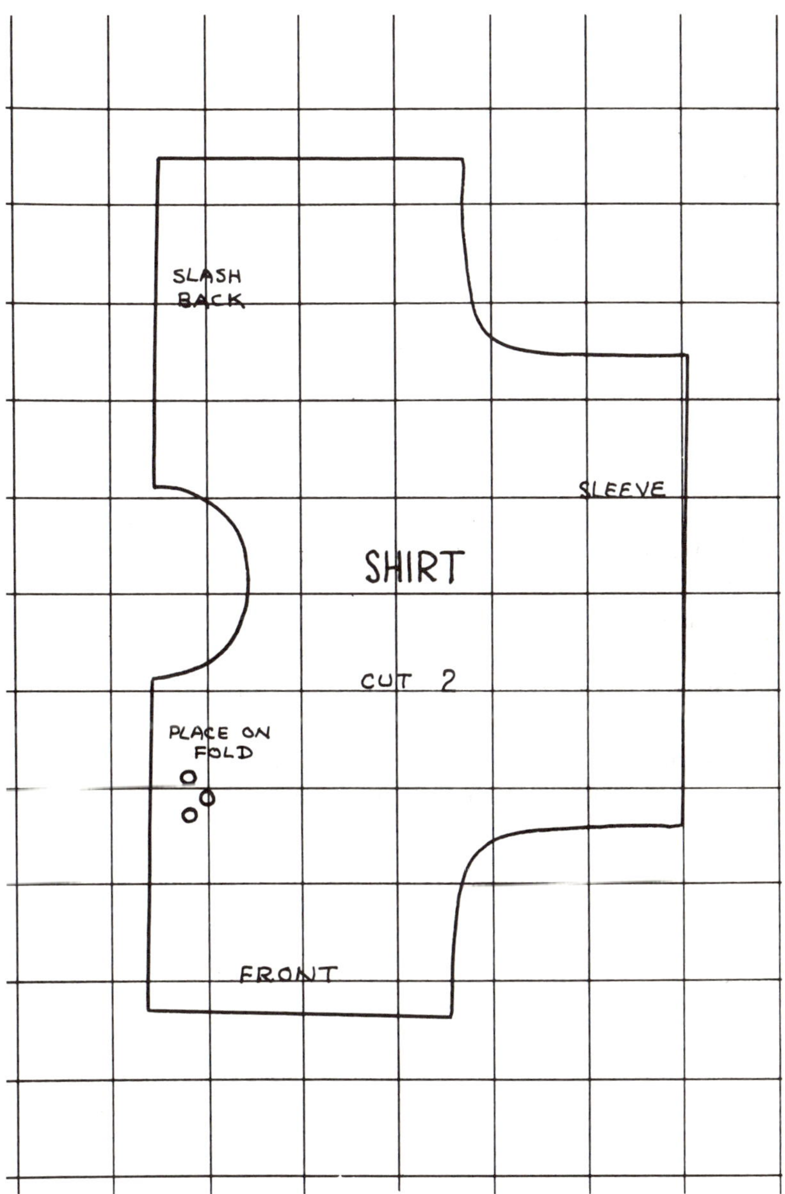


*Shirt pattern for Baby is to be laid on lengthwise fold of material.*

Wrap a thin stick with a scrap of cloth to pad it well, then after packing the body stuffing firmly and evenly, until it is almost to the neck, insert the stick and bury it in the stuffing, so that it will reinforce the neck between the head and shoulders. Continue packing the stuffing around it. This is most important, since otherwise the head would be floppy.

Make sure that the stuffing in the body is well packed into every curve and angle, and if necessary, press it down with a wooden spoon handle or a smooth stick as you go, making it firm.

After the head stuffing is completed, stretch the two edges of the opening together and sew securely.

### *Dressing*

This doll does not wear shoes, so at this point bend the feet to a natural position and hold them in place with several blind stitches at the darts shown on the pattern. These darts are not to be cut out.

Cut out and seam the shirt at underarms and sleeves. Turn rightside out. Sew snap fasteners at the neck opening, or close with buttons and buttonholes.

Cut out overall pieces as shown and seam as you did the shirt. Turn rightside out. Place snap fasteners on the shoulder pieces.

After the rest of the doll is completed, make the hair by threading a large darning needle with the black yarn. Sew rows of loops directly on the head, making the rows about one-half-inch apart. Begin at the crown of the head and continue out to the hair line. These loops are not to be cut.

# 7

# *The Crone of Threadneedle Street*

The utmost in realistic detail is to be found in a type of doll that the British call *pedlar* and Americans *peddler*. These dolls are alike in only a few respects: they are women, elderly, they wear mob caps, black bonnets, black dresses, and red shawls or capes. Each one carries a basket or has a tray suspended around her neck in which are the objects they are to sell. Their wares consist of pins and needles, tiny reels of cotton, jewelry, buttons, slippers, shoes, pots and pans, dishes, doll-size silverware, and dolls. In fact, they carry all of the articles that peddler women once hawked along the streets of London and up and down country lanes, or at village fairs. Because of the very nature of these dolls and their merchandise, there are never any two exactly alike, particularly among the older ones. It is clear that the owners of these dolls took great pains to outdo everyone else.

During all of its recorded history, the streets of London have been famous for noise and action, and in the 1700s, when peddler dolls first became popular, the city was lively and loud with the cries of hawkers and peddlers calling their wares, offering everything from cockles and mussels to Banbury tarts and needles and pins.

There were also men peddlers, tinkers, and the travelers who jogged through country lanes in the horse-drawn wagons in which they also lived. They, however, are not as fascinating and colorful to the doll owner as are the peddler women. These dolls are definitely not children's toys, but ones seeming to have special appeal for the more sophisticated ladies of fashion, who were fond of protecting and dis-

*Mrs. Murgelmouse without her black bonnet to show her needle sculptured face more clearly, and her white wool hair.*

playing them in the drawing room under a glass dome. There they were certainly what we call conversation pieces, and probably objects of envy among their high-born owners as they sipped their India tea.

Most antique peddler dolls are now in museums or private collections and seldom appear on the market, so if a dollmaker wishes to own one it is imperative that she make it, remembering that this is not a treasure for children to play with, but only to look at.

Our Mrs. Murgelmouse is dressed in the traditional costume of the

*Mrs. Murgelmouse peddles her wares, wearing a red shawl and black bonnet, an umbrella over her arm in case of rain.*

classic darlings of the past. She wears the crimson shawl, black dress, and a black bonnet on top of a lace mob cap, and carries a tray heaped and spilling over with beads, dishes, medals, and even a tiny doll, with an umbrella in event of rain.

Fortunately, Mrs. Murgelmouse has no need for a conventional body, and therefore needs nothing under her dress but a stiff petticoat or a wire frame, since only her head, hands, and feet are exposed.

This doll's head is made in needle-sculpture, a technique not original with this dollmaker, but certainly well worth experimenting with and not often described. As is also true with apple-heads, this is a method of dollmaking that even nonartists can amaze themselves with, and can make effective and unusual dolls by using it.

Needle-modeling is ideal for making old-people dolls, as are apple heads, allowing the dollmaker to depart from the conventional doll image in a purely creative way.

For Mrs. Murglemouse, patterns for the head, hands and feet are not given, since it is impossible to do so. The patterns for the clothes must be adjusted to fit your particular doll—an easy thing to do.

The head, hands, and feet are made of sections cut across the leg of a discarded nylon stocking, beige or tan-colored, and are stuffed with the versatile polyester fiber I have found ideal for making dolls because it packs smoothly under the stocking skin.

Her underwear is simplified, for she wears only a modest pair of pantalets. It is well known that doll-lookers always pick up a doll, then lift her skirts to investigate her underwear, and are disappointed if there is no lace nor tucks.

Underskirts are not really necessary for her, since she can be permanently wired to a conventional doll stand, or be supported by a cone of cardboard. Thus, the pantalets are useful in covering the wire framework that holds her together.

This doll is about twelve to fourteen inches tall, a good size for a peddler doll.

### *Materials*

One nylon stocking
Coathanger wire bent to make a hairpin shape about eleven inches long
White wool or yarn for hair
Blue, black or brown beads for eyes
Four pipe cleaners for arms
Florists' wire for tying framework
Scraps of fine lace, ribbon, sheer muslin
One-quarter yard bright red cloth for shawl
One-quarter yard soft black cloth for dress
Scrap of black felt for bonnet and shoes

### *Method—Body*

1. Cut a four-inch-wide section from the leg of a nylon stocking and in it place a wad of polyester fiber filling about the size of a large egg. Fold in half, crosswise, and gather both ends, making a sort of soft pad (a).

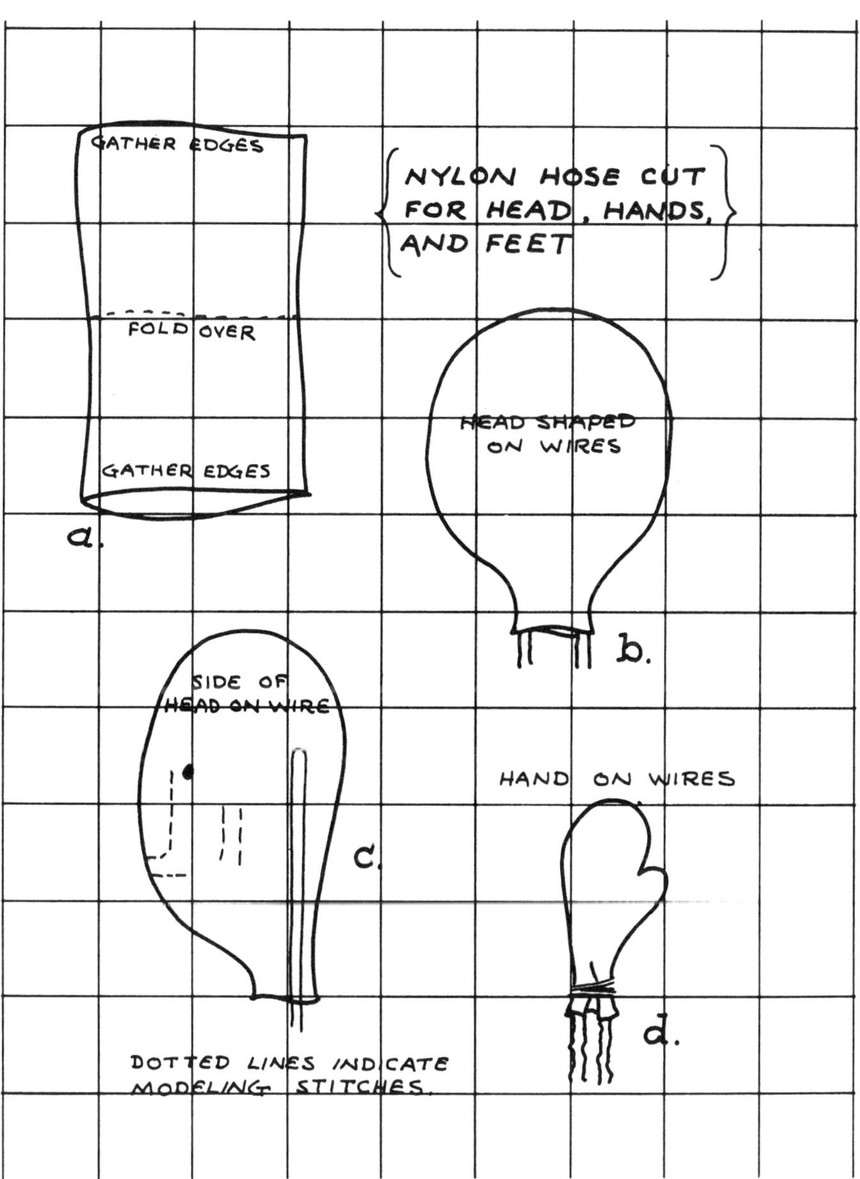


*Patterns and methods for making old lady's head, hands, and feet.*

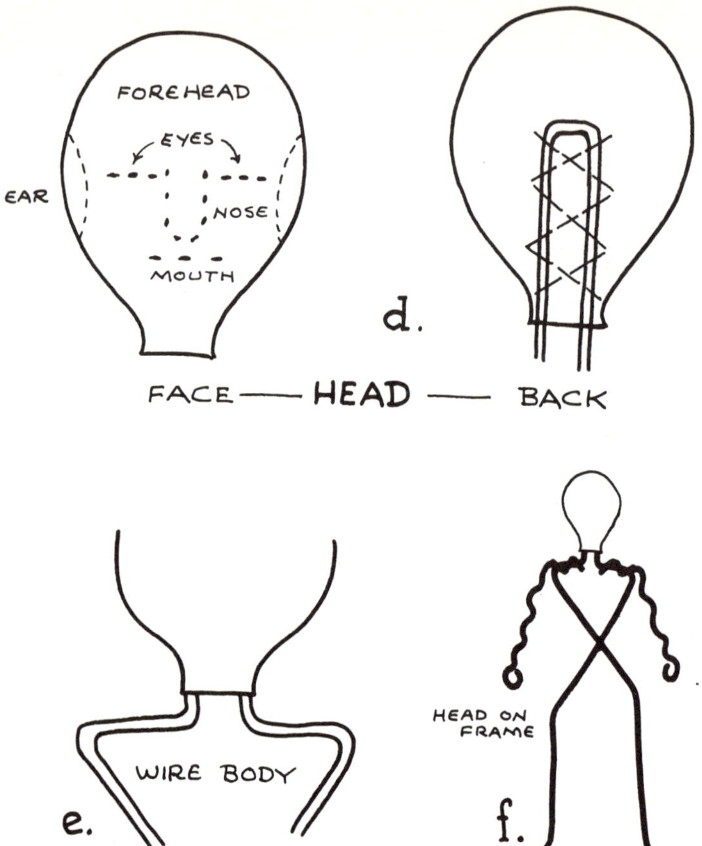


*Further details for assembling old lady, with diagram of stitching to create features of face.*

2. Sew the bent body wire to the back of this pad securely, so the front of the head will be egg-shaped and the neck will extend down over the wire as in the diagram. The head should be similar to (b).
3. Place two pencil dots halfway down on the face. This will be where the eyes are made.
Read chapter 1 carefully, for the placement of features.
4. Mark dots as in (c and d) on the face.
5. Thread a needle with thread that matches the color of the stocking. Run it through the head from the back to the eye dot. Now insert the needle back into the face about one-eighth inch from the eye dot. Pull the thread tight enough to make a depression for the eye. Repeat for the other eye.
6. Using the sketch (d), pinch the face between your thumb and

finger to form the nose, then the mouth, then the ears, for each feature taking one or two stitches to hold the shape. The ear should be about the same length as the nose, and directly in line with it.

7. The entire neck will be covered later, and so will the back of the head, so work simply for the front and side effect.

It is difficult to illustrate the exact way to do this modeling, so experiment. Each doll will be different, anyway.

8. For the hair, unravel a little of the wool or yarn and glue it directly on the top and sides of the head without trying to make a part. It is only necessary to have the hair show from the front, since the bonnet covers most of the head.

9. With pliers, twist the body wires (d and f). Hold the wires together at the waistline where they cross by winding a few twists of florist's wire around them to hold them firm.

10. Take small wads of the stuffing and pack it firmly between the wires of the torso.

11. Glue or sew a small bead in each eye depression. Mark the eyebrows with two or three short outline stitches of white or gray thread. Couch a line of red thread on the mouth depression to cover the modeling stitches. Tint the cheeks lightly with rouge.

12. Twist a double strand of the four pipe cleaners and wire them in the center to the center of the back of the neck at shoulder level. Bend the outer ends of the wires into loops to form bases for the hands.

13. Pad the hands with small wads of stuffing, then cover with a piece of stocking cut as in d. Repeat the same method for the feet.

14. Cut the rest of the nylon stocking into strips about two inches wide.

15. Pad the entire body with more of the stuffing to make it lifelike. Wrap the arms, first, with nylon strips, making a smooth skin. Wrap each leg the same way. Now, beginning at the neck, wrap the body. Fasten all ends securely and smoothly.

The doll is now ready to dress.

### *Dressing*

In using the patterns given here, some adjustments will be necessary, so it is a good idea to test them first by cutting out a tracing made on tissue paper. Pin this on the doll, and after making needed changes, cut the various pieces from the material, adding a one-quarter-inch seam allowance.

The pantalets are made of sheer white cotton, edged with one-inch-wide lace. Gather them at the top and sew onto the doll.

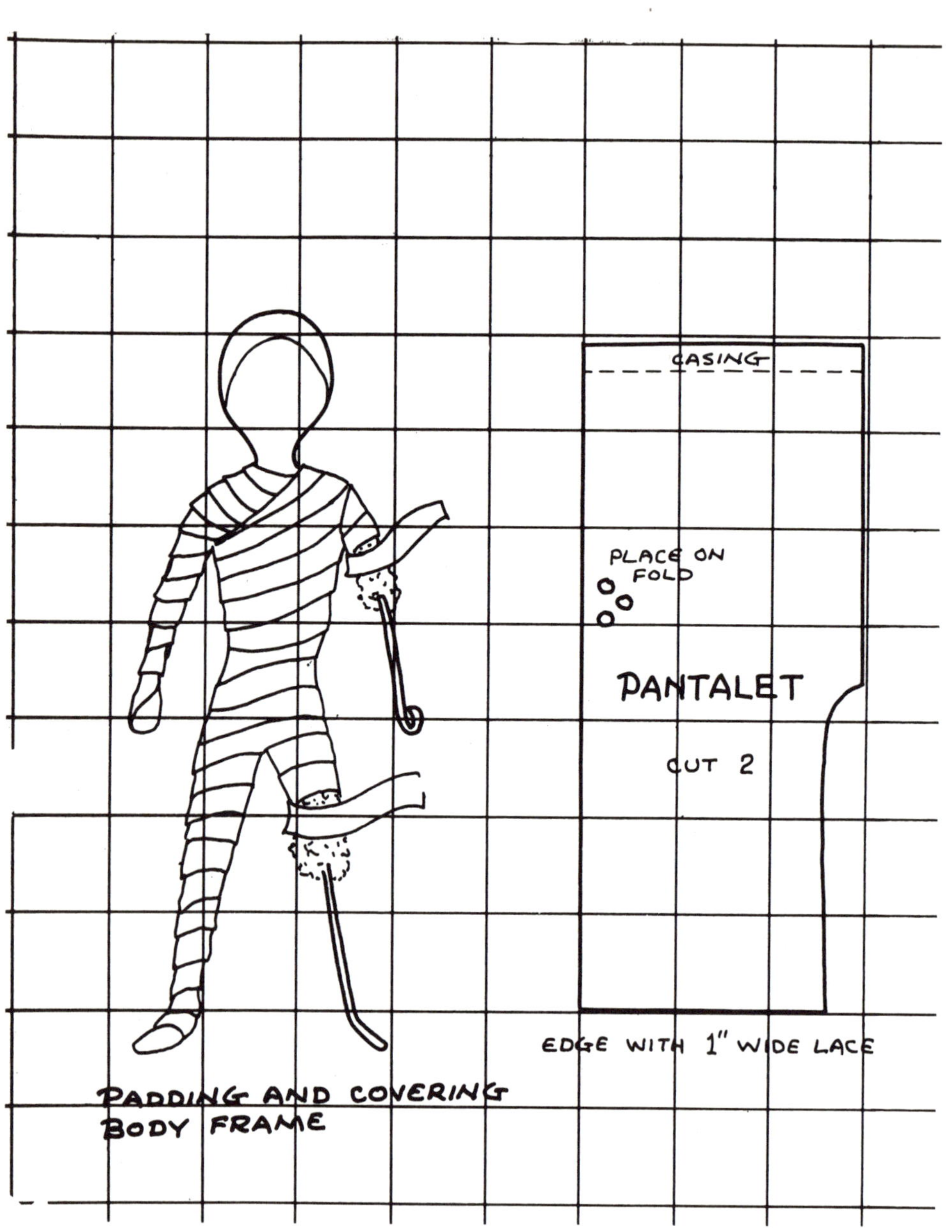


*Dressing the old lady doll calls for pantalets cut by this pattern, and a mob cap worn under bonnet, edged with lace.*

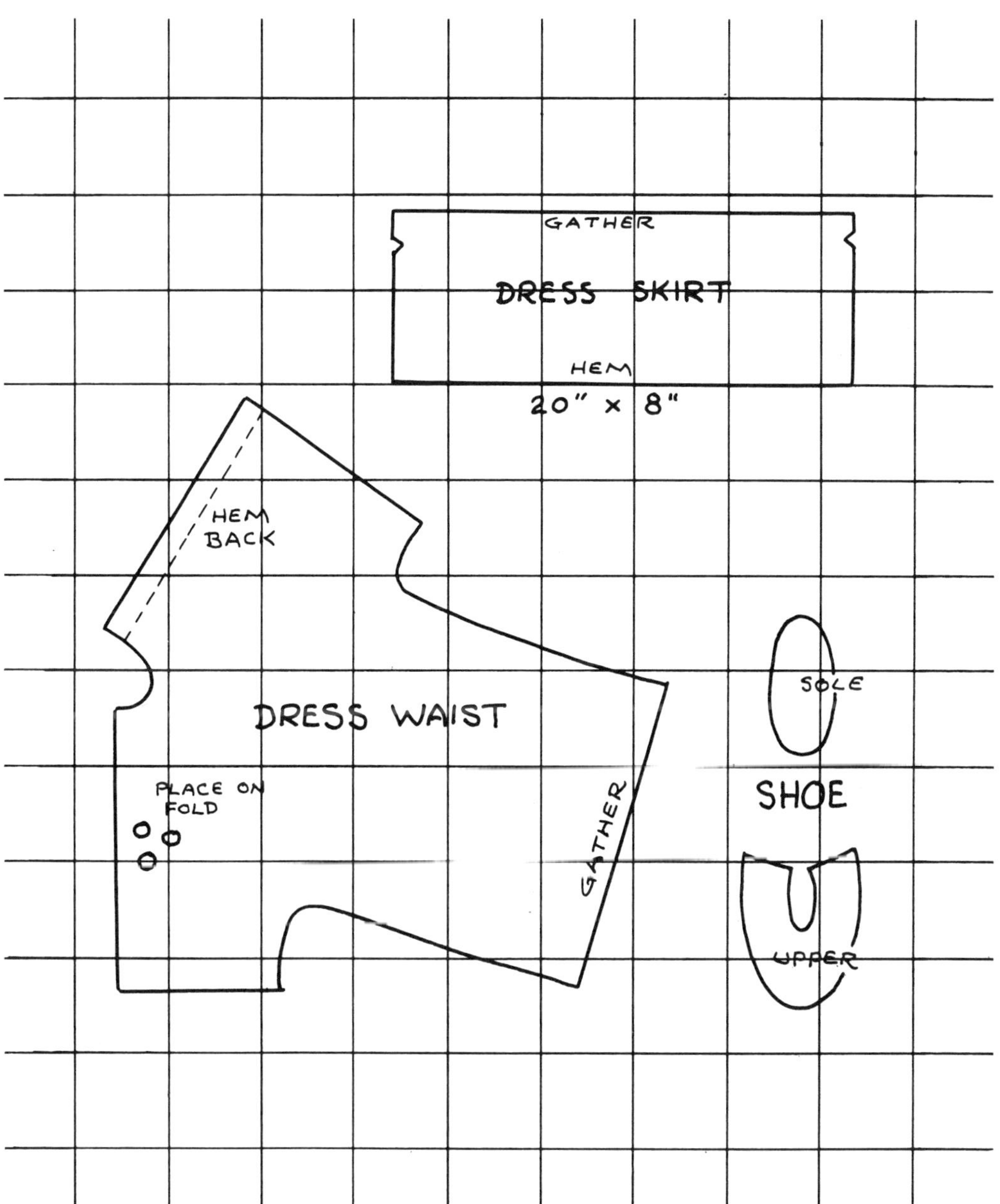


*Reduced pattern is for dress skirt, and full patterns are for dress waist and shoes.*

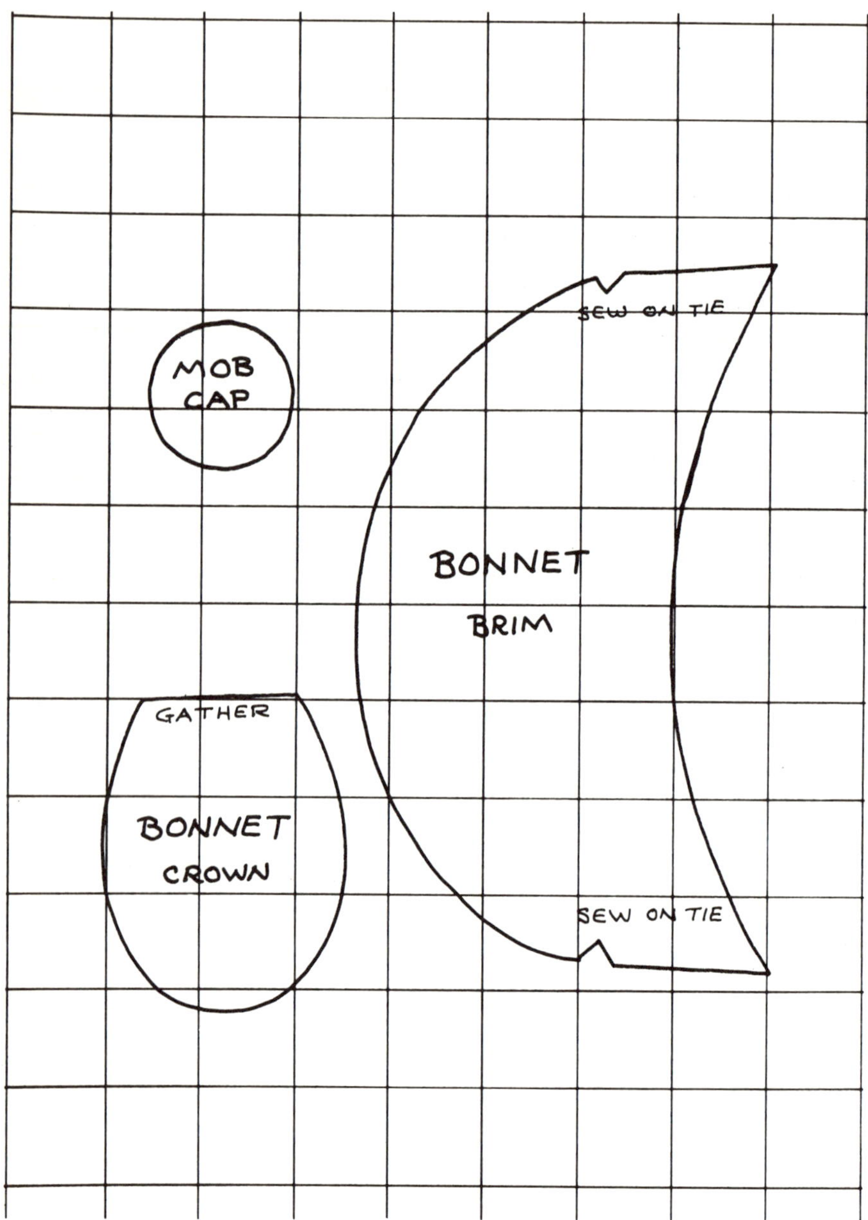


*The bonnet is cut from this pattern.*

The black dress is also sewn onto the doll, so no fasteners are used.

Make the red shawl by cutting a ten-inch square and folding it diagonally through the center. Fringe or narrowly hem the edges. Tack it together under the doll's chin.

Make the bonnet and shoes of black felt. The bonnet may be stiffened by cutting the brim double and inserting a layer of stiffening material, then sewing the edges together. Before tying on the bonnet, make a round mob cap by edging the sheer muslin center of the cap with a full ruffle of fine lace, then pulling it up into cap shape to fit the doll's head.

Mrs. Murgelmouse carries her merchandise in an oval tray suspended from her shoulders, but she could instead carry a large basket over one arm.

A peddler doll becomes a charming repository for your miniature toys, dishes, medals, favors, and buttons. She may also sell only flowers, hats and bonnets frothy with plumes and ribbons, or minute pastries, loaves of bread, and cakes, made of the dough mixture described in chapter 2 and painted realistically with acrylic paint.

Our old lady, as yours will be, is a challenge to the imagination and will be unlike any other doll.

# 8

# *Igloo Friends*

Visitors to our forty-ninth state bring home, when they can find them, dolls dressed as Eskimos. The least commercial of these are the ones made by the Eskimo people themselves, often in their mission schools. Unfortunately there are others made of plastic, with the obvious idea of attracting uncritical tourists.

I was fortunate in being asked by a native Alaskan to design and make true Eskimo and Tlingit Indian dolls, and I worked under this woman's direct supervision. These dolls, then, are authentic. One of them is a man—Wassilli-Wassilli, dressed in the well-known fur pants and parka. The other is his wife, who wears the summer parka, seldom seen on Alaskan dolls, made of bright calico and attached fur hood, just as the natives wear in the brief summer. The heads, hands, and feet of these dolls are modeled on a wire frame so that they may be bent to take any position. The fingers are made to hold a spear, harpoon, or a fine fat salmon as shown here.

### *Body*

The doll's body frame is to be completely covered, but in order to have the clothing hang realistically, the torso and waistline must be built up. It is also an advantage to have the doll able to stand on flat-soled feet sturdy enough to support it, even without a doll stand. These requirements have been taken care of.

*Eskimo dolls in their summer parkas. Authentic costumes like these add to the interest of a doll collection.*

*Wassilli-Wassilli displays a fine salmon he has just caught.*

This doll's body is essentially the same as that of the Indian's in chapter 9, and is based on the same familiar coathanger wire and the papier-mâché head and hands as described in chapter 2. However, Eskimo features are distinctive and the modeling is different. Cheeks are usually round, cheekbones are high, eyes slightly slanted, planes of the face flat, hair straight and black. Follow the sketch shown here as a guide. Eskimo women sometimes wear tattoo marks on their chins —a stripe down the middle when the girl is very young, and one added

*An igloo friend wears her summer parka and fur mukluks.*

on each side of it when the girl marries. Touches like this add interest and reality to the doll.

Hands may be made with wire fingers, as with the Indians, or molded of papier-mâché, or even of stuffed cloth.

The shoes are quite different than any others, as described later and shown in the illustrations, for they are really a part of the costume. With Eskimo dolls, costume is a main feature. Eskimo shoes are called mukluks. They are the same for both men and women, as is their winter

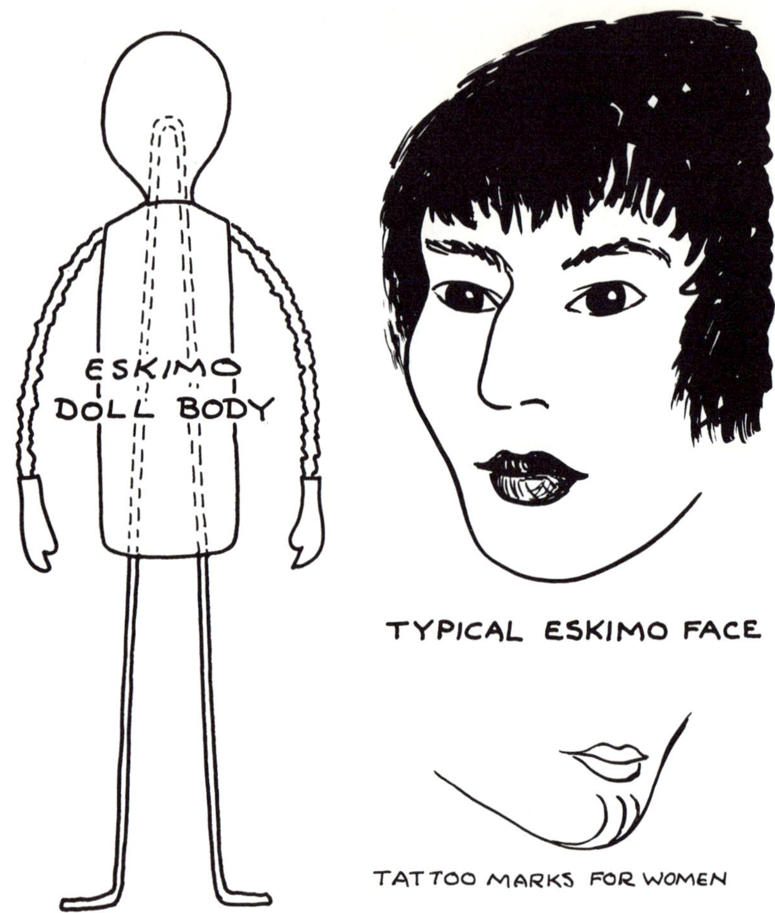


*Patterns for Eskimo body and typical Eskimo face, and for woman's face tattoo marks.*

costume. It is the women's summer parkas that are unique. They are made of brightly colored calico or cotton print trimmed with rows and rows of rickrack braid and with a fur hood attached. Often the women will let this fur hood hang down their backs and also wear a scarf tied over their heads when they go into the nearest village for gatherings.

Eskimos are happy people, and it is fun to work with their counterparts.

### *Method*

1. Straighten the wire from a coathanger and bend it in the middle to form a big hairpin, but do not cut the ends.

2. Mold the papier-mâché head directly on the bent part of the wire, referring to the sketch of a typical Eskimo face shown here. Since the doll will be from ten to twelve inches tall, the head should measure about two and one-half inches from the top of the head to the chin. Cover the wire below the chin to form the neck. Let dry for several days.
3. Paint the heads with acrylic paint tinted a light tan. The eyes, of course are always brown or black, and so is the hair, which may be made of fine wool yarn or of strands of hair from a black wig, glued on the head.
4. Make arms and hands by using four pipe cleaners twisted together

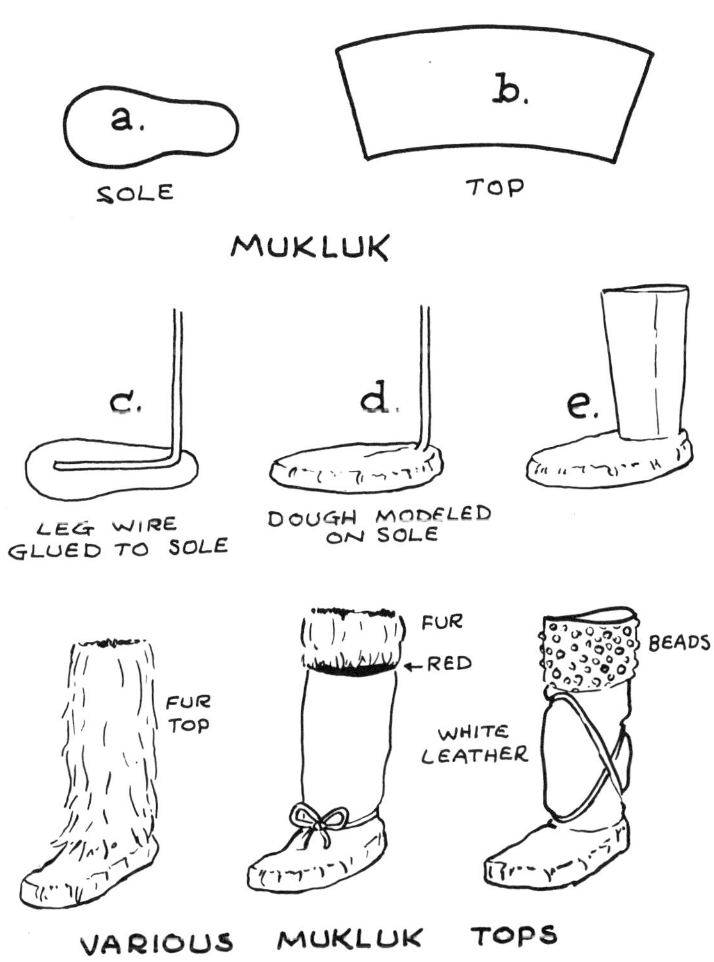


*Various styles of Eskimo mukluks are built on same leg and foot foundation.*

and bent into loops at the ends, then wired in the center to the body wire at the back of the head and below the neck.

5. Make the hands of papier-mâché or use the type described in chapter 9 for making separate fingers of wire.

6. Finish the body of the doll by wrapping the body wires with strips of cloth as far down as the hands to cover a firm layer of stuffing, then wrap the entire body with one-inch-wide bias strips. Make this covering as smooth as possible, fastening it securely, even though it will be completely covered with the clothes.

7. Measure the doll from the top of its head. At eleven inches cut the body wires, being sure they are the same length. Bend the ends at right angles to make an armature for the feet, which should be one inch long.

8. Cut two mukluk soles from pattern a, using medium-weight cardboard. Glue the foot wires to these soles. Let dry. Shown in c.

9. Mix a batch of bread crumb and glue modeling dough as described in chapter 2 and with it model mukluk soles as in d, over the cardboard and around the base of the wire.

10. While dough is still damp, cut two mukluk tops (b) from cardboard, fasten the back edges together and press the top down into the soft dough (e).

11. Allow to dry. This forms the complete foot in its mukluk and may be decorated in various ways, a few of which are shown, using beads, fur, narrow bands of color, or combinations of these, as you wish.

### *Dressing*

Add a narrow seam allowance when cutting out the clothes.

Ideally, real fur should be used for the winter parkas and for the woman's hood, but you may substitute fur cloth, which is easy to sew and looks quite real. Fur tails used to decorate the front of the man's parka may be made of a piece of thick white yarn dipped in black paint and twisted at the end.

The women's smmer parkas are cut from such tiny bits of cloth that no exact amounts are given. If you have no scrapbag borrow your neighbor's. Remember, the designs should be small and in scale with the size of the doll. It is possible to make these clothes entirely by hand, but no harm is done if you stitch the long seams on the machine. Any stitching that will show should be done by hand. It is permissible to use a selvage as an edge without trimming or turning.

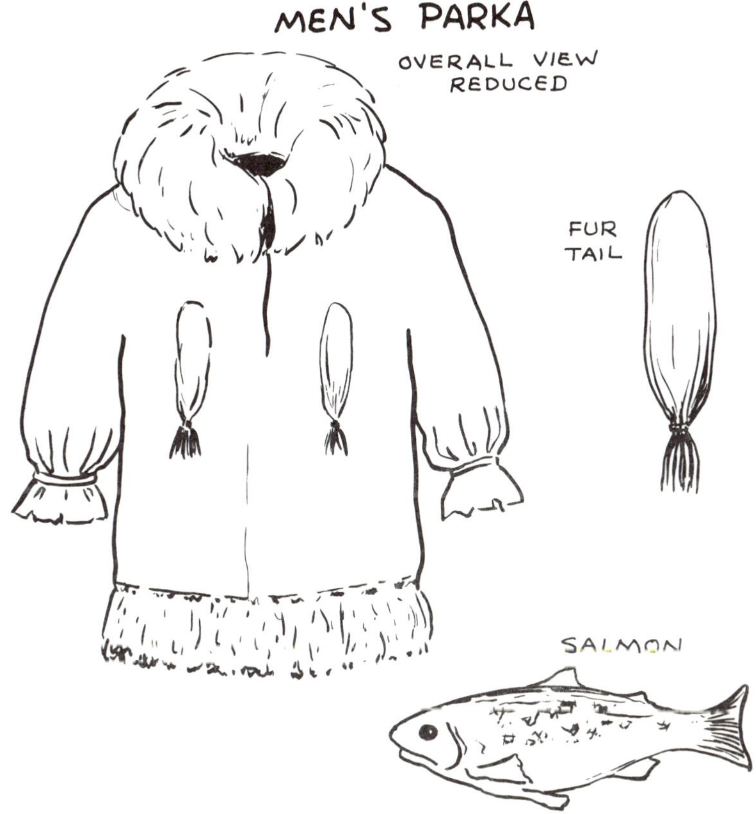


*Eskimo parka with attached hood is made of fur for both men and women. Salmon is molded from bread dough mixture, and painted.*

*Woman's summer parka is trimmed with rows of rickrack braid, but has no fur hood.*

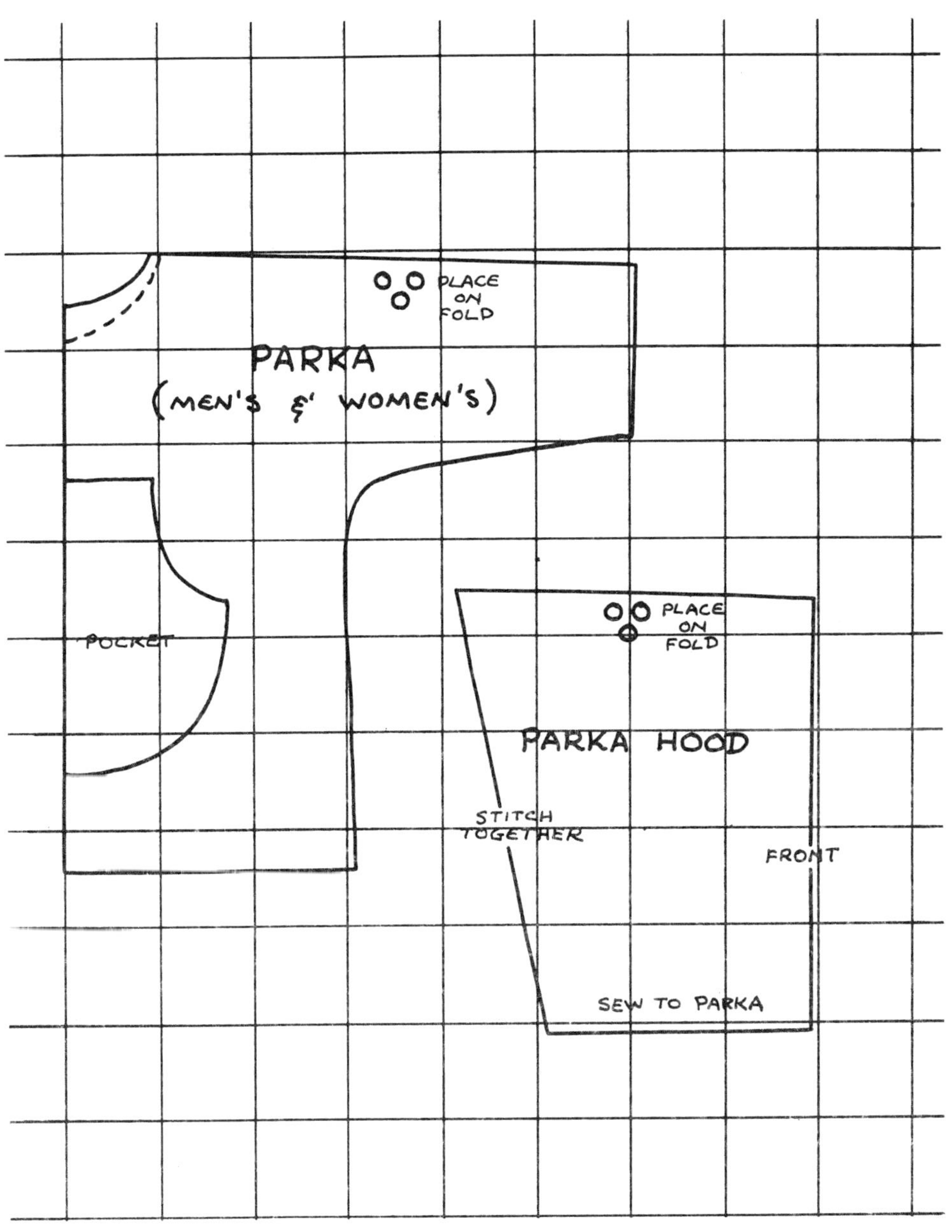


*Eskimo parka and attached hood is cut the same for both men and women.*

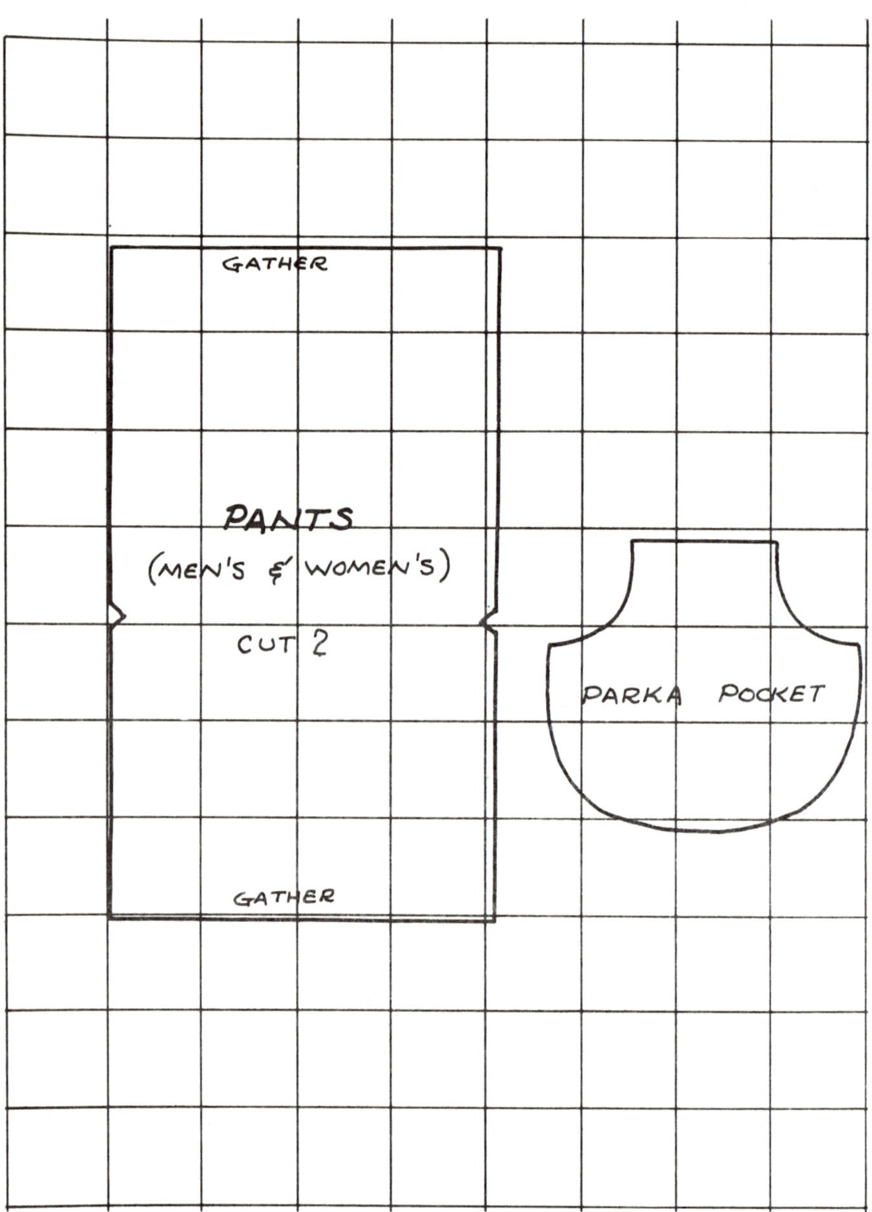


*Pants worn with parka are cut the same for both men and women. Parka pocket is attached to front of parka on both winter and summer styles.*

### *Accessories*

Eskimo dolls are particularly well adapted to being part of shelf displays and exhibits. See what your library offers in the way of illustrations of Eskimo artifacts. Visit museums and study the real objects, then test your skills in reproducing them for your dolls. A good beginning is to make our Chinook salmon from the bread dough mixture, painting it realistically with acrylic paint. Or make a harpoon, a spear, even a kayak or an igloo.

These dolls can become a researcher's delight.

# 9

# *Off to the Potlatch*

The Tlingit Indians of the American Northwest are handsome, well-built people with strongly marked characteristics. Before demoralized by the white man, these people lived in permanent villages of solidly constructed cedar planks and beams, each house with its tall totem pole in front, and corner posts also carved in totemic designs. The people were divided into three clans, the Raven, the Wolf, and the Whale, and their unique headdresses are elaborations of their tribal symbols. They celebrated outstanding personal and tribal events with an elaborate gathering known as a potlatch, when men of the village brought out their brilliant and distinctive costumes and head decorations, which they donned after journeying to a neighboring village by boat. These visits and the gifts brought to the hosts were later returned by the visited, so that there was an endless succession of festivities. The costumes worn by the Tlingit men are so intriguing and colorful that they offer a dollmaker a rare chance to produce a doll of distinction.

Tell your librarian what you have in mind and ask her for reference material and pictures for your project, since while the following costumes and designs are authentic, they are only a beginning.

These figures are not for the dollmaker in a hurry, for their making requires hours of painstaking, detailed work, but he can be certain that the result will be well worth it.

The patterns given here are for dolls about ten and one-half inches tall, the preferred size for collectors' dolls. All materials are inexpensive and easy to find, while much of it is straight out of the scrap

*Tlingit village chief dressed in totemlike headdress and Chilkat blanket. His wife wears native costume of dark blue decorated with typical design in red.*

bag. Begin with the following materials and add others as called for: coathanger wire, straightened out with a pair of pliers, a small roll of florist's wire, white glue, paper towels or newsprint, tissue paper, acrylic paint in colors suggested in earlier chapters, a pressed paper (not plastic) egg carton, a medium-sized watercolor brush, and a small bowl or pan to hold water.

When it comes to costuming the dolls, look in a salvage store for an old black wig to provide straight black hair for your Indians. You

*Another Tlingit man with a headdress decorated with ermine tails. His red fringed shirt is ornamented with pearl buttons and beads. His staff of office also carries a totem figure. In his nose is a characteristic nose ring.*

can also often find small beads, shabby bits of fur, and even scraps of thin leather there. If you use felt for costumes, buy the small squares of it in red, blue, yellow, or white, for you will need only a little. Browse through craft and hobby shops but be prepared to pay top prices there. Part of the fun in making dolls is to see what you can devise for little or no cost.

The Tlingit chief, clad in his Chilkat blanket and animal headpiece, is shown here with his less glamorous wife, but their bodies are the same and their shirts cut from the same pattern.

*View of the same Tlingit man from the rear, showing depth of fringe on blanket that is covered with black, yellow, and light blue designs.*

*Side and front views of Tlingit Indian figure, showing his raven headpiece and the ermine tails hanging from it down his back.*

Before making the doll, read chapters 1 and 2 carefully, since you will use the methods and the mixtures described. Mix up the suggested amounts of both papier-mâché and bread dough and store until you need them.

## *Method*

1. Twist the hook from a wire coathanger and discard it. Straighten

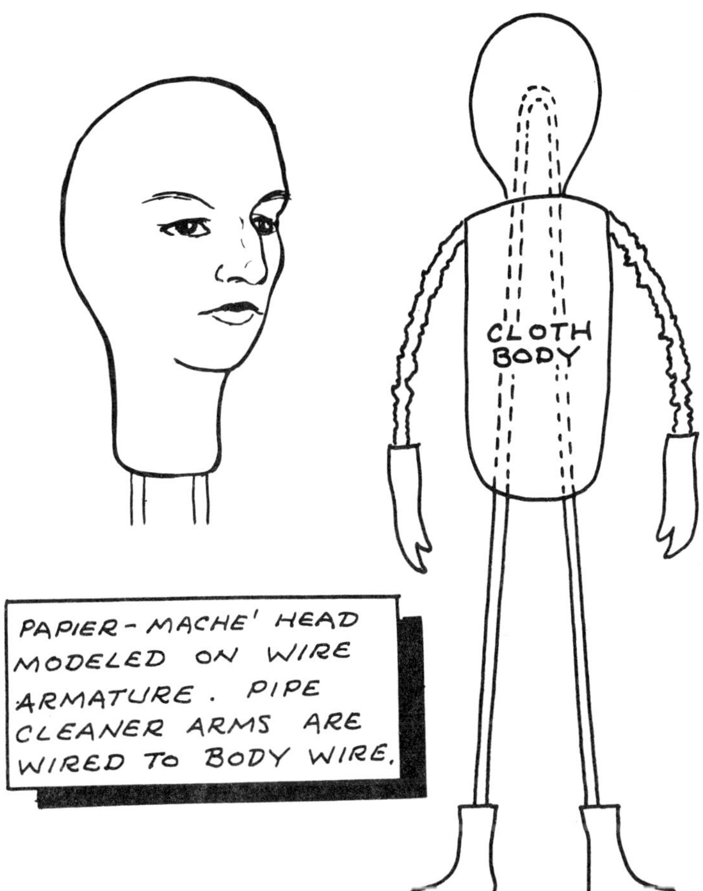


*Cloth body for the Indian dolls is made on a wire frame, and the head is modeled from papier-mâché, then painted.*

the wire with a pair of pliers and bend in the middle into a sharp loop. This wire will be the basic armature for the doll. Do not cut it until the head is completed.

2. Make a core for the head by tightly wadding newspaper or paper toweling around the bend in the wire in an egg shape.

3. Wind several narrow strips of paper around the base of the core to form a foundation for the neck.

4. Using the papier-mâché mixture, build up the head and neck over the wadded paper. Model the facial features. Set aside to dry.

5. Measure the doll from the top of its head. At ten inches, bend the wires at right angles and cut the bent portion off, making the foot armature one inch long.

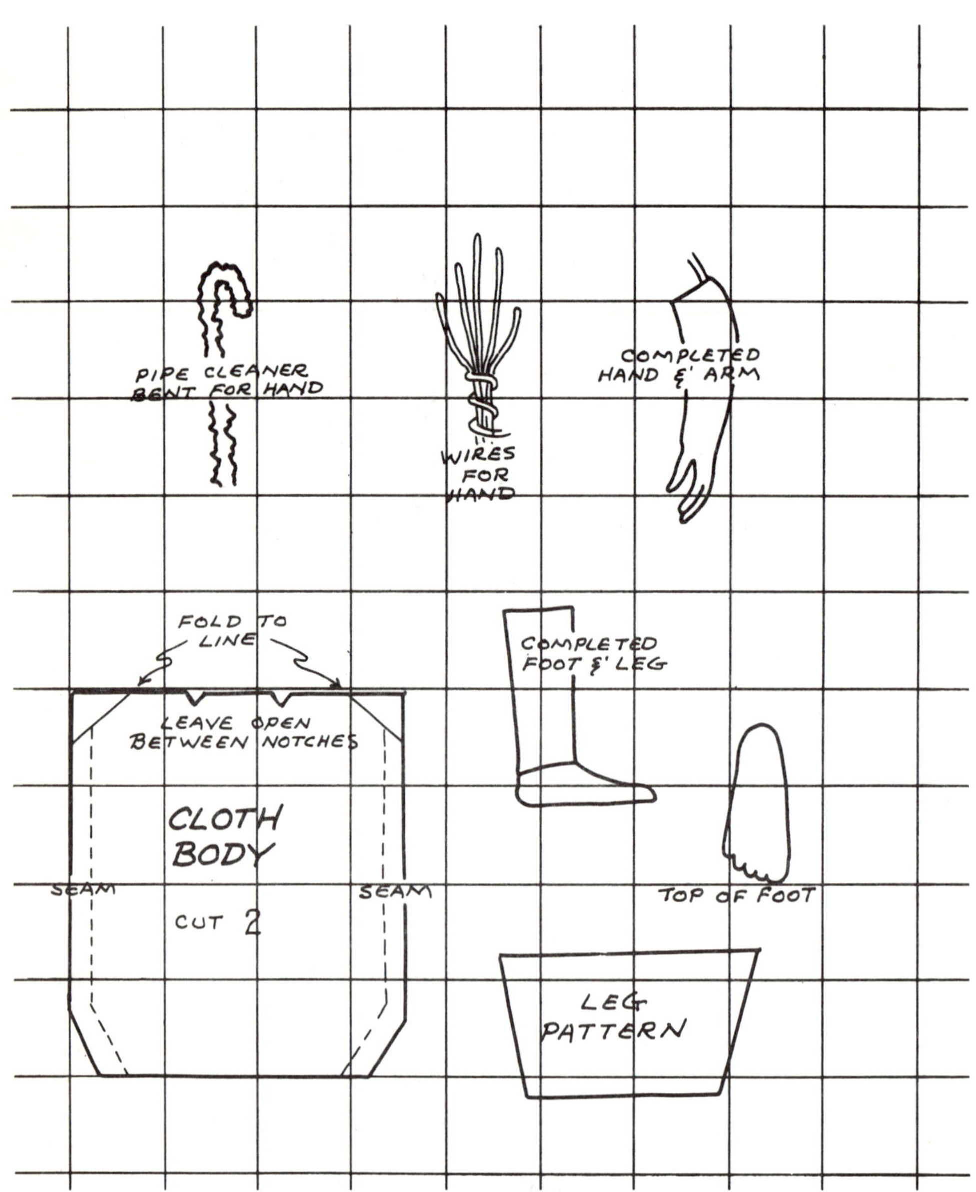


*Details in construction of doll body.*

6. Using the pattern for the sole of the foot, cut two from medium-weight cardboard and glue the foot wires to them. Let dry.
7. Bind two pipe cleaners together at the ends and in the other ends make a half-inch loop to form bases for the hands.
8. Cut three-inch lengths of the florist's wire and cover half their length with narrow strips of tissue paper dipped in white glue, binding two wires together for each finger.
9. When dry, place five fingers for each hand on top of the loop in the pipe cleaners. Spread the fingers slightly apart, then bind the wires to the pipe cleaner at the wrist.
10. Cover the entire hand and arm from fingertips up about two inches, with narrow strips of paper. Glue well and smooth the surface.
11. Cover entire head and neck with narrow tissue paper strips, making the surface as smooth as possible. Let dry.
12. Model the tops of the feet with bread dough, directly on the cardboard soles, shaping the toes. While the dough is still soft, cut two leg sections from thin cardboard and glue them around the leg wires, then press the small end of the resulting cone down firmly into the soft dough. Let dry.
13. Paint entire head, neck, arms, hands, and feet with acrylic paint tinted a pale tan. Dry.
14. Cut cloth body (two pieces) from firm cloth and stitch along dotted lines shown in pattern. Slip over doll's body, turn in neck edge, and sew snugly around arm and leg wires.
15. Paint on the features with a fine brush. Dry.
16. Cut several strands of hair from a black wig and glue them on top of the head, shoulder length. The back of the head will be covered with the headdress and need not be covered.

Make women's hair the same way, except that the entire scalp is covered. Tlingit men often wear a nose ring. Make one out of the wire and glue into the nostrils. The ring should be about one-quarter-inch in diameter. The doll is now ready to dress.

### *Dressing*

Tlingit men wear soft leather pants, fringed, and while we might use thin, soft, leatherlike chamois-skin, it is just as well to use tan-colored felt instead. Cut from the pattern shown and whip seams together with self-colored thread. Make the fringe in narrow strips and sew to the pants legs invisibly. Traditionally, these Indians are always barefooted.

The women wear narrow dark cloth skirts. Their shirts are exactly

*Typical styles of men's and women's clothes that are varied in many ways.*

the same as the men's, and both are decorated with a large appliquéd totem figure or a bead design. Use felt for the appliqué. The bottom of the shirt and lower edges of the sleeves are fringed. Another favorite shirt decoration is made with tiny white pearl buttons, sewn down the front, as in the illustration.

### *Headdresses*

Head masks or ornaments are totem figures, representing the wearer's clan. They sit on top of the head and are generally fastened on with leather thongs. For our purpose, glue works best.

A section cut from a pressed paper egg carton forms a good base, already shaped, for a headdress, and may be painted in bright primary colors. Sometimes a few strands of hair or fur may be added, or beaks made from the bread dough, or a variety of ornaments. Some suggestions are shown here.

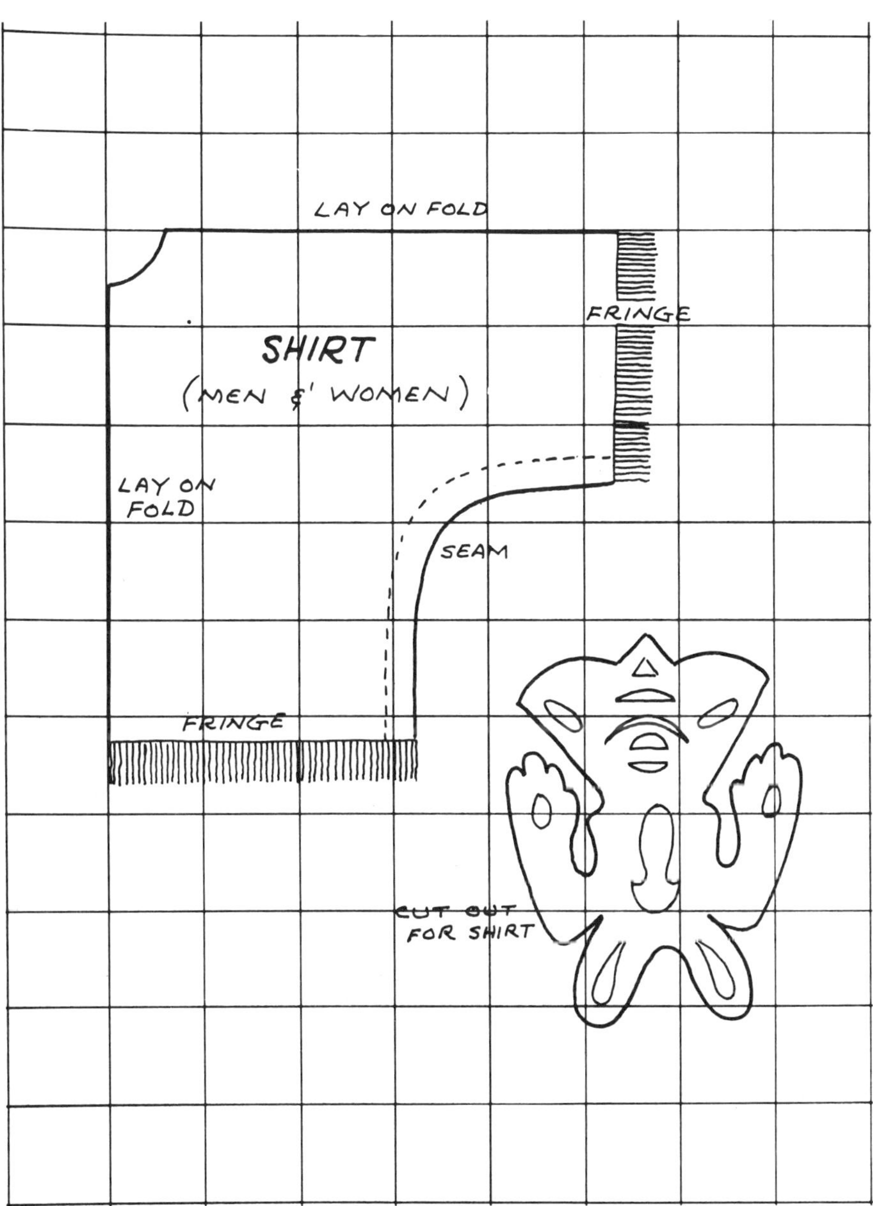


*Pattern for Tlingit shirt has an appliqued figure on the front. Both men and women wear this garment.*

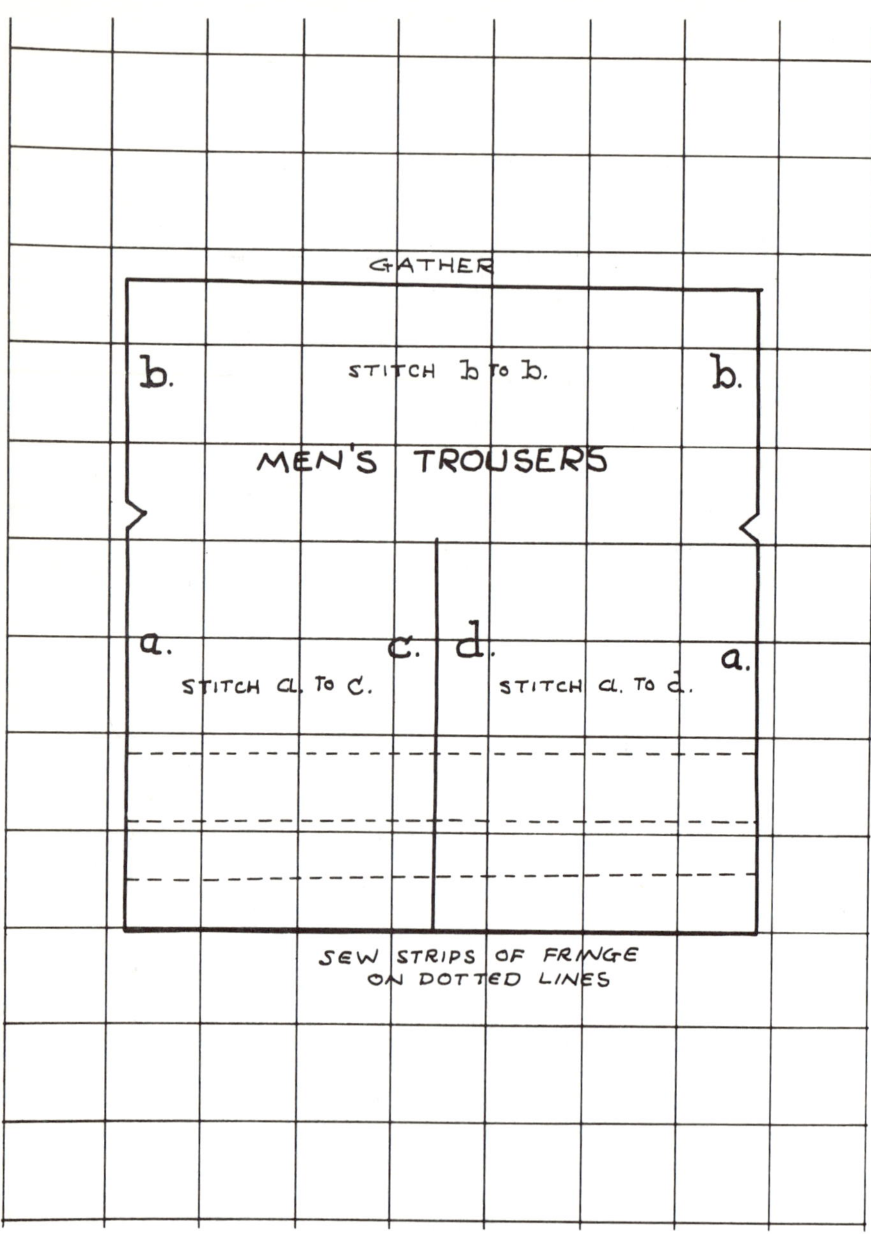


*Pattern for man's pants cut in one piece, and seamed at back to the notch, then the legs are sewed separately.*

## DESIGNS FOR HEAD MASKS

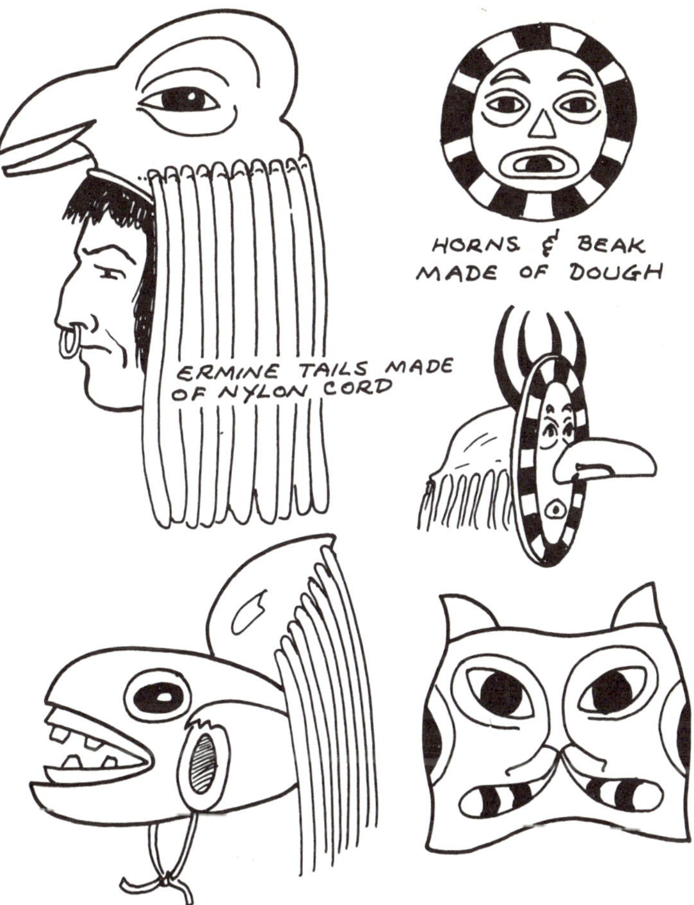


*A few of typical Tlingit headdresses.*

### *Blanket*

The Tlingits make and wear the fabulous and elaborate Chilkat blankets, made by weaving together cedar bark and goat hair. Designs vary, but the colors are always the same: a cream-colored background, black lines and figures, much pale yellow, and light greenish-blue. The real blankets are handwoven, of course, but for our dolls we have selected Osnaburg, which is the right color, has enough body, and is smooth enough to take paint well. Use the pattern but allow an extra two inches on three sides for fringe. Stitch around the pattern line on

*Chilkat blankets are made by the Northwest Indians in an endless variety of designs. This one represents a whale.*

the sewing machine and pull out all threads from the edge to the stitching. Make a narrow hem at the neck edge and sew a heavy cord to the top edges for tying on the doll.

Since these are not play dolls and are therefore not intended to have the clothes removed, the body structure is left uncovered as described, while the cloth section is used simply to form a base for the doll's clothing.

The same patterns for making the doll may be used for making entirely different kinds of dolls of other tribes, races, and nationalities. Because of the flat, cardboard-based feet, the dolls can be made to stand. Also, arms and legs are easy to bend to whatever position is desired.

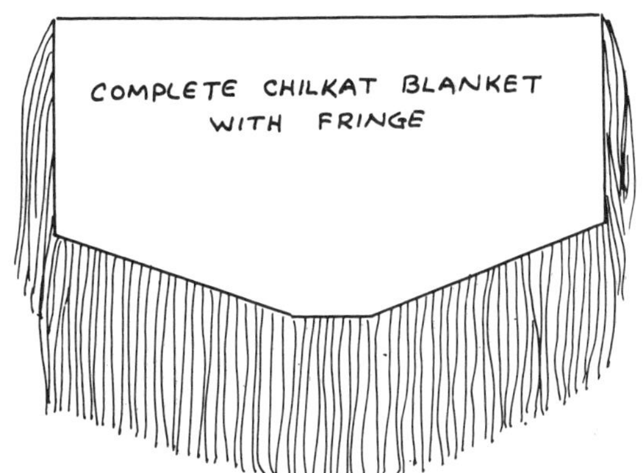


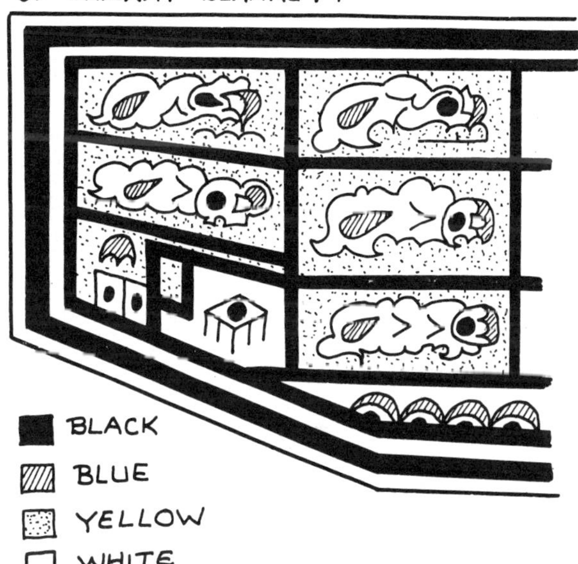


*Chilkat blankets are made of cedar bark and goat's hair, but these dolls wear blankets made of cloth, painted in typical pattern. The long fringe at bottom and sides is so long it almost reaches ground.*

# 10

# Dollhouse People

There are times when it is desirable to have a smaller doll than is to be found in toy departments, for a dollhouse, perhaps, or with a train layout or in military scenes or dioramas.

It is a mistake to think that small dolls are quicker and easier to make than are large ones. On the contrary, the making of a tiny doll calls for more patience and care than is sometimes realized. On the positive side, however, the amount of material required for making and dressing a miniature is almost too small to measure, so this is an ideal way to use the scraps of felt, lace, cloth, fur, and the various oddments a dollmaker accumulates, at the same time producing dolls that cannot be duplicated commercially. The methods given here are quick and simple, and the results are fun to keep, sell, or give away.

### Patterns

Every one of the dolls described in this book may be reduced to smaller size by ruling a sheet of tracing paper into one-inch squares and tracing on it the patterns in the book. After deciding the size you wish the doll to be, make another grid of smaller squares and repeat on it the outline on the first grid.

Our miniature people, Mr. and Mrs. Covington Goodby, are scaled to the conventional dollhouse size—one inch to one foot, and are therefore about five and one-half inches tall.

*Mr. and Mrs. Covington Goodby are dressed in their best for a dollhouse party.*

*Mr. Covington Goodby as a civilian. Both dolls are made the same way, except for the heads.*

*Mr. and Mrs. Covington Goodby are small people who could be made even smaller. The bodies are made the same of the common materials found in any kitchen. Mrs. C. is not yet dressed.*

## *Materials*

A batch of the bread dough mixture given in chapter 2 for each doll
One or two pipe cleaners for each doll
Two barbecue skewers or round toothpicks for each doll
Scraps of felt, lace, sheer batiste, soft woolen, etc. for clothing
A small piece of pelon or interfacing for skirt
Fine yarn or embroidery floss for hair
Acrylic paint
White glue

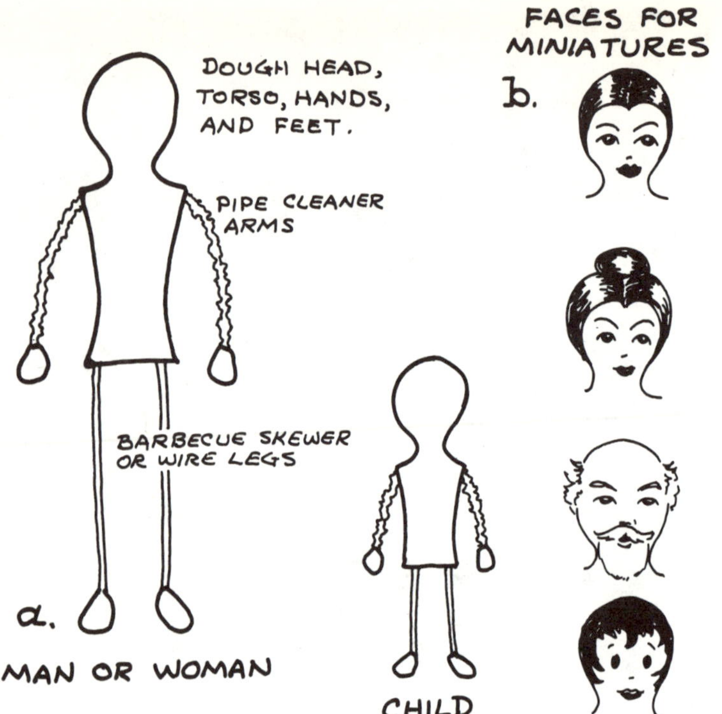


*Miniature dolls can be made by shaping heads, bodies, hands, and feet on wire or pipecleaner frames, then painting them. Children are made the same way, but in scale with their elders. Heads and faces may be made more natural if wool is used for hair and beards.*

### *Method*

Unlike some of the dolls in this book, these miniatures are not made on a wire framework. Instead, the head and upper body are molded of the bread dough and the wooden legs and pipe cleaner arms are inserted into it.

1. Knead the dough until smooth, then shape it as shown on a, making the body about one-half inch thick and the head slightly thicker and more round.

2. Immediately insert a pipe cleaner into the dough at the shoulders, pushing it down well. Smooth the dough to conceal this insertion.

3. Dip the tips of the pipe cleaners in white glue, then roll small bits of dough for hands directly onto the arms.

4. Push two barbecue skewers into the body section after first dipping the ends into white glue. Make feet on the other end of the

wires just as you made the hands. Let dry thoroughly, which may take several days.

5. Paint the body with acrylic paint, using white, tinted with a small amount of red and a touch of yellow. Let this dry, then paint on the features with a very fine brush—00 or 000.

6. The last step is to glue on the hair. Fine yarn or several strands of embroidery floss are good to use. For old people, bits of white or grey wool yarn may be used.

### *Patterns*

The patterns for these miniature dolls may be used as shown, or they may be used merely as basic patterns. For example, if you are making costume dolls, it is a simple matter to make a fluffier skirt, or a straight, floor-length style; replace the puff sleeves with tight, straight ones; make a hat; cut a cape by marking off a circle or a segment of a circle sliced down one side. Men may be given white collars, or white ties and tails, or be dressed as cavaliers with long curls and knee breeches; clad as Pilgrims; Santa Claus; or Christmas tree ornaments.

The easiest way to alter patterns is to pin and snip them right on the doll. Tissue paper, cleansing tissue, or paper towels are soft enough to work with in this way, and anyone can fit a pattern, we insist.

### *Dressing*

I decided that these small dolls would be easier to make and dress if their clothes were sewed directly on the bodies rather than closed with buttons or snap fasteners, which would be bulky. So, if you want them removable, just pin them on the dolls.

Mr. Goodby is a Victorian gentleman, as his handlebar mustache indicates, and his costume tells us that he is in a branch of the service where he wears a dress uniform and medals on his chest. Using the same patterns, he could instead wear white pants and a striped blazer, and in addition carry a straw hat.

In making this pair I used felt for Mr. Goodby's clothes and in this way simplified both seams and finishing. Felt edges may be joined on the outside by tiny over-and-over stitches and be almost invisible. His tunic is made of light blue felt, his pants of dark blue. A one-eighth-inch-wide strip of red felt was tacked over the outside seam of one leg

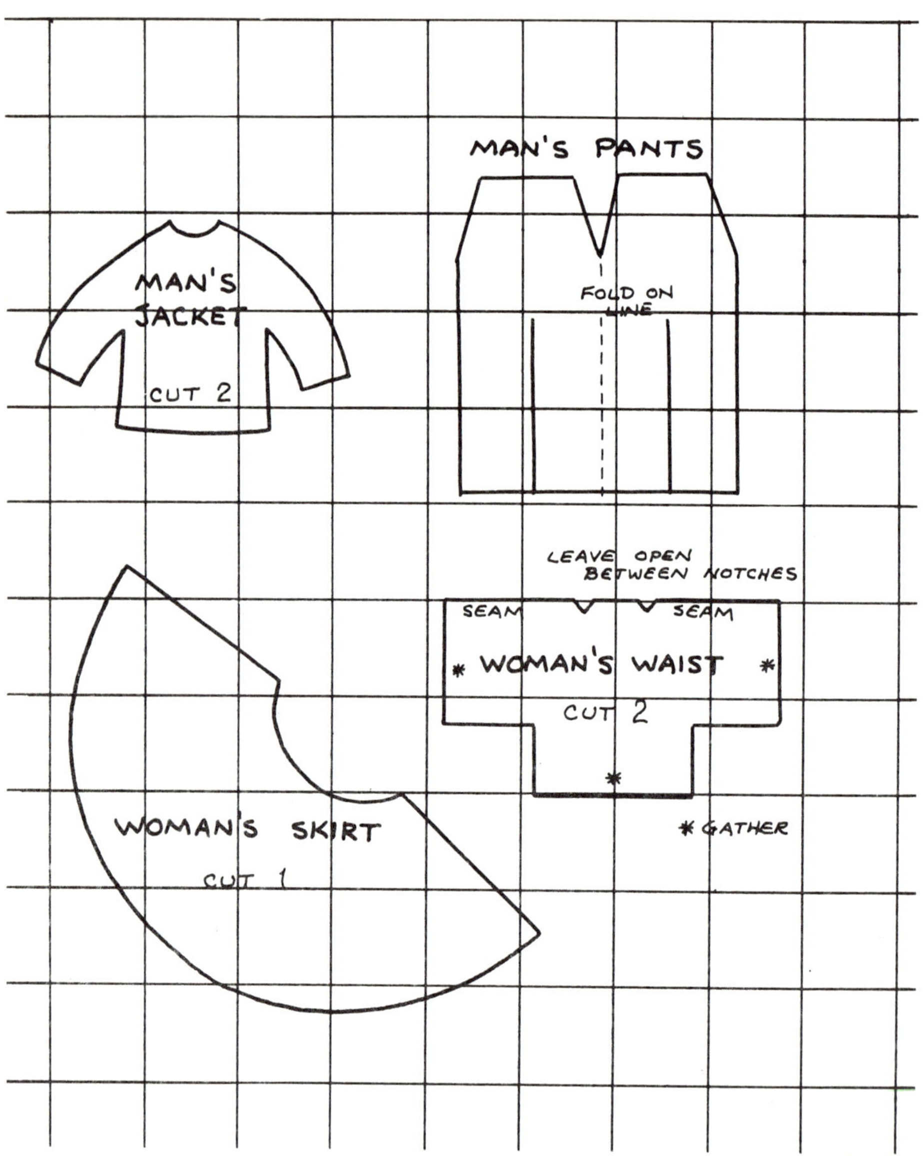


*Patterns for men's and women's clothes may be varied by using these patterns as basic garments.*

to make a stripe. The underarm seams were first joined, then the top slipped over the doll's head and the shoulder and sleeve seams were joined, right on the doll. The pants, cut in one piece, were first folded lengthwise on the dotted line, the doll slipped inside, then the side seam and the darts sewed up. A narrow strip of black felt was sewed at his waist for a belt.

Mrs. Goodby is modishly gowned in a lacy flounced dress with puffed sleeves. Her yellow hair is made of embroidery floss twisted into a pompadour and invisibly stitched in place.

Instead, she could have been made into a modern woman wearing a long skirt or pants suit, and her hair could have been left hanging loose or trimmed into a short length. She could be a queen or a peasant, old or young, ancient or modern. A costume doll is the delight of most doll collectors, and a miniature costume doll is particularly desirable because of the minimum of shelf space needed for display.

After Mrs. Goodby was completed, her skirt was cut from a piece of white interfacing, such as pelon, and rows of lace were gathered and sewed to it. Before being sewed on the doll the waist was made, also of lace. A wad of cotton was pushed up under the waist to fill out the bust, then the bottom edge gathered closely at the waistline. The completed skirt was fastened on the doll and its back seam was closed. A narrow ribbon sash tied around the waist covered the raw edges.

This pair of dolls can be said to be dollmaking at its simplest, especially for people who don't like to sew.

# 11

# A Good-Luck Voodoo

In all lands from early England to the present-day islands of the Caribbean, we find versions of the voodoo doll. They may be called fetishes, talismans, and mascots, as well, but all share a common characteristic: each figure has human aspects. The little figure made of wax is perhaps the most familiar one, and the way it has often been used is well known. If someone wishes to destroy an enemy he will stick pins into the figure, and that person will die or become tortured with pain. Perhaps this satisfies some obscure human urge, since the practice is so universal.

During the time I was doing some research on the subject of voodoo dolls, a national political convention was going on, and during a commercial break on television wax images of the opposing candidate were offered for sale. It was suggested that if you wanted your man to win, sticking pins in his opponent's image would bring that to pass. Someone must have put a stop to the advertising, for it was never repeated. However, in browsing through the stock of a nearby toy shop I found the two dolls for sale. No such use was suggested for them on the package and it is to be hoped that no evil use was ever put to the dolls. This story confirms the durability of the superstition.

I told the proprietor what I had heard on the air and remarked that I was having no luck in finding a voodoo doll. He looked at me quizzically and asked, "Would you tell anybody if *you* had one?"

This man's attitude is characteristic, for most of us have deep inborn fears about the things that we can't understand, and to even talk about a thing may bring it to pass.

To some of the mountain people of the American south—descendants of Elizabethan immigrants who settled there long ago, there is still belief in the magic of human talismans, and of course the voodoo dolls of the West Indies duplicate those made by their ancestors in Africa, the same place where New Orleans voodoo rites originated. There is still much that is not known about these rites, but it seems likely that rather than being a distinct voodoo cult, the secret ceremonies vary with the people themselves and that just as there is no set form to them, they are the spontaneous expressions of emotions common to man.

Apparently straying far from the subject of dolls, these references to cults and superstitions demonstrate the scope of the subject of dolls,

*Ancient Peruvian dolls found in a mummy bundle along the Peruvian coast with faces and clothes made of tapestry are now in the Traphagen School of Fashion, New York City.*

*This goodluck voodoo doll is so mysterious she won't tell her name, but she brings pleasure and happiness.*

and point out places where an interested student of the race can take up a different angle of the behavior of man.

As was said earlier, there is no beginning and no end to the subject of dolls, and this is given emphasis when viewing the artifacts found in and near the caves where pre-Neanderthal men lived in Europe before the Ice Age. The so-called Venus figures, whose use is still and possibly will always be unknown, suggest that they might have had uses such as we have been discussing, and while they can only prove that early man was fascinated by his own body, they stir the imagination.

We can certainly go no farther back than that until some archaeologist unearths, probably in Africa or Asia, an object fulfilling a similar purpose. Until then, we must look a little closer to our own time for magic dolls.

The pair of Peruvian dolls, which the American Museum of Natural History has dated as having been made in the tenth to fourteenth centuries, are not the oldest dolls that can be considered to be fetishes, but because they were found in a mummy bundle along the coast of Peru, it is fair to assume that they were placed in the bundle for the same reason the early Egyptians placed tiny human figures, or *ushabti* in the tombs of their mummified nobles. They were the servants who would attend the deceased in another life, and so also may this man and woman, made entirely of wool tapestry, have been intended to protect and care for the one who had died. In this way, they also become talismans.

In a different way, the ancestor dolls of the Orient were tokens of love and remembrance, and the figures would be given an honored place in the midst of the family, so that they would not forget to revere them. Ancestor dolls, and also fetish and voodoo dolls were almost always left without features, for fear of offending the gods. The good-luck voodoo shown here has eyes and mouth, but no nose, which is rare.

This voodoo doll is an exact copy of a West Indian voodoo that I was allowed to hold in my hands and was given permission to cut a pattern from. The only restriction was my promise that it should be used only for good luck—not evil. I was assured that the doll will sweep away bad luck with her broom of twigs, that she will make your cake rise and your true love serenade you by moonlight, bringing you only good and beautiful things.

The entire doll had a feeling of having been made for use, not to play with or to be admired. Those who are returning to earthy things and manners will perhaps place her at their doorway or beside a fireplace, or quietly tuck her in their luggage when they go on a journey, since she is only about ten inches tall, and is soft and uncrushable. She could be made smaller by reducing the size of the patterns.

To make a voodoo doll of your own, first trace the pattern in the book on a sheet of paper and cut out the pieces.

### *Materials*

One-eighth yard black broadcloth for the body—or use percale
Four-inch wide strip of black cotton print having a small figure for the blouse
Six-inch square of cotton cloth for head scarf—black broadcloth

Small piece of a different patterned dark calico for blouse
Scraps of red felt for shoes
Scrap of white muslin for pantalets
Narrow lace to edge pantalets
Small scrap of red, figured cotton for two pockets
A tiny cross about one-half-inch long on a short string of small beads
Few strands of pale blue and bright red sewing cotton
A twig about five inches long for broom handle
Broom straws or shredded palm leaves for broom
Stuffing—preferably polyester fiber

## *Body*

Cut the body section from a double fold of the black percale or broadcloth, adding extra for seam allowance.

Cut four pieces of the red felt for shoes.

Seam body, leaving top open for stuffng, then turn rightside out.

Stitch the shoes to the legs, then stuff the body lightly through the head opening. Close the opening with overcasting.

Mark the fingers by making long stitches of black thread on the end of the arms.

Mark the eyes and mouth with two or three single stitches of red thread. There is no mark for the nose.

This completes the body.

## *Dressing*

Cut out the pantalets and sew up the seams and edge the lower part with lace. Gather the top and sew directly on the doll.

Make the petticoat from red material and edge it also with lace. Gather the top and sew directly on the doll.

Cut out the dress skirt and sew the two patch pockets at each side halfway between the top and bottom. Gather the top and sew it directly on the doll.

Make the waist of the dress and sew it also on the doll, its lower edge hanging loose.

Gather the sleeves at the wrists to make ruffled edges.

Hang the rosary around the neck.

Make the head scarf and tack it on the back of the doll's head.

Make the broom by winding a few turns of the pale blue thread

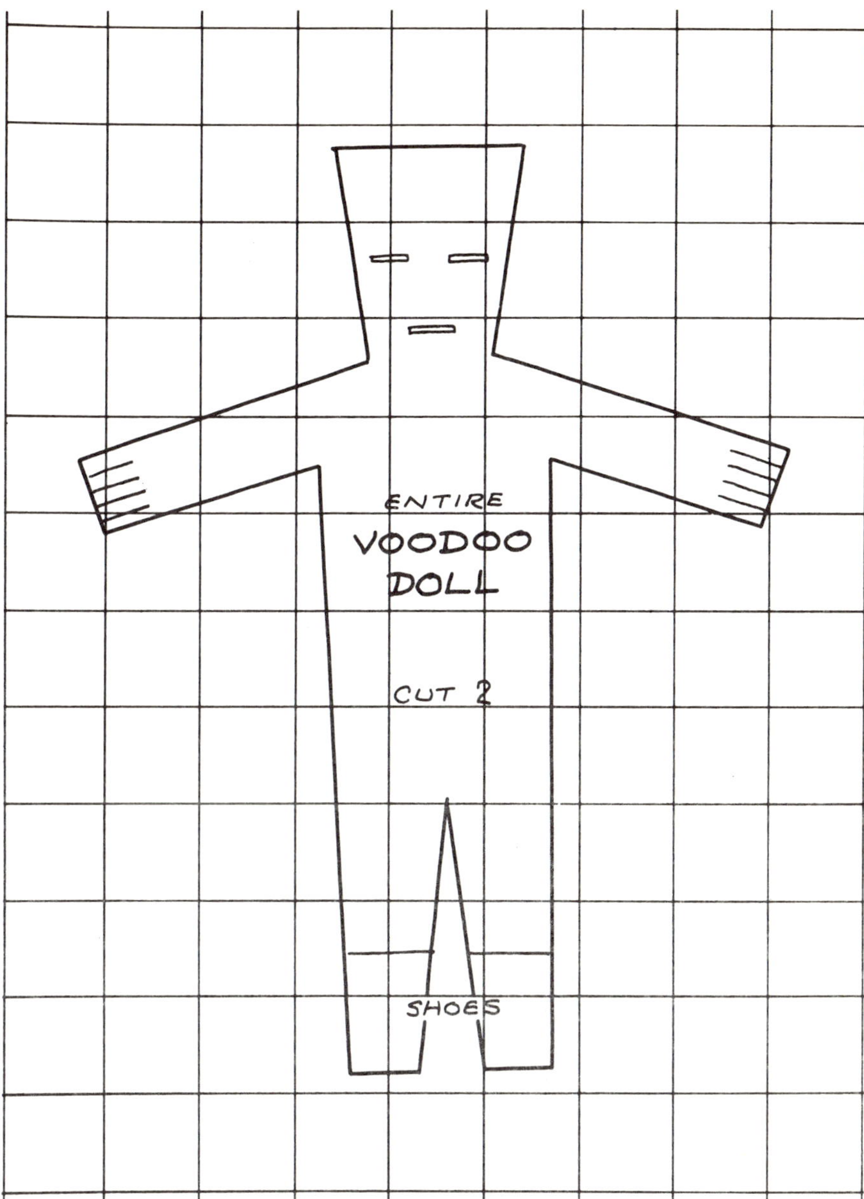


*Using this pattern, cut front and back of doll the same. It is the entire doll.*

around the straws to hold them in place on the stick. Sew the broom in place in the doll's hands in a sweeping position.

The original doll was made very crudely, with long stitches and unfinished edges and seams, but you may want to be more precise. This doll is made exactly like the original except for those differences.

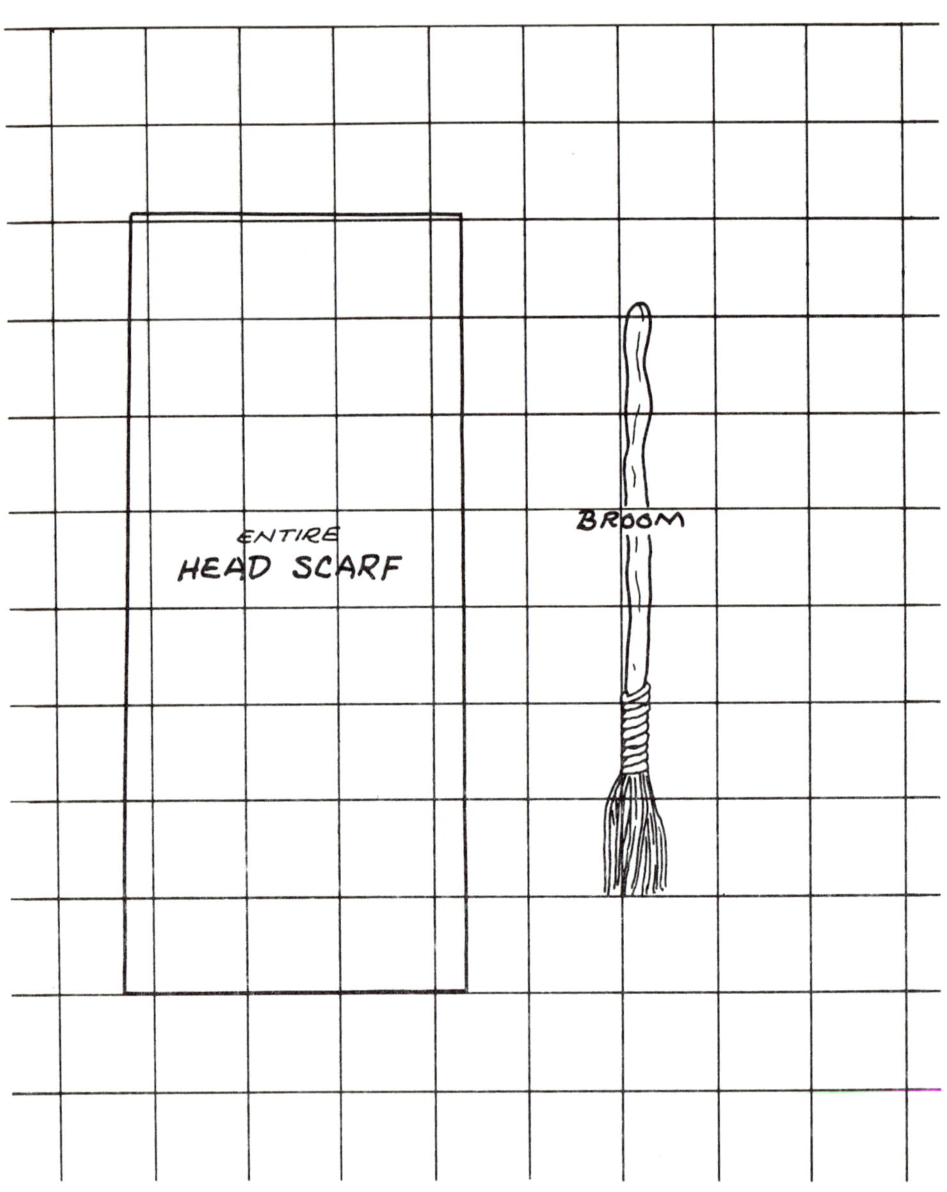


*Details of the voodoo doll include her head scarf, and a broom made of a twig and bundle of straws.*

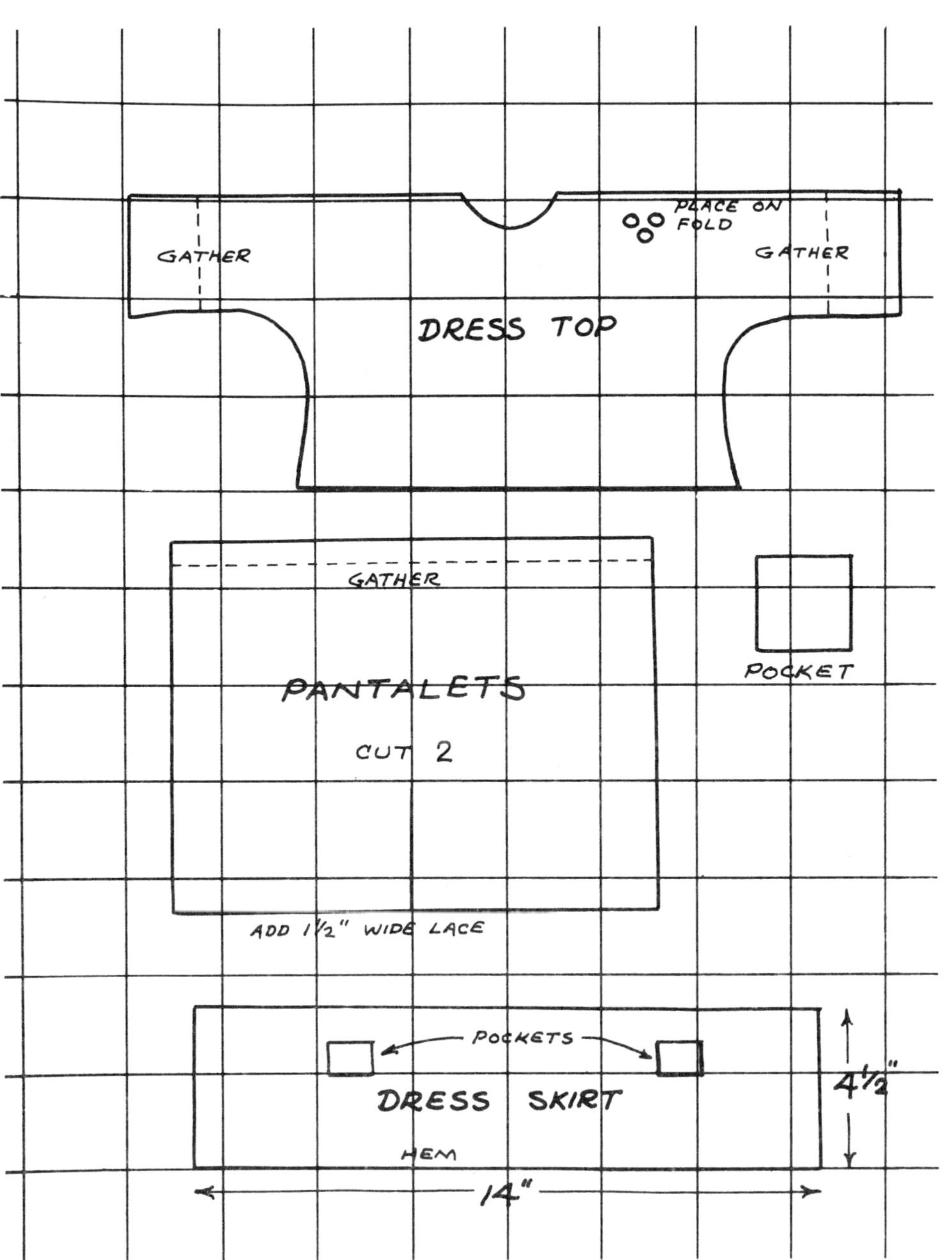


*Voodoo doll's costume is cut from scraps of printed cotton cloth of several patterns. Pantalets are made of white cloth.*

# 12

# *Paper Dolls, Old and New*

For generations, paper dolls have been enjoyed by little girls, their mothers, and grandmothers. Methods of making them and overall effects vary from time to time, but some of the old construction ideas are worthy of revival and adaptation to the present-day interest in the not-too-remote past. This chapter was prepared and illustrated after the discovery of a trio of 1880 paper dolls that had unusual appeal because of their history and the fact that they could be placed in innumerable positions, unlike the rigid and unimaginative paper dolls we usually see. Briefly, these dolls could *do something.*

Raphael Tuck made some of the first dolls on the market, which were colored by hand. They are rare prizes for collectors, as are the paper dolls that soon followed, published in various women's magazines. The Letty Lane, then the Betty Bonnet series appeared in the *Ladies Home Journal* from 1908 through July 1915. They were printed in full color and showed the little girls in their dresses, coats, hats, and accessories. Collectors of old magazines seldom if ever find copies of the *Journal, Delineator,* or *McCall's* that have not had the doll pages removed. If some remote attic should yield an intact copy, leave the doll pages in place, and remember that their value is greater if uncut, and still greater when bound in the magazine.

Early in the century the Dennison paper company sold packages of doll makings, consisting of a colored, lithographed paper doll, enough crepe paper to dress her, and paper lace to trim the dress, together with instructions for making a doll stand to hold the doll erect. While

*Jointed Victorian paper doll is dressed in crepe paper and paper lace.*

these dolls were attractive, their popularity was probably largely due to the fact just mentioned; they called for something more than a mere cutting-out process.

The 1880 dolls illustrated here were printed in Germany on heavy white cardboard. As may be seen, the heads and shoulders, gloved arms and hands, and legs and feet were lithographed in color, and while the names were not printed on the figures, the dolls represented famous actresses of the time: Lily Langtry, Emma Eames, and Nellie Melba. These dolls were packaged unassembled, to be put together with tiny metal fasteners and then dressed. Unlike the Dennison dolls, no material seems to have been supplied, and the buyer could and did make clothes of paper, silk, lace, braid, and velvet as desired. In dressing

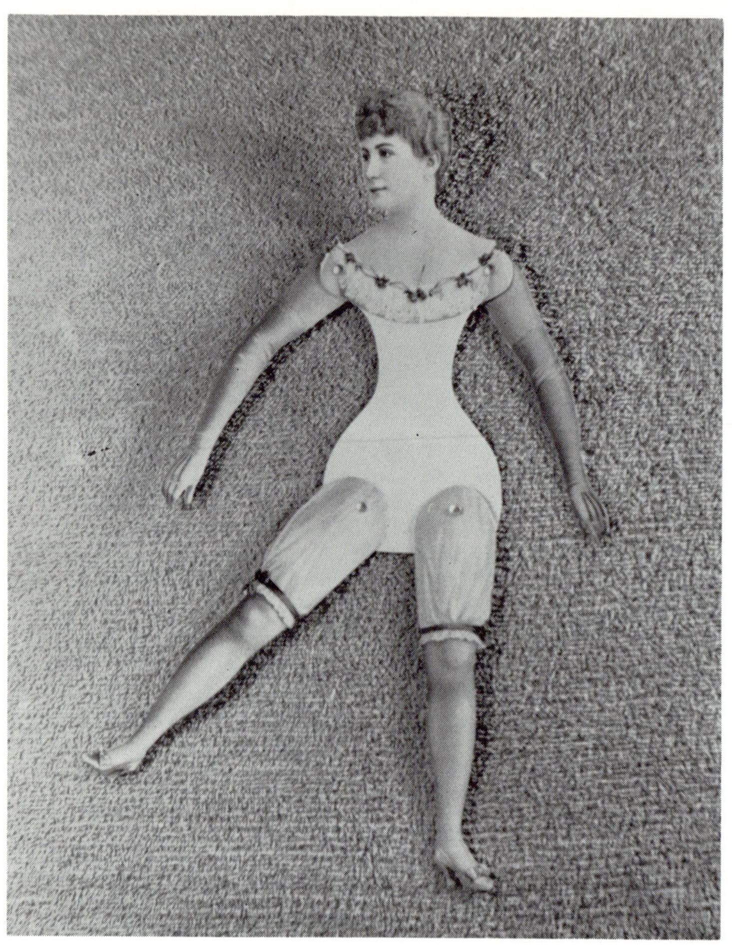

*Lily Langtry paper doll of the 1880s is printed in color. She is from a set of three famous actresses.*

them, it seems a pity to cover up the charming details of their modest, lace-trimmed panties, chaste ribbon-run corset-covers, and elegant long gloves, so in showing them, one is left undressed. The other, Lily Langtry, is stylishly gowned in pink and turquois-blue crepe paper, ruffled and gathered, and pasted on a white paper dress shape as a base. If her frills are not to be crushed, she may be framed in a shadow box, behind glass. Nothing could more suitably he hung on the walls of a Victorian bedroom.

A doll of this type could be dressed in short ruffled skirts as a dance-hall beauty, and thus more of her printed person would be left exposed and the arms and legs moved to various positions. At least, the arms can be left uncovered so they can be moved, and if skirts are wide, the legs can also be made to do high kicks.

Tracy, the modern version of this doll, is shown here both undressed and wearing a pants suit, with a long formal dress besides, but it is left to the dollmaker to add accessories and to make other clothes, for above all others, paper dolls are a challenge to the imagination.

To make the doll, trace the pattern pieces onto a piece of tissue paper, then onto fairly stiff Bristol board or poster board. Mark the lines and color the doll with felt-tip pens. Watercolor paint or even crayons could be used. Fasten the pieces together with one-half-inch brass paper fasteners, pushed through at the dots marked on the pattern.

When dressing the dolls, trace around the body, adding tabs at the shoulders to hold the clothes in place. Other tabs, as at the sides, can

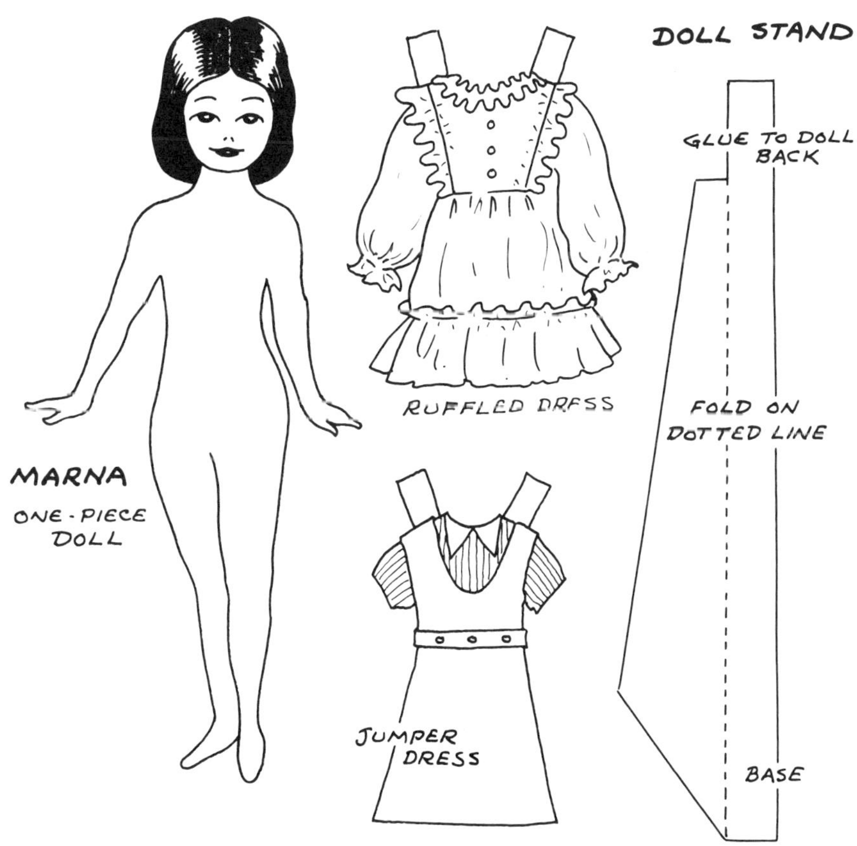


*A one-piece paper doll can be held upright by gluing a cardboard stand to her back.*

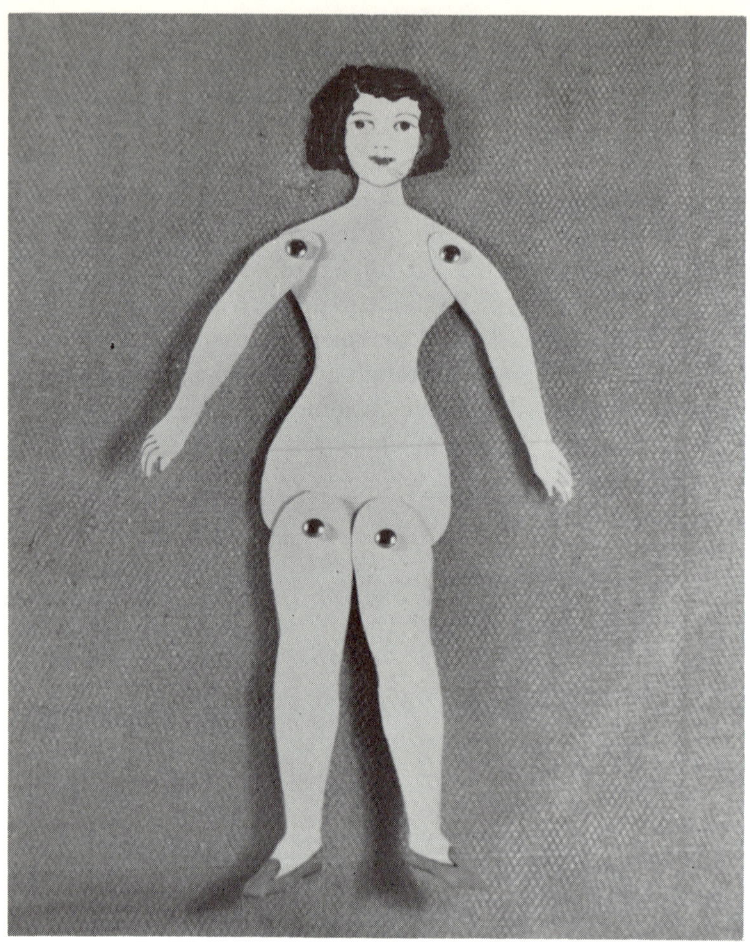

*Modern paper doll is put together with small paper fasteners so she may be placed in many positions, just as paper dolls of the 1880s were made.*

be added. Clothes may be cut from or decorated with pieces of gift-wrap paper, or can be made entirely from sheets of colored craft paper —the kind that comes in packages of assorted colors. While it is possible to make clothes for paper dolls from cloth, or to add scraps of lace, beads, fur, or embroidery to the paper, some dollmakers refuse to use anything but paper. Try both, for the search for materials is one of the charms of making these dolls.

Another variation is to cut out and paste on a head from a colored picture or photograph on the paper body. This was done with the Tracy in pants suit. Heads so used must be carefully chosen, so they will be in scale with the body. Mail-order catalogs are full of suitable heads, as well as a source for designing doll clothes. There are also small

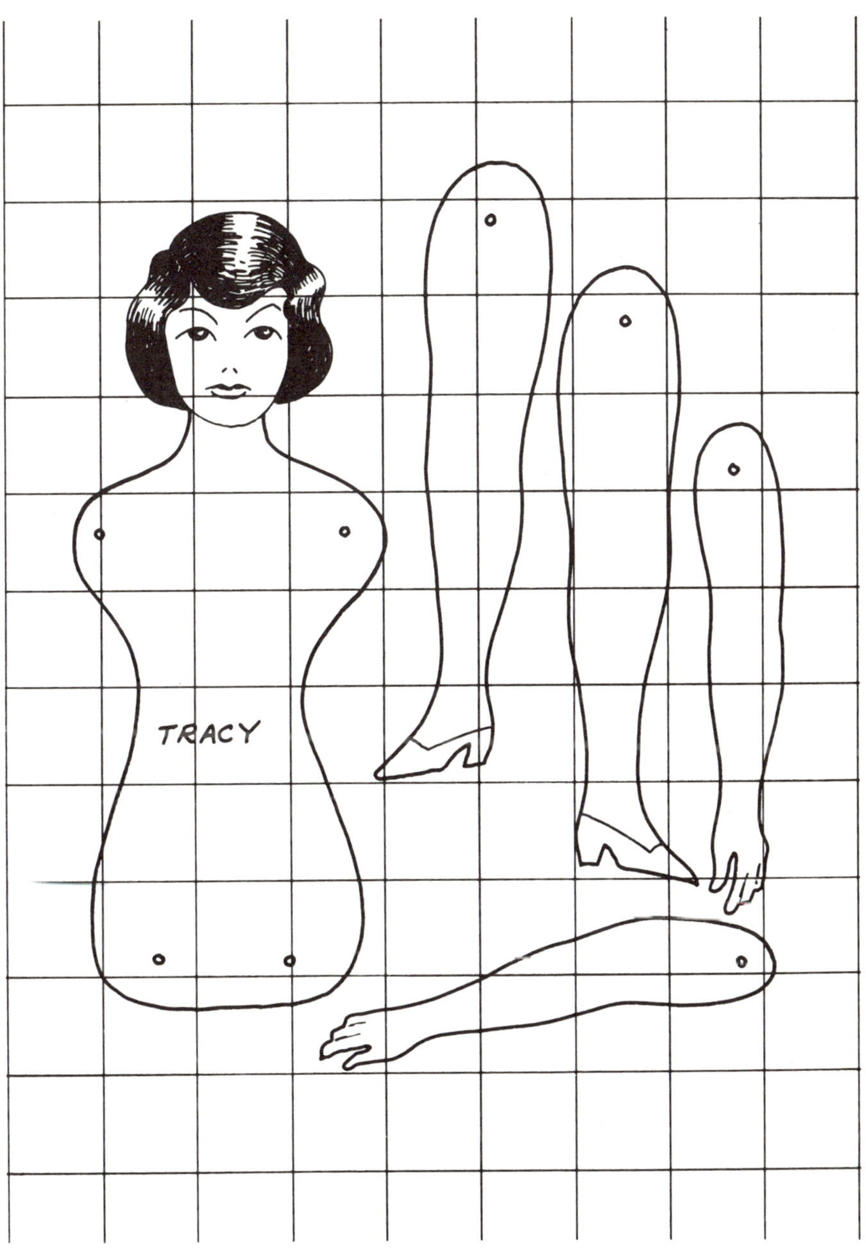


*Pattern for a jointed paper doll to be cut from lightweight cardboard and painted. Dots indicate where paper fasteners are to be inserted to hold body together.*

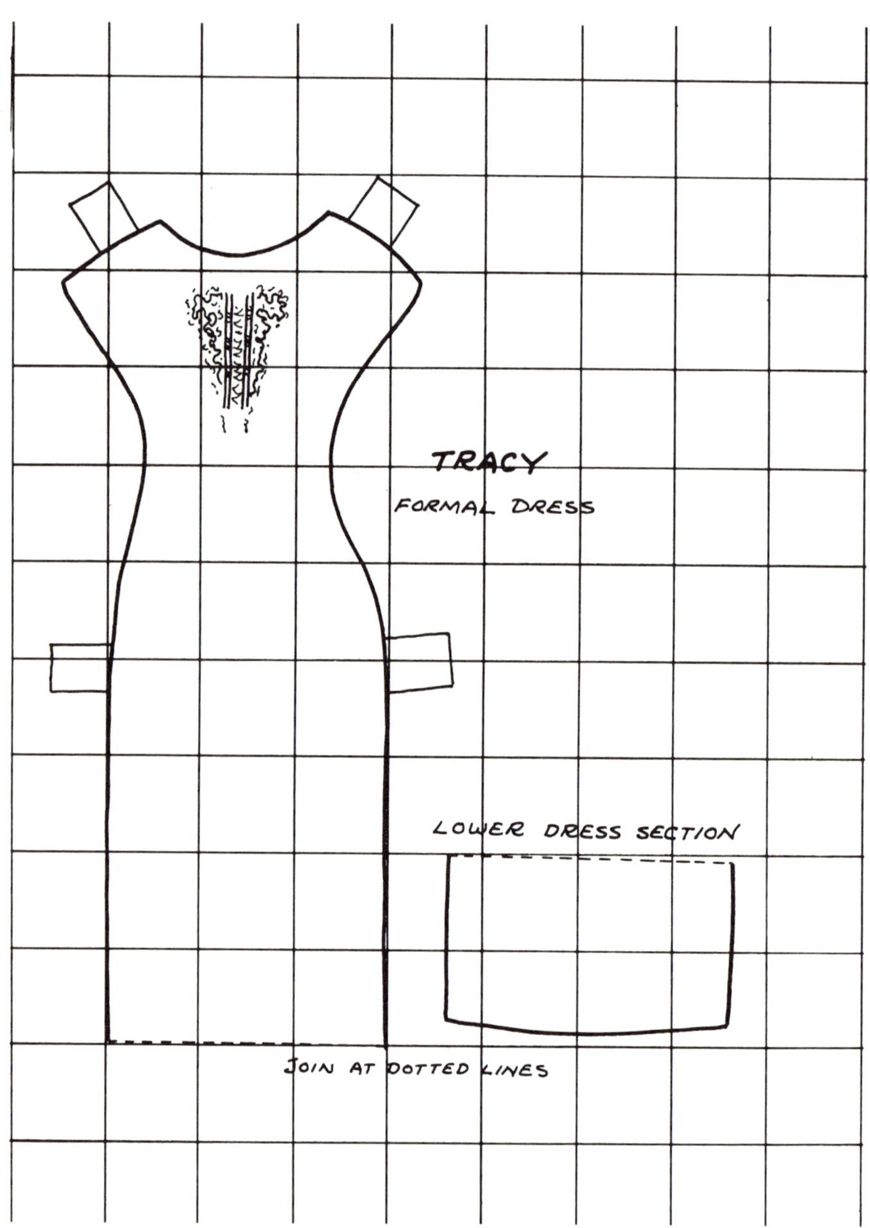


*Formal dress for a jointed paper doll may be trimmed as you wish.*

*Paper doll wears a pant suit made of craft paper.*

colored prints, copies of paintings, to be found in hobby shops. Just be sure the size is right. In the same way, you can turn a family photograph into a doll by cutting out the entire figure and mounting it on cardboard.

Another possible use for paper dolls is to make your own paper doll books for children to color, similar to, but more personal than, those made commercially. Make them on sheets of drawing paper, marking the features with a felt-tip pen, and using no color on either the doll or its clothes. In this way, the child does the coloring, so the design should be uncomplicated.

It is also best to draw the doll fairly large for the same reason. Pages of the book could be the nine by twelve sheets of craft paper, bound together between covers of stiff cardboard. This is an excellent idea for making gifts for children in hospitals.

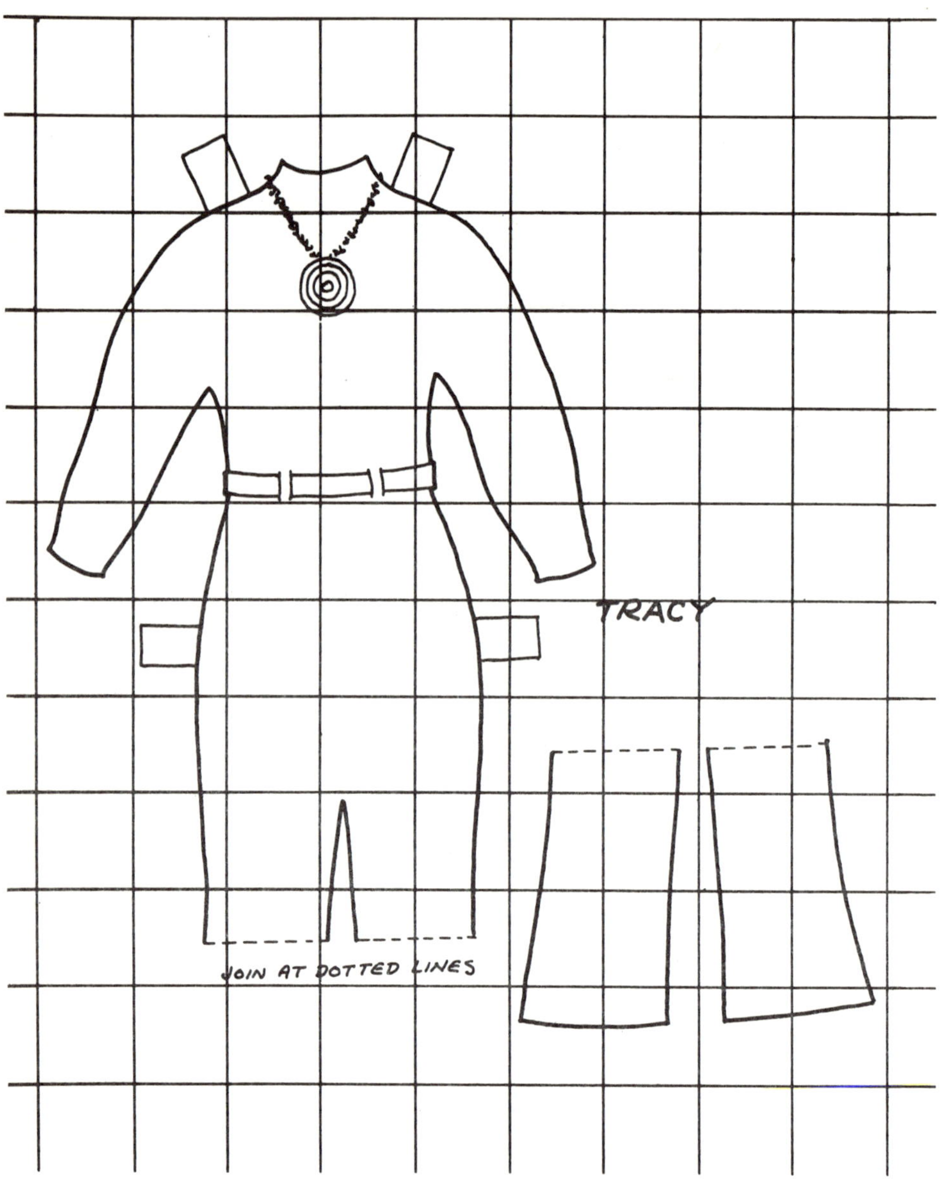


*Pantsuit pattern for the jointed paper doll. Join the two sections of the legs when cutting.*

Paper dolls in suitable sizes become attractive Christmas tree ornaments, or may be turned into gift tags.

Tiny doll shapes may be traced onto plain stationery and turned into note paper.

The paper doll collector has few of the storage problems suffered by other doll collectors. Such a collection is ideal for the doll lover who lives in an apartment, since you can stow quite a number of them in a flat box or a drawer, certain they will not bend or break. Your grandmothers often kept their paper ladies and gentlemen between the pages of a magazine or mail-order catalog—one of the staples of family living in the past. The furniture pages could be cut out to furnish a paper doll house for the dolls, also cut from the illustrations. They were splendid sources for men dolls—gentlemen in top hats and Prince Alberts—not often easy to find, and now words of unknown meaning to later generations.

As may be seen, the drawings and photographs in this chapter may be copied, but preferably should be used to fire your own imaginative dollmaking. They are by no means the final word about paper dolls.

# 13

# *Dolls of Clay and Cloth*

Doll collectors—and it takes only one or two dolls to qualify you for the title—often get their start with a doll from their own childhood, or if not that, a pink bisque or glazed china inherited from a mother or grandmother. The more perfect and unblemished by time this doll is, the more it is sought by other collectors, but this is far from saying that it was the most-loved by its original owner. A cuddlesome rag doll is a personal treasure more often than is a pristine wax or a marble-fleshed fashion model. However, if you are making a sample of dolls of different materials for your collection, you will certainly want to include either a pink bisque or a glazed china. Pottery shops often sell copies of old china dolls made from the original dolls, but why reproduce someone else's doll? Design and make your own and proudly put your initials on its shoulder, so that someday a collector may look you up in a doll directory. There are many doll types you can make, but why not begin with an ancestor? If you like doing research, here's your chance. Libraries burst with sources—in fact anything ever painted or photographed has potentials for costumes, to say nothing of the actual garments found in museums. Dugald MacDonald, my own ancestor, I dressed in his authentic tartan and kilts, with a Glengarry bonnet tipped over one eye. His sprig of heather is one I picked many years later from the banks of Loch Katrine.

You may be a Mayflower descendant and decide that your ancestress, Truth and Honor, would be an inspiration for *your* descendants,

*Red-haired, freckle-faced Ginger was the first of my ceramic dolls.*

*Ceramic doll made from an old French print. She has a cloth body but china head, arms, and legs.*

*Bonnet doll made from a photograph of a child shows how ceramic dolls may be used in portraiture. Bonnet is modeled directly on head.*

so you'll research costumes of the seventeenth century and dress her authentically.

When you or your daughter, sister, friend, grandchild, graduates from high school or college, make a doll in her image and dress it as that person was dressed. (A wedding gown, a favorite costume, as a gift or for yourself.) The doll can be made to look as much like the wearer as you can contrive, although creating resemblances comes easier to some craftsmen than to others. You can at least duplicate the hair style.

Newcomers to the doll world should understand that a ceramic doll is one made of clay and then baked or fired, in a kiln (pronounced *kill*), or oven. Clay is part of the earth and is found everywhere. In order to make it strong and enduring it must be heated many times hotter than your kitchen oven will get. Unless you have a kiln of your own, look for a school that will fire for you, or a hobby or ceramic shop. They charge moderately for the work.

Some ceramic dolls are made without glaze and are called bisque if pink, parian if white or very pale pink. Glazed ceramic dolls are either glazed pink—called pink luster—or white. It is the white ones that are described in this chapter, and they are made by pouring liquid clay (slip) into plaster-of-Paris molds, as will be explained.

Collectors, as has been said, favor dolls from eight to ten inches tall, a size large enough to dress effectively and small enough to fit into the average display case. These dolls are that size. The children are smaller, but in scale with their parents.

These dolls are of course in the round, and cannot be made by pattern, as are other dolls, so you must work on your own, up to a certain point, using the pictures and sketches only as models. Original ceramic dolls such as these are made as some of the early dolls were made, with ceramic heads, arms, and legs, and cloth bodies. Once dressed, all the cloth portions are covered.

Begin your doll by making a sketch according to the proportions given in chapter 1. This will determine the size of the head you will model. However, clay shrinks about ten percent when it is dry and is fired, so allow that much more when modeling. Also, assuming that you will want to make more than one doll from the mold, add another ten percent for that shrinkage.

Take a lump of modeling clay of the nonhardening kind, and shape a head. If you have no modeling tools, use instead an orangewood stick, a loop of fine wire, or even a paper clip to model the features. Look at the head from all sides and upside down, making it symmetrical.

Next, model one arm and one leg, because it is not necessary to have a right and left for a doll this size. Smooth all the surfaces as perfectly as possible.

You will next make plaster casts of the pieces you have modeled and you will need strong, smooth pans or boxes about an inch deeper than the thickness of the doll head and wide enough so there will be a margin around each part of at least an inch. The sides of this box should be straight. Grease the box thoroughly and tie it so the corners will not open. Nothing is more messy than runaway plaster bursting through open seams.

Plaster-of-Paris can be bought inexpensively in most hardware and paint stores by the pound, and five pounds will make several molds.

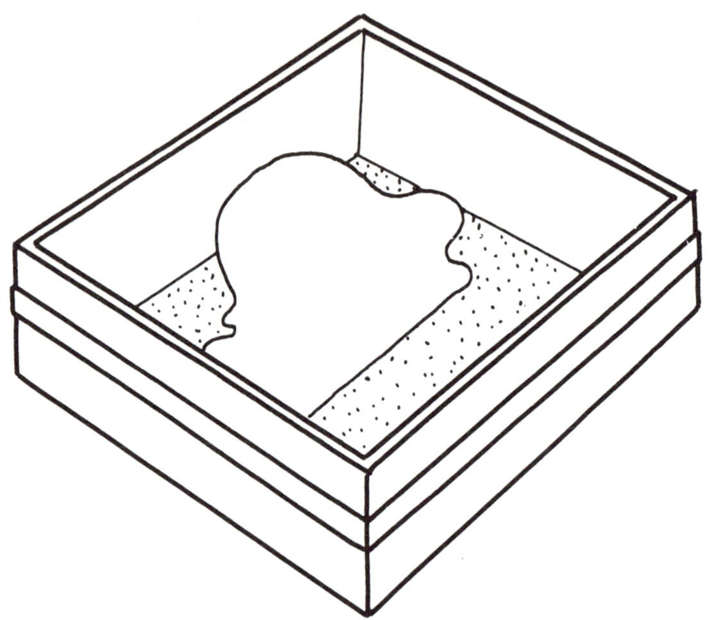

*Model for head is in place in mold after first half has been made.*

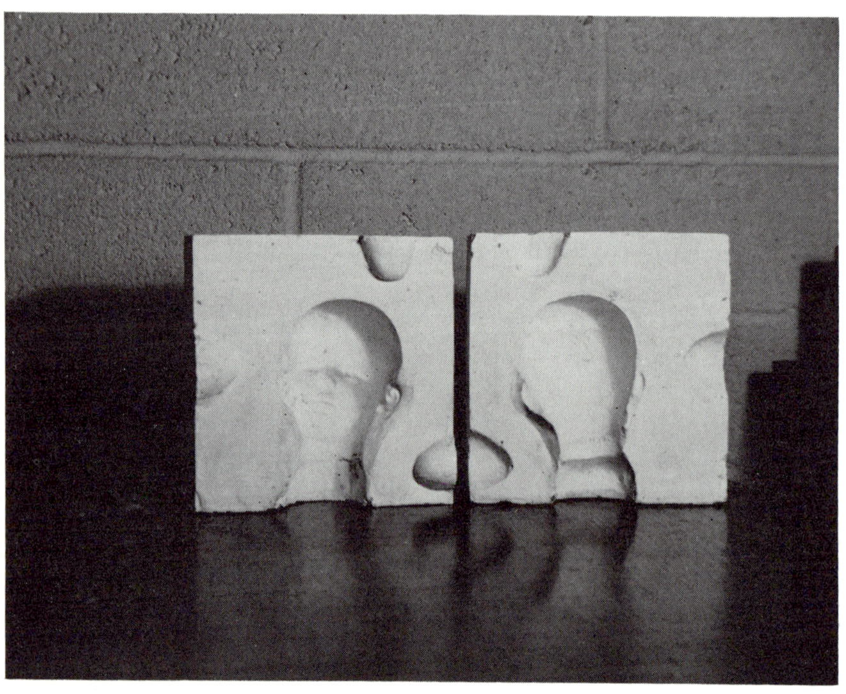

*Mold for doll head shows the locks cut in three sides to keep halves from slipping out of line while in use.*

Be sure to keep it dry till used. You will also need a glass, china, or metal mixing bowl, and a flat stick for stirring.

Put your greased box on a sturdy level surface. Place a cupful or two of water in the mixing bowl. Into it slowly sift, without stirring, enough plaster to form a small mountain rising out of the water. The mixture will be thin. Stir it just enough to mix well, then let it stand until it begins to thicken. Work fast now, and pour into the mold and jiggle gently to even the surface. Let stand until it begins to feel warm and is quite firm. This first layer will raise the pieces above the bottom of the mold. Place the parts you have modeled on top of this plaster and pour a second batch of plaster over the first, exactly halfway up the sides of the pieces being cast. Jiggle to get rid of air bubbles. Let stand till hard, that is, for several hours. With the tip of a teaspoon, scoop out four holes the size of half a marble in the corners of the plaster mold. Grease them well and also grease the top surface of the hardened plaster. The holes, when filled as a part of the top layer, will act as locks, holding the mold in position. Mix more plaster and when it begins to harden pour it into the mold, being sure that it reaches every part of the surface. Jiggle gently to eliminate air bubbles and to level the surface.

Allow to harden for several hours or overnight before separating the two halves of the mold. Do this by gently sliding a thin knife between the two parts of the mold. Remove the clay models and rinse off any bits of plaster so the clay can be used again. Allow the casts to dry for several days.

To use the mold, hold the two parts together with a wide rubber band or soft string. Pour liquid clay or slip into the opening up to the rim. This slip is available already prepared from hobby shops, and is sold by the gallon. It is better to buy than to make it, for other chemicals must be added to the raw clay to give it the right consistency. As the moisture from the slip is absorbed by the plaster mold, more slip must be added to the first pouring to keep it up to the rim. After a few minutes, tip the mold slightly to see how thick the rind of clay is inside the mold. When it is about one-eighth inch thick, pour the remaining slip back into the jug and turn the mold upside down to drain. As soon as the clay inside the mold loses its gloss and is dry enough to hold its own weight, separate the mold and gently lift out the casting. While it is harder to make a good casting the first time a mold is used, it can be done. If the casting sticks, try again. Sometimes a slight undercutting in the original model will need to be corrected before a casting comes out perfectly.

Allow the casting to dry to the leather-hard stage, when it will be ready for trimming or fettling, with a modeling tool. Trim away the

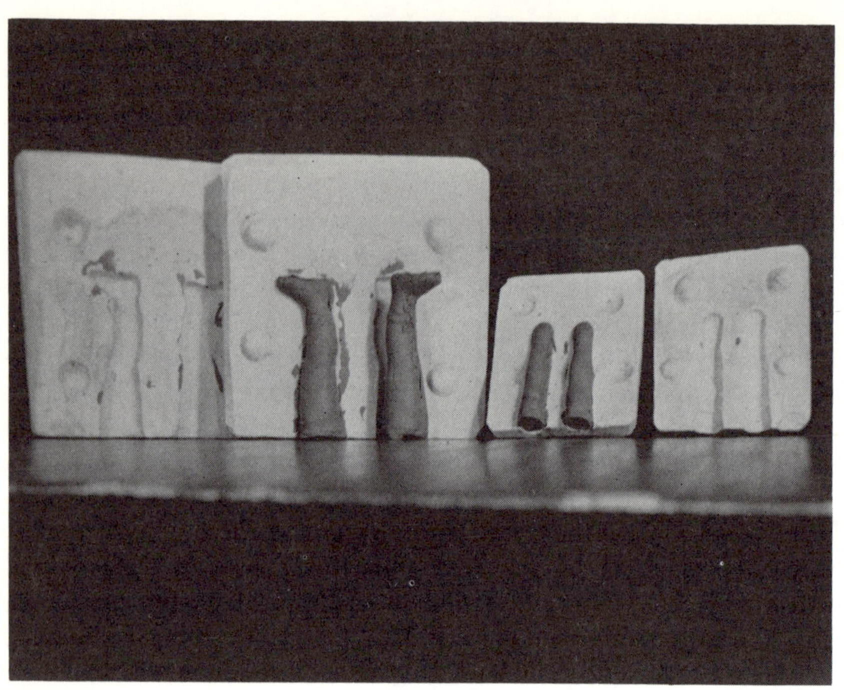

*Plaster molds are opened when clay slip has become hard enough, and removed for finishing.*

*Doll head is removed from plaster mold and is now ready to trim away seams and irregularities.*

seam line where the two parts of the mold met, and all irregularities. Now sponge lightly with a bit of damp cotton or an elephant-ear sponge, being very careful not to rub out fine details of the modeling. On the heads, make a small hole in the clay at each corner of the shoulders, using a match stick. These will later be used for sewing the head onto the cloth body.

On the arms and legs cut a thin groove around near the top. These will be used when sewing on the cloth sections. Dry the pieces thoroughly and fire or have someone else do it. After firing, the surface is dull and porous and must be glazed. For this, dip into or spray with clear, transparent glaze and fire again. First make sure the holes in the shoulders are not filled with glaze, and that the grooves in arms and legs are also freed from glaze.

You now have an all-white glazed doll head, arms, and legs. The arms are finished, but the head and legs must be painted. A really fine doll's features are always painted with overglaze color (china paint), not colored glaze, using the finest of brushes. Ceramic suppliers carry both liquid and dry overglaze color, which has an endless shelf-life, and liquid color that is already mixed. Dry color is mixed with turpentine on a palette or a piece of glass, with a palette knife until it is smooth. An oily medium is traditionally used for this but has a tendency to run except when applied thinly, but is almost a must when tinting a doll's cheeks.

Do this first, rubbing a small amount of medium into the palm of your hand, then rubbing a small pad made by placing a bit of cotton in the soft silk into the color in your hand. Tap the pad on the doll's cheeks as if applying rouge, blending the color at the edges and centering it high on the cheeks. Paint the eye-color next, using either the blue or the brown. Do not make the black pupil of the eyes until the second firing.

Now color the mouth, using a thin wash of red. It is better to apply thin coats of color than to use only one, for the paint will peel if too thick. Overglaze color may be painted and fired many times if needed to get the desired effect. Now paint the eyebrows—a short, straight line on these small dolls, and also a short, thin line to mark the top of the eyes. Two important don'ts must be mentioned here: do not, ever, paint eyelashes on a doll, and do not, ever, paint pink nostrils.

Brush a thin tint of color for the hair, repeating for the second firing. Delicate color is always more attractive than heavy, harsh shades.

If the doll is to be in costume, refer to books of costumes for shoe styles and paint the selected ones on the feet. Some old china dolls had cobalt-blue garters painted on their legs, and the oldest ones wore

*Victorian lady and gentleman shown without clothes illustrates method of attaching heads, arms, and legs to the cloth bodies.*

*Family of Victorian dollhouse dolls made of glazed china. Man and woman have stuffed cloth bodies, while children are all ceramic.*

slippers without heels. Modern dolls may wear painted slippers or sandals, or even go barefooted.

Overglaze color must be fired in a lower temperature than that for bisque or glaze, and reds and pinks in particular fire out completely if the kiln is too hot. If the firing is done in a ceramic studio they will of course take care of this.

After all the ceramic parts are completed, make the cloth body. Again, the patterns given here can only be approximate, since each doll head mold will create its own size. To adapt a pattern to your own doll, measure *inside* the shoulders to get the size of the body at the top, then using this measurement make a test pattern of the body, and try it out in cloth. After stuffing this test body, adjust it so that the head will fit snugly on it. When the pattern is corrected this way, cut the final body from a piece of firm muslin or sateen, adding a seam allowance. Turn rightside out and stuff tightly with clean sawdust, then close the open top with overcasting. Sew the arm and leg sections at the side seams and attach to the ceramic arms and legs as shown in

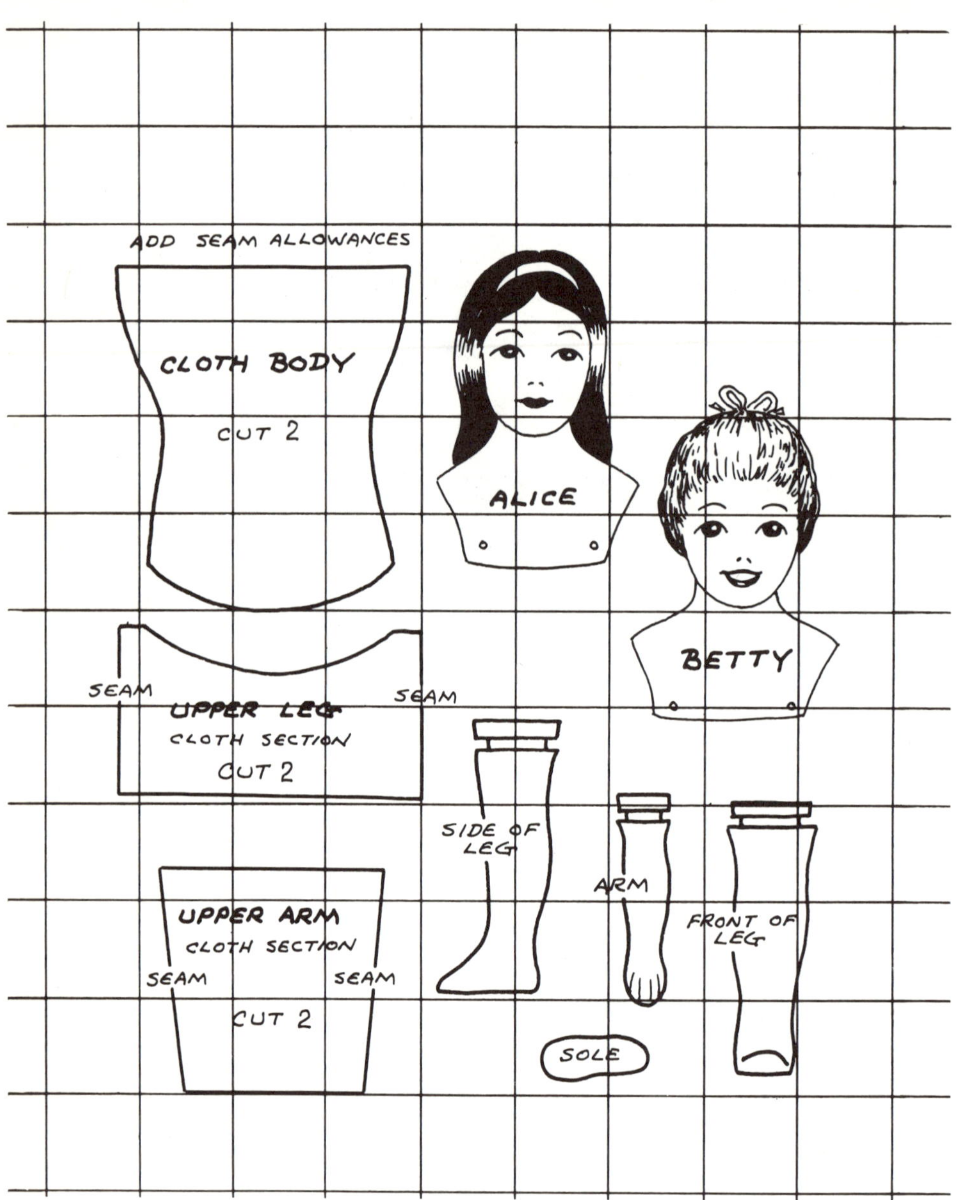


*Ceramic head designs for Betty and Alice and arm and leg ceramic pieces. Cloth body, arm, and leg patterns are made of cloth.*

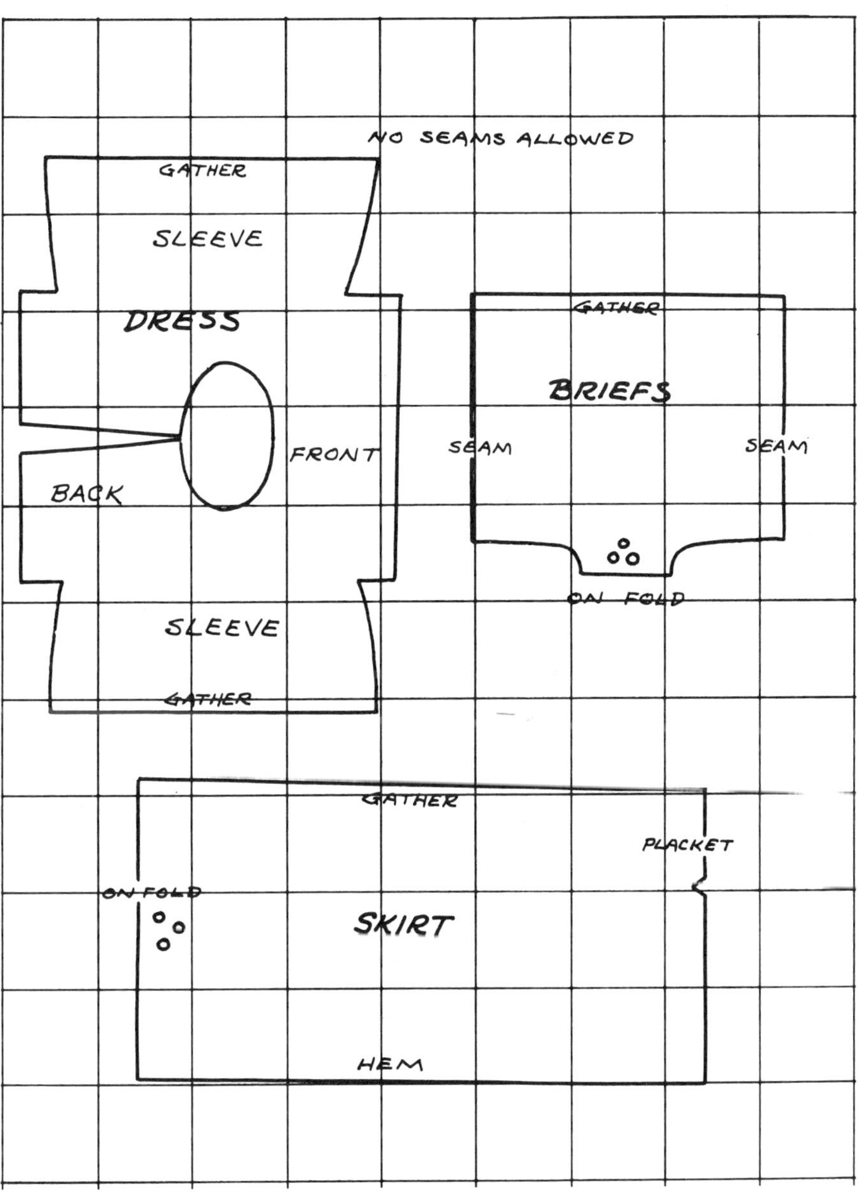


*Patterns for dress and underwear for Betty and Alice.*

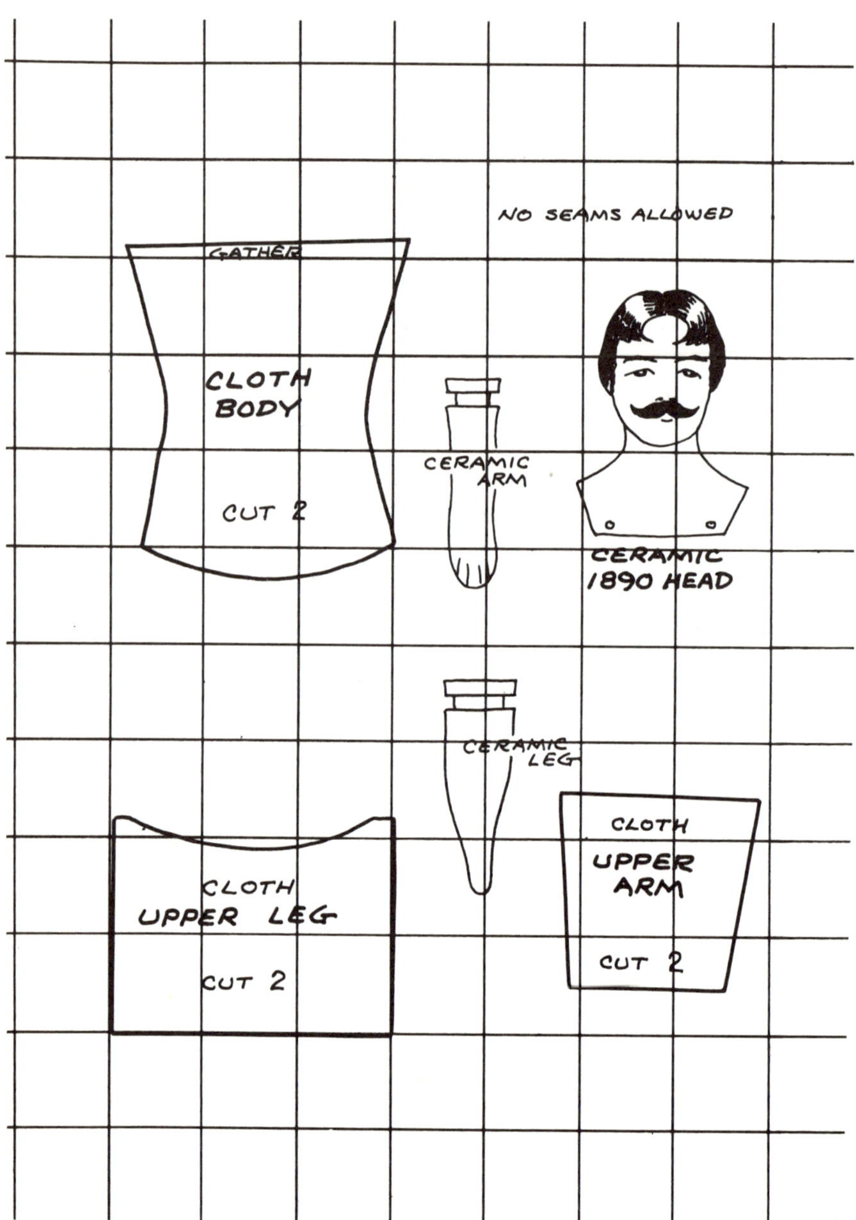


*Ceramic head and body patterns for Victorian dollhouse man.*

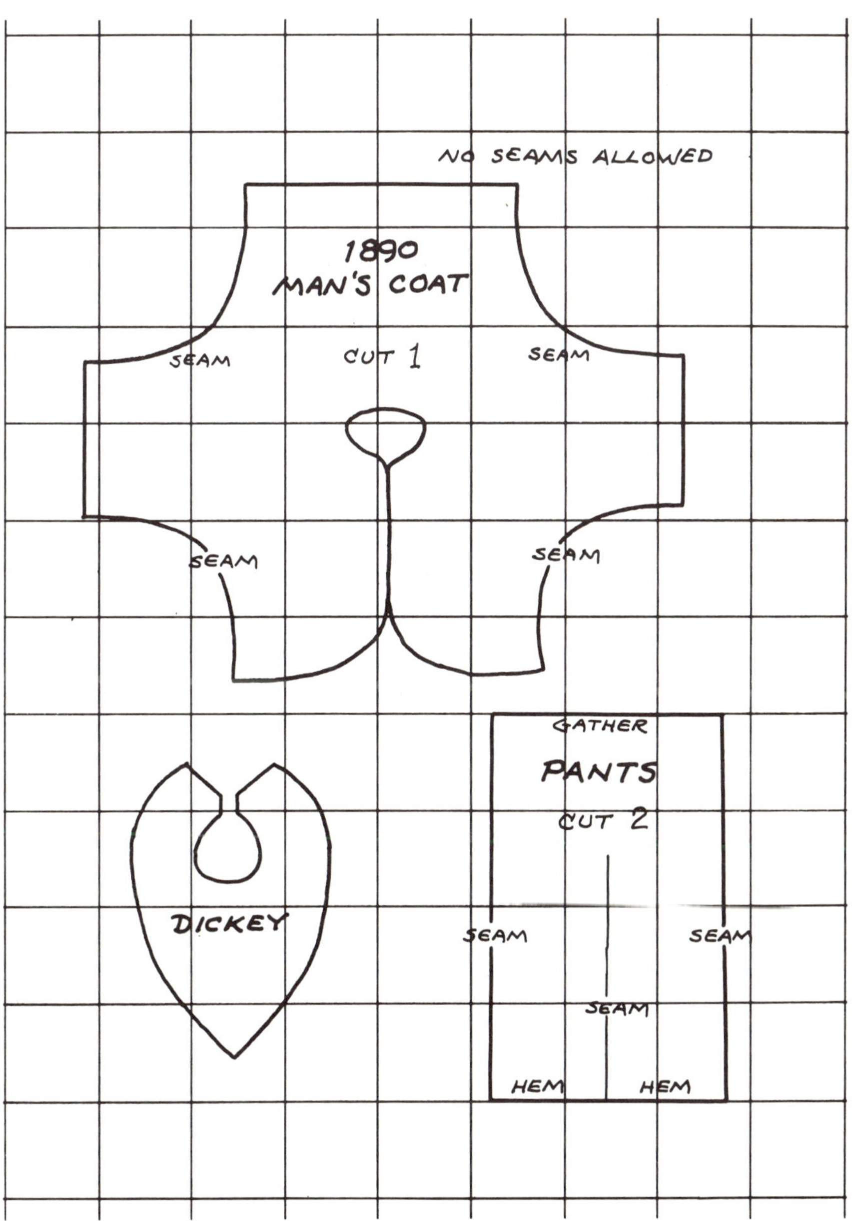


*Patterns for clothes for the Victorian dollhouse man.*

*Brown-eyed Betty and Alice in Wonderland were made in a small electric kiln in my kitchen. Their bodies are cloth, stuffed with sawdust.*

the illustration. Wrap several times with thread in the grooves, and fasten the thread securely. Turn rightside out.

Do not put stuffing into the arms of small dolls like this, but stuff the cloth sections of the legs, then turn in the edges and whip together. Sew the arms to the top of the body section, and overcast the legs onto the lower part. Push the head down onto the body and sew it in place, using a long needle and strong thread. Run the needle clear through the body from one hole to the other. Fasten invisibly.

The suggested use of sawdust is obvious: it is clean, easily obtained from a lumber yard or a home workshop, and will last for years. Other stuffing materials may be used, but after making thousands of ceramic dolls, I still prefer the sawdust.

As always, use only fine, soft materials when dressing dolls, and as was true of the body patterns, the patterns for clothes given here can only be approximate, since clothes must be fitted on the dolls themselves.

Some people enjoy making dolls more than dressing them, but dolls this size are easy to handle—neither too small nor too large. It seems paradoxical, but the smaller the doll the longer it takes to dress it, and while it is not recommended that doll clothes be made by machine, for large dolls, long inside seams may well be machine-stitched.

It is possible to make a group of dolls, all in the same mold, as has been done for collections of museum figures of First Ladies, and the Boston Museum of Fine Arts mannequins, where costumes, rather than the doll itself are stressed. By changing the hair and eye color alone, the figures look different.

Advanced ceramists may attempt making bisque dolls rather than glazed ones, but it is not recommended that beginners do so. A good bisque doll must be smooth of surface, perfect in all details, and is entirely outside the hobby-shop class. These dolls are made of a high-fire clay of the so-called stoneware type, since it is fine grained and smoother than the low-fire clays. It is also trickier to paint bisque, because colors sink into the surface quickly and cannot be simply wiped off with turpentine if corrections are needed, as on a glazed surface. Bisque dolls are extremely attractive when well done and will present none of the glaze problems that often perplex the dollmaker when the glaze is either too thick, too thin, does not fit the clay and crazes. Also it requires a second firing.

If you insist on trying out a bisque doll, here are a few suggestions. Make or acquire the most perfectly detailed plaster molds possible. Strain the slip through a fine screen to eliminate coarse particles. First, fill your mold with pink slip. After a few minutes, pour out and refill with white slip and allow it to build up to the usual thickness. This conserves the more expensive pink slip and is the way the German and French dolls of the last century were made. Incidentally, most of those doll heads were made by families as a cottage industry, which should encourage today's home craftsman.

The plaster molds are of course a necessity for making ceramic dolls as described here, and they can also be used for making papier-mâché doll parts, particularly for larger dolls than these eight-inch ones. The molds themselves must be thoroughly greased before using that material, for otherwise the paper will stick to the plaster. Once the casting is dry, it can be finished the way it was described for the Eskimo and Indian dolls in chapters 8 and 9 by covering the surface with strips of paper dipped in white glue.

It is also possible to make all-ceramic dolls, as the 1890 child shown here was made, but have no illusions, you will have to solve serious problems in firing the glazed dolls, otherwise they will stick to the kiln. Tiny arms and legs must be designed so they can be sus-

*All-ceramic child with attached arms is less than three inches tall.*

pended on wires similar to bead racks, then later fastened to the body with wire or elastic. Personally, several years ago when making ceramic dolls commercially, and after many frantic attempts, I gave up the project, and the child shown here is the only survivor. I pass the patterns and designs illustrated here to anyone who wants to try them, but for myself, I decided that there were better ways to make two-inch dolls than of glazed china.

The lazy dollmaker will find "greenware" doll heads, cast from old dolls, in many supply shops. What you do is to take the head home, trim it, fire, glaze, and paint the head. This isn't creative dollmaking, so at least scratch the word COPY and your initials on the back before firing, so that no uninformed person will be deceived into thinking it is an antique. Of course, as always, be sure to initial your doll, adding the date. It is astonishing to see common, familiar things suddenly termed *antique* by a younger generation.

# 14

# *Making and Dressing a Costume Doll*

Dollmaking generally includes doll dressing, as I have detailed in previous chapters. However, dressing dolls can be done by those who perhaps do not wish to construct them, or who want to make clothes for a doll already at hand. This chapter will offer a few suggestions for doing both, with the hope that you will boldly design your own doll costumes, as well. The doll shown here is exactly the size of a Barbie doll, that teenager who revolutionized the doll manufacturing business to the point where every manufacturer was forced to meet the competition by introducing his own model the same size. Clothes that fit one, in other words, fit them all, as do the clothes shown here.

Doll collectors have their own names for certain dolls, and these are listed as teenage fashion dolls. What is the difference between a fashion doll and a costume doll? A fashion doll is one dressed in clothes in style at the moment, while a costume doll wears clothes of some other time or place. The exact moment a fashion doll becomes a costume doll is as hard to determine as when an outdated object may be called an antique, in spite of the one-time 1890 deadline.

Assuming that the doll to be dressed is also to be made, and in the proportion of the teenage dolls, it must be from ten to eleven and one-half inches tall. There are many permanent-finish cotton fabrics being made that are ideal for doll bodies, and I have chosen a pale pink broadcloth, closely woven but not bulky, and for stuffing used the polyester fiber—ideal for small dolls.

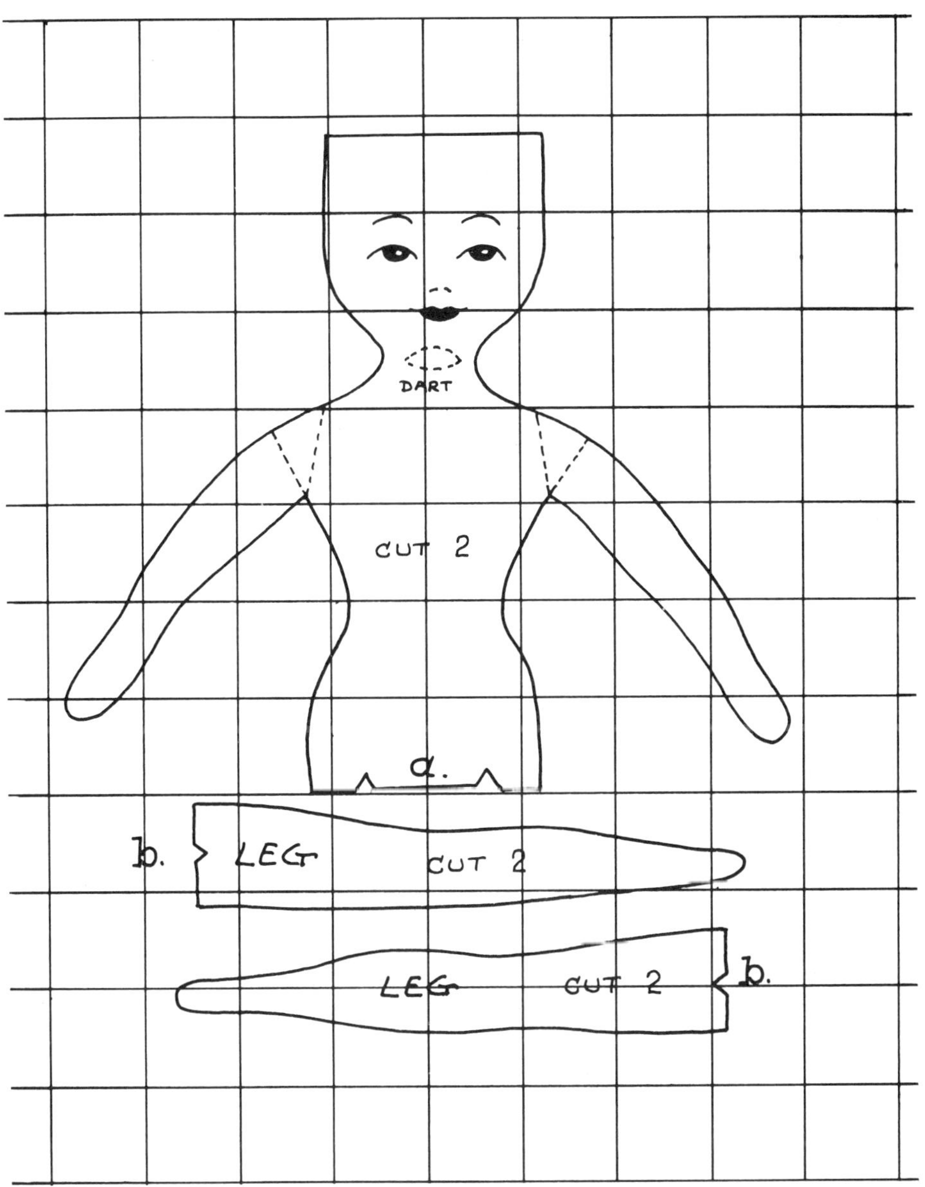


*Pattern for teenage costume doll.*

Trace the pattern in the illustration onto tissue or tracing paper. Reread chapters 1 and 2, before going further.

Trace the pattern on a double layer of the broadcloth, using pencil, lightly. Baste the two pieces of cloth together with long stitches up the center of the body, arms, and legs, just to make certain that they stay together during the process of stitching the seams. Now sew the body together all around the outside, except for the top of the head. Leave that open. Sew, either on the sewing machine or by hand, directly on the penciled line, making fine, even, close stitches. Use thread the same color as the cloth. Make a slash up into the armpits and between the legs. Overcast several times at these points for reinforcement. Trim carefully all around the doll, about one-eighth inch away from the stitching. Make a tiny dart under the chin, as shown in the drawing, to shape the face.

Turn the doll right side out. This is a tedious business on a small doll like this, but is easier to do if you don't hurry. A darning needle is often helpful in stubborn places.

Stuffing the doll comes next, and is also a test of your patience. Stuffing must be packed in place as tightly as possible, and this is easier to do if small wads of it are added at a time. It is helpful to push each wad in place as you add it, using a small, smooth stick. I use a wooden chopstick for the purpose. Begin this stuffing with the feet and legs. At the dotted line run a tight row of small stitches across the leg. Leave about one-eighth inch unstuffed, and again stitch across the leg.

Continue the stuffing by first filling the hands and arms. Pack stuffing as tightly as possible, just as for the legs. As soon as the first dotted lines are reached, stitch across the arm, then leave one-eighth inch space, run another line of stitches across the arm.

Continue stuffing the body of the doll until you reach the chest section. Wrap a matchstick with the fiber and bury it in the stuffing between the chest and the top of the head to reinforce the neck. Also, mold the bust area and stuff so it will be emphasized, since these dolls are not flat-chested. It is also possible to mold the head slightly as it is stuffed, making it round and natural looking. Run a line of gathering stitches along the top of the head pieces, and when the head is full and rounded pull up the thread and overcast the edges flat to the head. This will be covered by the wig, but should be smooth for a base. The doll is now ready for its face.

Mark the features lightly, then embroider them with a single strand of colored thread. Remember that the tiniest changes make a great deal of difference in the doll's expression.

The wig may be made of either fine yarn, embroidery cotton, or

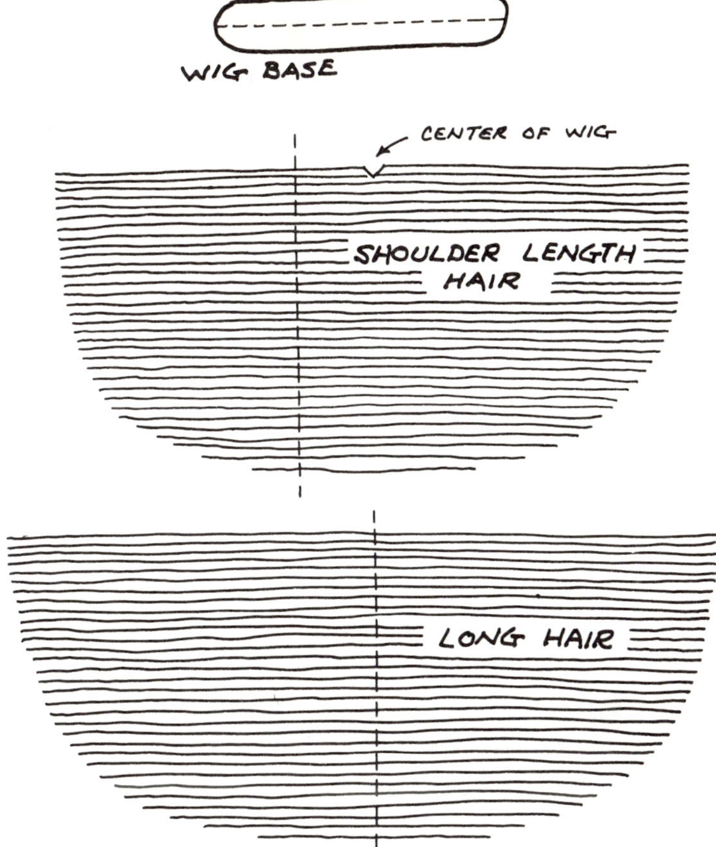


*Outlines for making teenage doll wigs of yarn, indicating part with line of stitching.*

strands cut from an old wig. If the part is to come in the center of the head, sew hair to a narrow strip of the body material with a line of backstitches made with flesh-colored thread; if the part will be on one side, place the reinforcing strip off center. When attaching the wig to the head, sew invisibly at both ends of this strip, then make several holding stitches into the head with color that matches the wig. In this way the scalp will not show through the hair.

Shape the feet by bending the foot up for about one inch and tacking it securely to the instep, then fastening securely.

Feet as small as these may more easily have slippers indicated by painting the feet with a little acrylic paint, or by covering the soles and sides with satin stitch done with embroidery cotton.

*Teenage costume doll wears crocheted bathing suit.*

Making clothes for dolls this size will be one way to use all the tiny scraps you have been saving. Small pieces of brocade, satin, silk, velvet, lace, and ribbon that hardly seemed worth saving may well be just the thing here. If you were born to be a packrat, rejoice. As an example, the two-inch bit of lace forming the lace collar for the medieval lady was at the bottom of my doll-dressing box, where it had been for a dozen years.

In selecting a costume for your doll, don't confine yourself to the familiar Colonial dame, Pilgrim mother, or Gibson girl styles. Instead try a Greek or Roman woman, an Egyptian, Cretan, or even a copy of your great-grandmother as pictured in a family daguerreotype. With

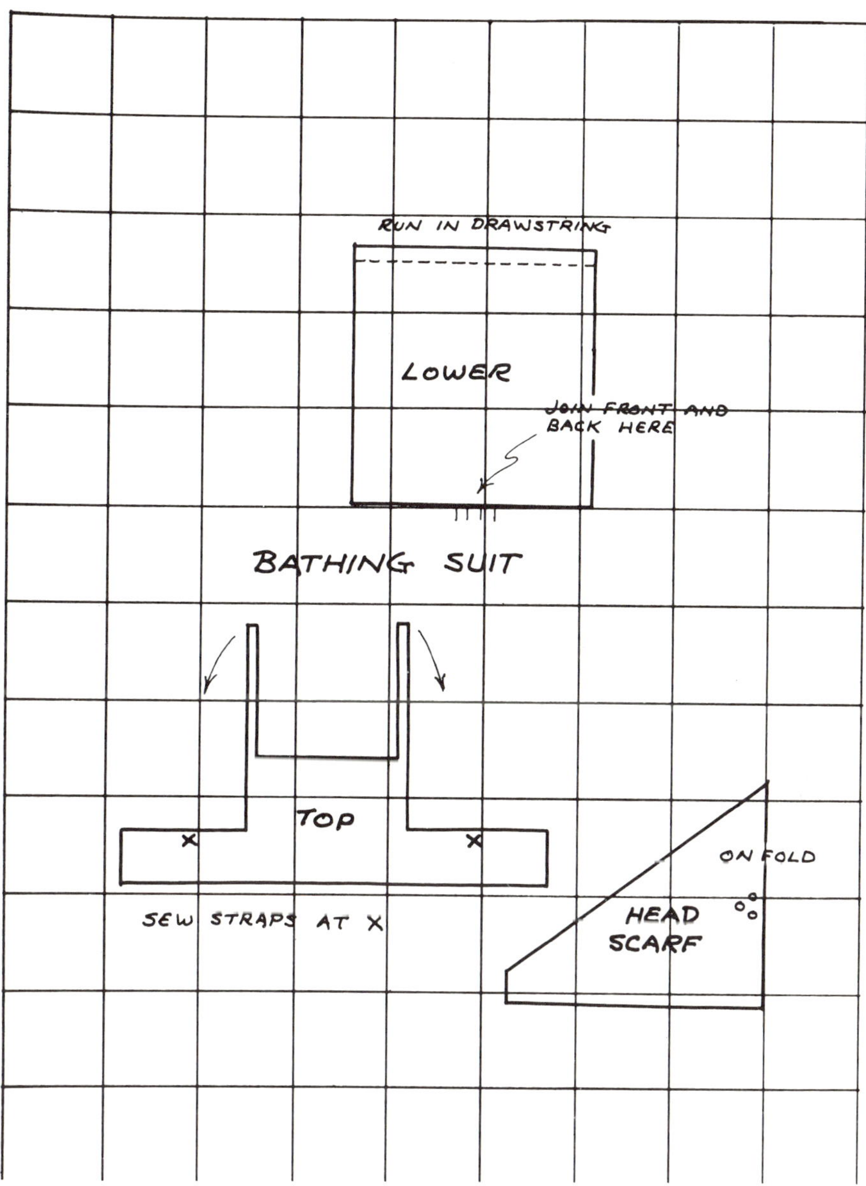


*Bathing suit pattern for teenage costume doll is crocheted or used with knit fabric.*

the handful of patterns here, you can change them into numerous styles to dress the doll you have made or one bought in a store.

It is not necessary to make underwear for dolls this size and style, in fact it is likely to make them look too bulky, so we can go ahead with a few examples of costumes.

The first dressing project is the simple one of crocheting a bikini-type swim suit. Use fingering yarn or Baby yarn, and a No. 1 steel crochet hook. Use the drawings to check for size and shape. For the top section:

Chain thirty-six.

In the second stitch from the hook make a single crochet. Repeat to the end of the chain. Chain two. Turn. Repeat first row. Break off yarn. Fasten yarn in the eighth stitch from the end of strip. Chain two. Make double crochet in next ten stitches. Turn. Chain two. Repeat last row. Without breaking yarn, chain nine for shoulder strap. Attach to back of strip. Make the other shoulder strap the same way. Fasten with a snap fastener.

The pants section is made by crocheting a chain of thirty. Join without twisting. Make single crochet in each stitch, then continue until there are fourteen rows. Break off yarn and join the front to the back with three stitches. Make a chain of thirty-six stitches and run through the top edge of the pants. When on the doll, pull this draw-string up and tie at the back.

Make a head scarf by the pattern to use with this costume. Finish all edges with a tiny rolled hem.

### *Cardigan Sweater*

This is also made of fingering or baby yarn but is knitted, using No. 3 needles. The gauge is seven stitches to one inch.

For the back: cast on twenty-six stitches. K 1, P 1 for one-half inch.

Knit in stockinette stitch (knit one row, purl one row) till piece measures two inches. Cast on twelve stitches at each end of row and continue in stockinette stitch till piece measures three inches. Knit twenty-two. Cast off six stitches for back of neck.

Attach another length of yarn and K 22. Continue in stockinette stitch for four rows. On each front edge cast on four stitches. These will make the front bands of the sweater. One side is worked P 1, K 1, P 1, K 1; the other side just reversed. Continue until the wrist measures two inches.

Cast off twelve stitches at each side edge. Continue until piece

*Teenage fashion doll wears hand-knitted cardigan sweater and wool pants.*

measures one and one-half inches. K 1, P 1, for one-half inch. Bind off.

Sew the fronts and back together on the wrong side and sew three small buttons to the left front.

### *Pants*

The slacks or pants shown on the doll are made of felt or light-weight soft material. All seams are allowed. Slash at the back for about one inch for a placket. Fasten with snap fastener. A piece of soft ribbon is tied at the neck for a scarf.

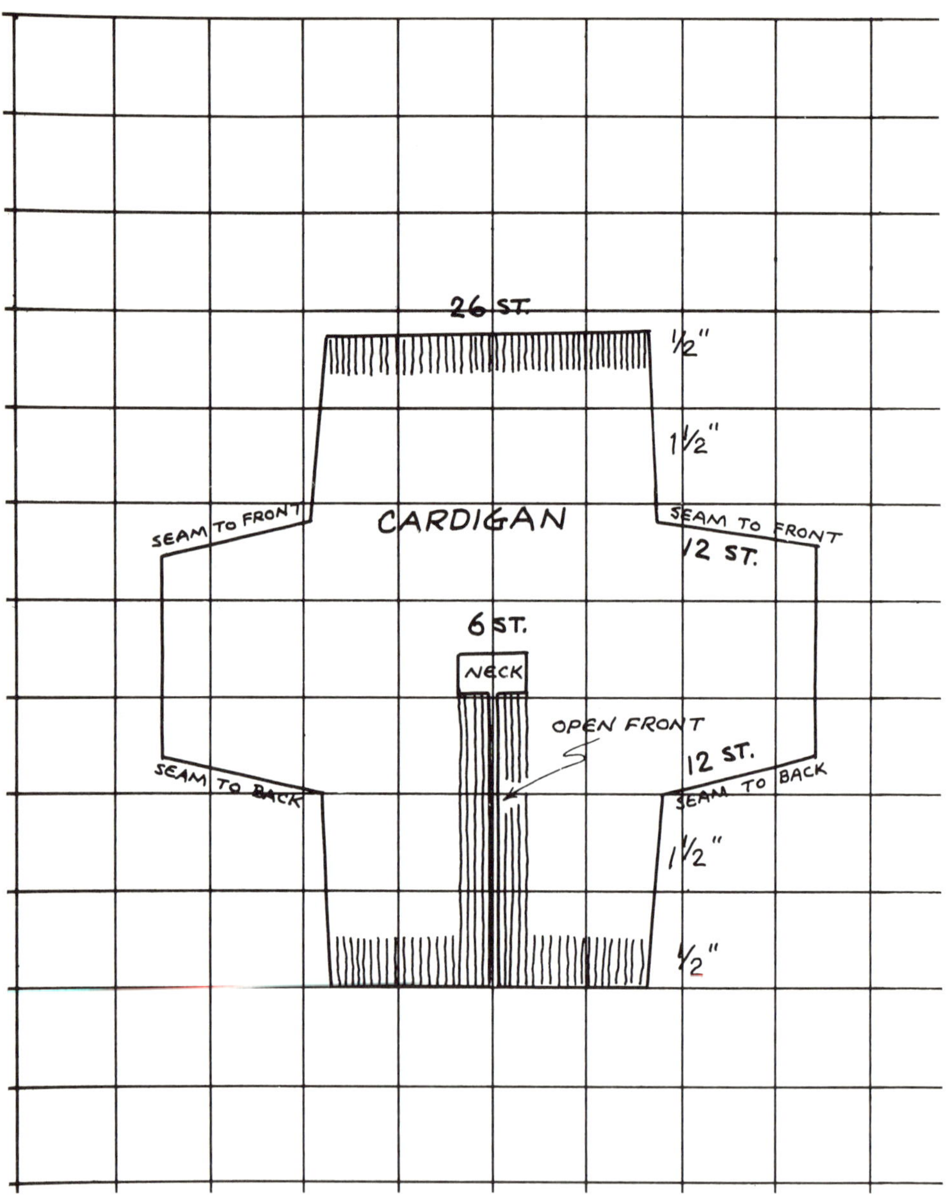


*Cardigan sweater pattern for teenage doll may be used by knitting or crocheting garment to fit it.*

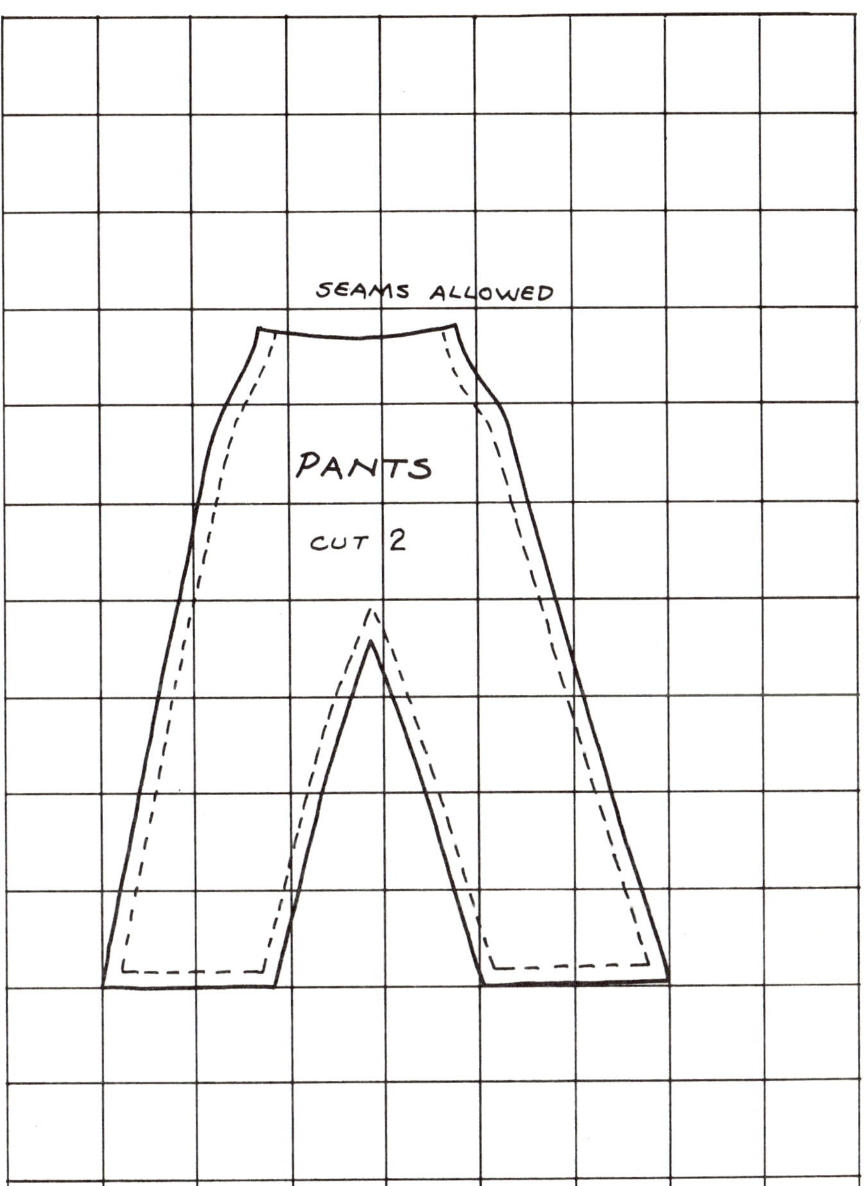


*Pants pattern for teenage doll.*

## *The Queen*

This is a basic pattern, and many changes may be added to create glamour. It is also well adapted to other types of costume by adding sleeves, making the skirt narrower, fitting it at the top, or in other ways using it to experiment with in dress designing. As worn by this doll, it is typical of the 1860 period when hoop skirts were in style. If you wish to cut a cardboard or crinoline foundation from the pattern, place the doll inside it before closing the edges and then either tape or sew them together with the doll in place. After the dress is made, slip it over the doll's head and arms. It is a good idea to use the selvage edge of the dress material for the bottom edge of the skirt rather than making a hem. Make the skirt, then the waist. Join them together on the wrong side and fasten at the back with snap fasteners.

*Queen in her taffeta and lace hoopskirt wears a crown sparkling with diamonds.*

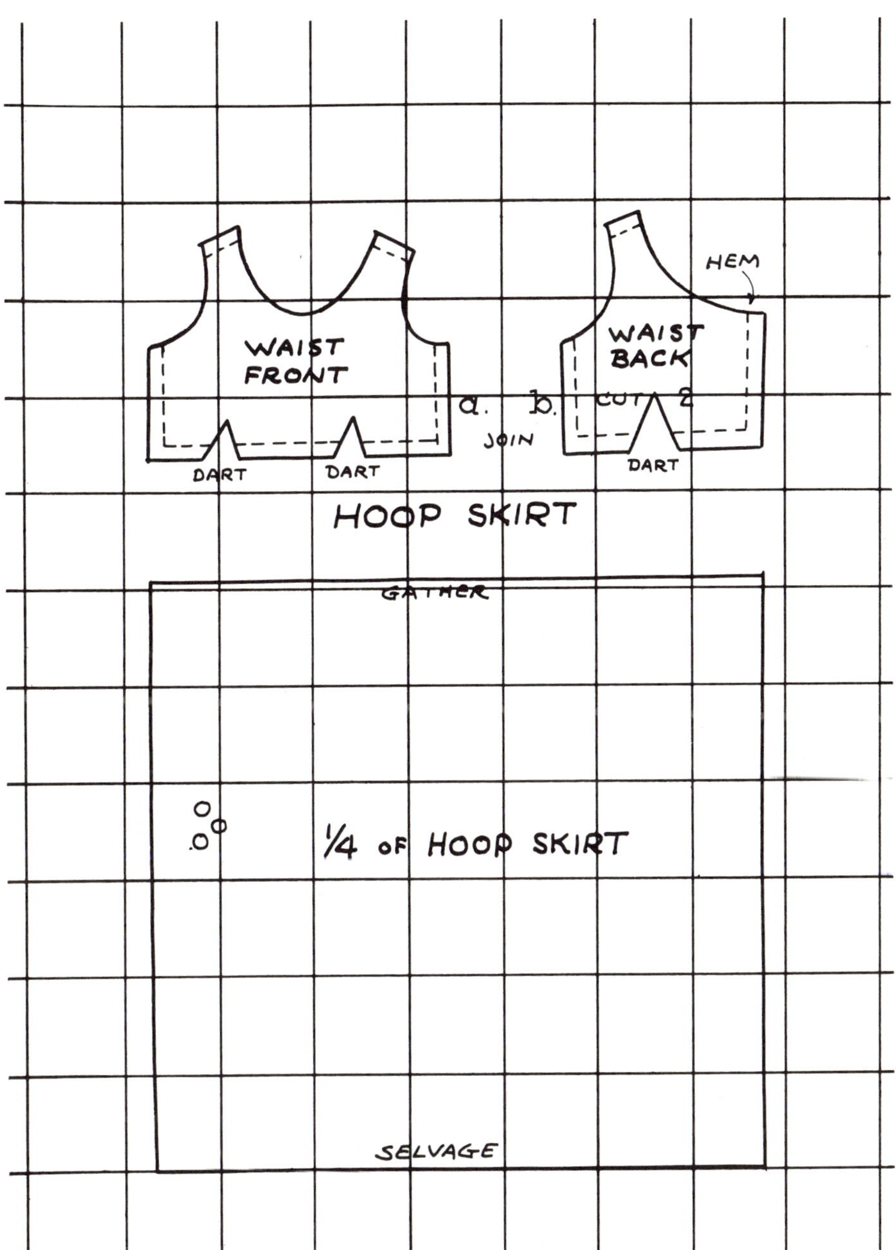


*Pattern of the Queen's costume as made in hoopskirt style.*

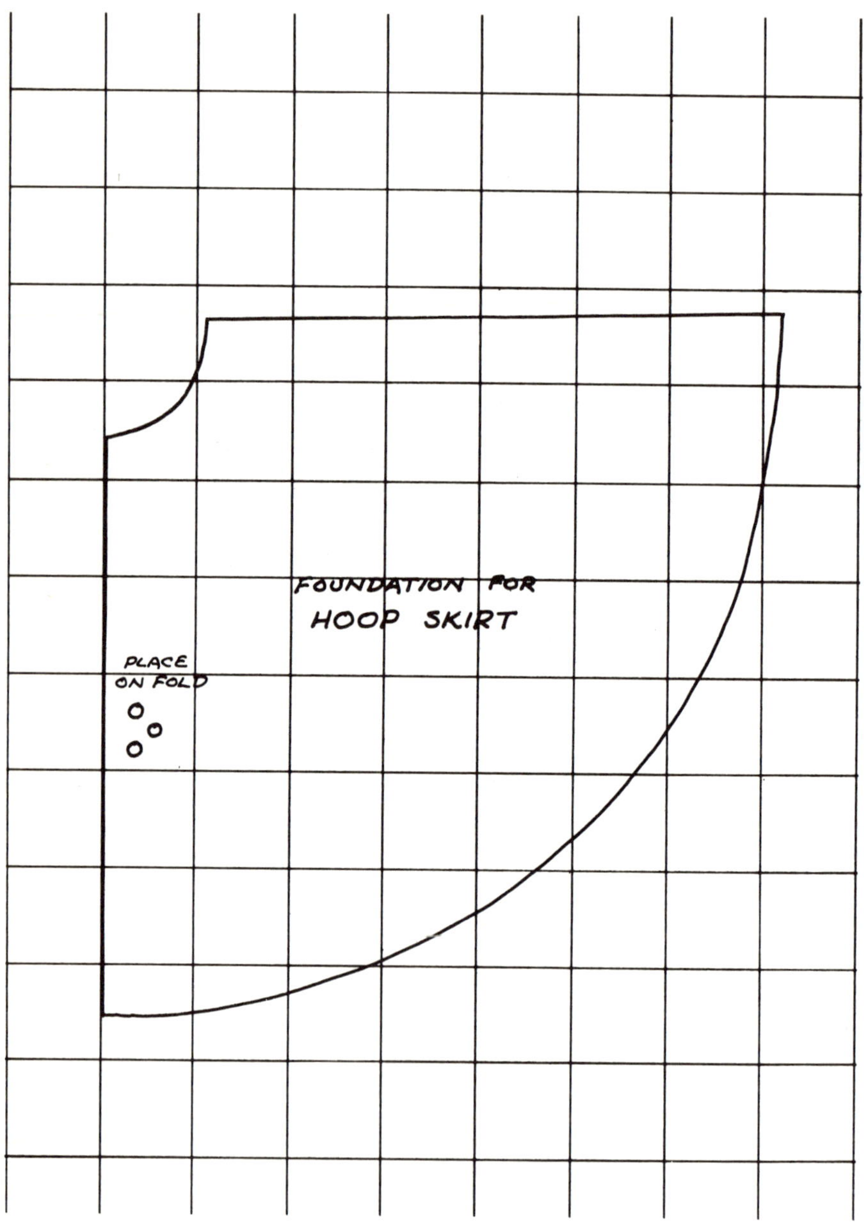


*Pattern for the display foundation for the hoopskirt costume.*

Gather a twelve-inch-long strip of two-inch-wide lace along one side to fit the top of the bodice and sew in place. The use of this flounce is authentic for the time and eliminates the need for sleeves. The same lace could be gathered and sewed to the lower part of the skirt for a flounce.

A section of discarded costume jewelry was just right to make the Queen's crown and was fastened to her hair with minute hairpins bent from fine wire. She could have had a high-backed comb instead of the crown, a lace mantilla added, or a wreath of small artificial flowers. Or perhaps a flowery bonnet.

### *Medieval Lady*

Dressing the doll in this costume gives you a chance to use small scraps of soft velvet, as was done here. For ease in making, this pattern is ideal, for a princess style with kimono sleeves requires the minimum of joining and seaming. The back is slashed for a placket and is fastened with a hook or snap fastener. Certainly no dress could be easier to make.

The conical headpiece, known as a hennin, is cut out of lightweight cardboard and the edges of it are securely taped together with the edges meeting but not overlapping. It is then covered with gift-wrap paper in a small design and glued at all edges. The veil is the sheerest possible chiffon or net, not hemmed, and is gathered tightly together at one edge and poked through the tip of the cone, then held in place with a few drops of white glue.

A strip of narrow ribbon is glued to the front edge of the hennin and the long ends allowed to hang down the doll's back.

Here again there are many ways to change this basic pattern, and to add ornamental touches as long as they are in keeping with the styles and materials of the fourteenth century. The veil, for example, may either hang down the back or be flung over the lady's shoulder, since old prints and paintings show veils worn both ways. This is another instance of how use may be made of the richness of libraries and museums when designing costumes for dolls.

If you are looking for still other ways to dress a doll, consider the variety of accessories there are, including hats. No patterns are given here because making them involves actual fitting on the doll, but methods are simple.

In modern days it is unusual to see a woman wearing a hat, but until forty or fifty years ago, hats were always worn away from home,

*Medieval lady is dressed in green velvet and beaded belt. Her hennin covers her hair completely.*

and perhaps there a woman would wear some other kind of headgear, a sunbonnet, or a dust cap, or even a "boudoir cap."

Those were the times when a woman could cure the blues by buying the most beautiful hat she could find. This was possibly one of the most utterly feminine ways of renewal, for hats were pretty things. Back in the 1900s, the mother of this woman may have appeared in a stiff-brimmed sailor hat, held on her head with long hatpins, to go with her shirtwaist having a starched collar like a man's but her daughters preferred the flower-covered confections that appeal to those who dress dolls.

Even earlier than the sailor hats were the gay little bonnets that the Empress Eugenie favored, and that reappeared later. They were

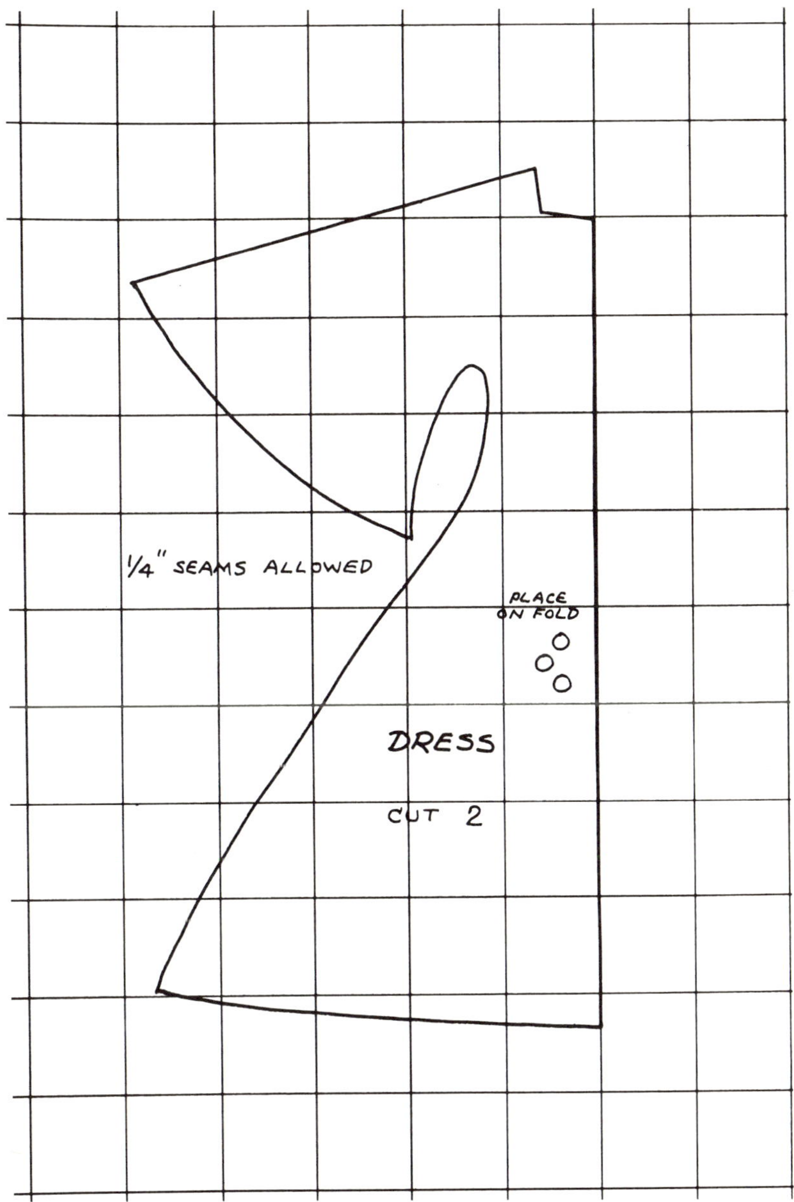


*Pattern for dress for the medieval lady, which is made of velvet.*

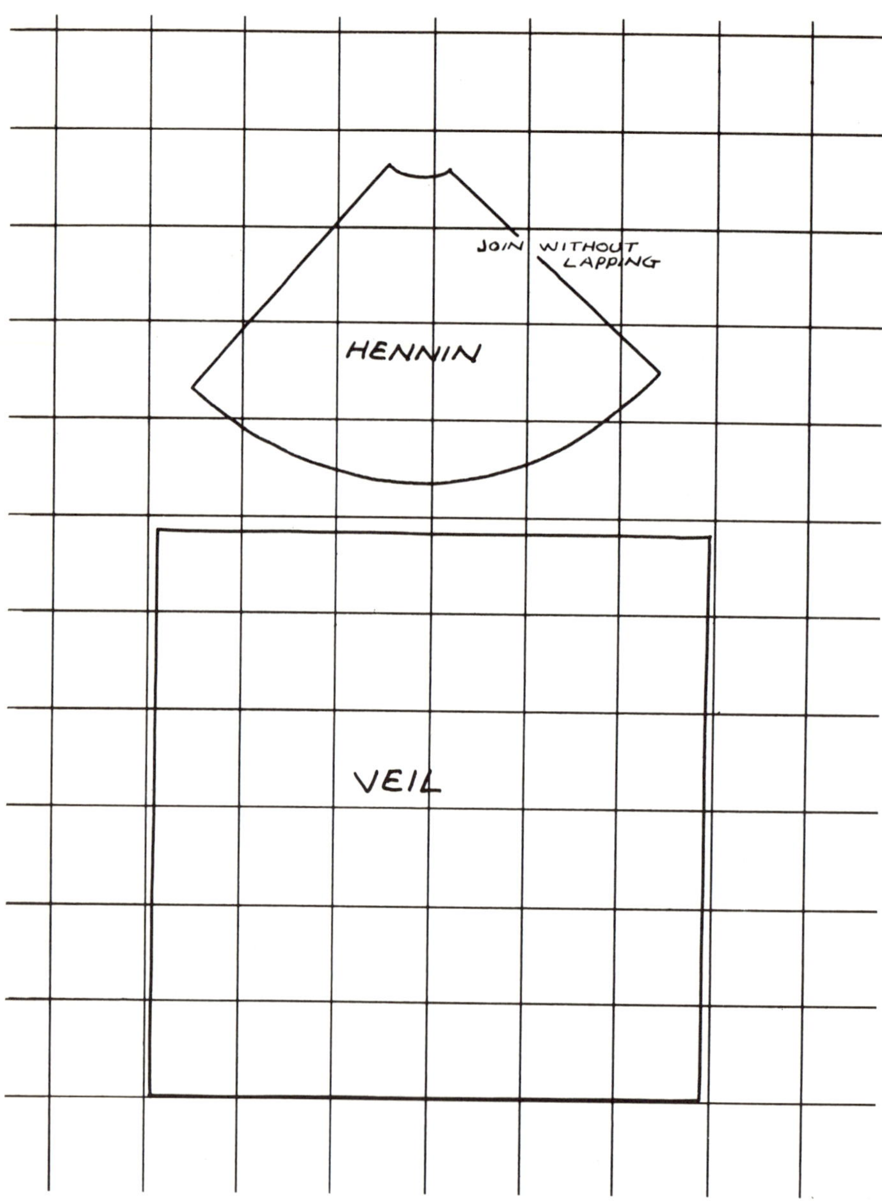


*Patterns for the medieval lady costume. Headpiece and veil.*

built on wire or buckram frames covered with silk or velvet. They had long ties for fastening under the chin, and were trimmed with flowers or tipped with feathers. It was correct to have the hat match the dress, and this called for a woman to have many hats.

In the latter part of her life, Queen Victoria was pictured in her widow's bonnet and veil, simple and somber, for at that period it was customary for a woman whose husband had died to go into deep mourning for a year. Deep mourning meant wearing all black, and no jewelry except jet. At the end of the year she might add touches of white, then gradually grays and lavenders. All women, widowed or not, adopted the Queen's type of bonnet automatictlly as soon as they reached the age of forty, admitting then that they were old ladies.

Turning away from the bonnet story, comes the day when wide-brimmed hats known as merry widows appeared. They dripped with long ostrich plumes or flowers, and swept off the face to reveal the wearer's profile against an elegant background of silk or velvet. Hats of this kind belong with Gibson girl styles, which included rustling taffeta petticoats covered with ruffles, bosoms padded with still other rows of ruffles, and skirts that trailed in the dust. These are attractive fashions for dolls, and the clothes can be adapted from basic patterns. As for the hats, make a brim out of a circle of stiffening material, cover with silk, cut a crown from the same silk, and gather to fit the opening for the doll's head. Trim it with small artificial flowers or the feathers you have saved.

Beside hats, there are gloves to make by tracing around the doll's hand and arm, allowing a very small seam allowance. Gloves may be made from silk or fine, soft leather. Victorian ladies wore their evening gloves almost up to their shoulders, and they usually also carried a fan.

To make a fan cut a small circle of gold or silver paper, then remove a pie-shaped piece of it about one-fourth the size of the circle. Fold the paper into accordion pleats. Hold the base together with one or two stitches of fine cord and tie knots in the ends. Hang the fan by the loop over your lady's arm.

Other additions to a doll's costume could include the little face veils worn both inside and outside the hats. For this a small piece of fine net can be turned into a veil. These were popular after World War I.

Also, don't forget the fur muffs, carried by both women and their daughters, to keep their hands warm in winter. Make them of scraps of fur, perhaps to match the fur toque she wears. Give your doll of this period a flair by pinning a bouquet of violets at her breast.

Summing up this sketch of clothes and accessories suitable for dolls, it seems fitting to turn now to the costumes and accessories of a tribe of the first Americans, the Hopi Indians.

# 15

# *Kachina Dolls*

To be authentic, Kachina dolls must have been made by an Indian of the American southwest, usually a Hopi, living in one of the villages in Arizona. It is the men of this region who carve the dolls from a piece of root from a cottonwood tree, then paint and decorate the dolls. Those who are not Hopi Indians and who have no access to cottonwood trees cannot make authentic kachina dolls, but they can make dolls that resemble the true ones. As an example, teachers sometimes wish to illustrate a project with these fascinating artifacts. Also, a doll collection often has a place for a kachina doll, or perhaps a dollmaker simply wishes to make one. It is then that a few guiding directions are needed.

But first it is important to explain the three meanings of the word *kachina.* The Hopi people have no written language, so it is impossible to discover how many generations have passed along the legends of the kachinas to their children, but it is probably from the beginning of their culture that they have performed the ritual dances and ceremonies that the kachinas inspire.

Hopi kachinas are the supernatural beings who live in the San Francisco mountains north of Flagstaff and are said to come down to the villages the first half of every year to dance, sing, and bring gifts. In this dry land rain is a blessing needed for life itself, and the kachinas are supposed to bring it. The men living in the various pueblos don their masklike headpieces, their costumes, and the body paint that identifies a particular kachina, at the time of the winter

*Old kachina doll now owned by Santa Fe Railroad, photographed soon after it had been repainted. It is almost a foot high, and is quite heavy.*

*Completed kachina doll carries dance rattle and wooden sword. His head mask is decorated with feathers.*

solstice, about December 21. There are more than 250 of these. When he turns himself into a kachina dancer, the man loses his own identity and assumes the characteristics of the kachina. He then becomes a participant in the rituals that end early in July with the ceremonial dances. The spirits of the kachinas return to the mountains at that time and the men to their regular pursuits.

Our understanding of the deeper meanings of Indian religions is faulty, for its advocates are vague about details, so it is only in a superficial way that we can either understand or describe exactly what kachinas are and what they can do. However, we do know that one of the activities of the kachina dancers is to leave with the children of the pueblos the kachina dolls made earlier by the men and designed to be placed in the family hogan to familiarize the children with the various kachinas. They are not sacred idols, and one need feel no sense of desecration in making one. Neither are they toys, in our meaning of the word. Some are more elaborately dressed than others. Some are made in dance postures, some as if the dancer were waiting for his time to join the others, but they all have common characteristics. The head sections represent the masks worn by the real dancers, and most of them wear a kilt-type garment held in place with an elaborately decorated belt or sash.

Early kachina dolls were painted with natural earth colors, but modern ones are more varied, and the paint is tempera, or poster paint.

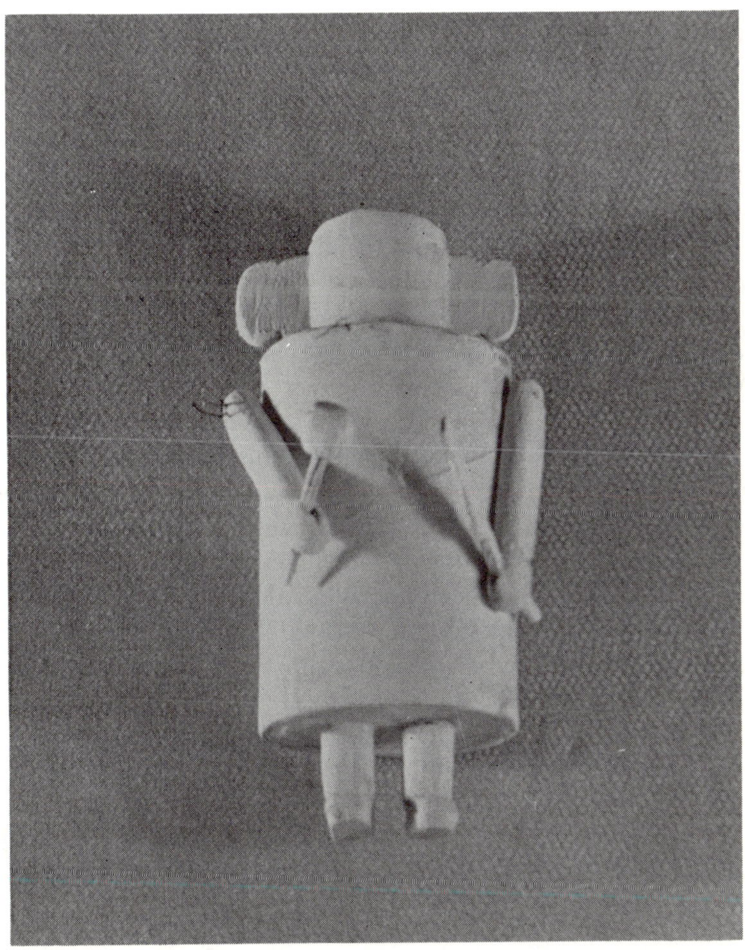

*Balsa wood kachina doll carved and ready for painting.*

Lacking cottonwood root, a simple substitute for us is to make our kachina from a chunk and small pieces of balsa wood or pine. Balsa is for sale in most hobby shops and is easy to work with a jackknife or hobby knife.

Today's Indian trading posts and craft fairs display kachinas of many sizes, but the one you make from our pattern is a satisfactory shelf size—about ten inches high. Aside from a square piece of balsa wood about twelve inches long, you will need a few scraps or pieces of one-half-inch balsa for the arms, legs and feet, and rattles. Poster paint in red, white, black, yellow, and blue is applied with a medium-sized watercolor brush and a small liner for details. The poster paint is clean and easy to use and may be purchased in either the dry form to be mixed with water, or already mixed in small jars.

To make the kachina, block out the head and body on the large piece of wood and smooth it well with a carving knife and fine sandpaper. Carve the arms and legs from the smaller pieces of wood and finish them in the same way. With a sharp point like an awl or icepick make small holes part way through the top of the arms and into the top of the legs and corresponding holes an inch or so deep into the body. Brush both surfaces with white glue and push a short piece of wooden toothpick or matchstick into the holes to act as dowels. This helps to reinforce the joint. Allow the doll to dry overnight.

Paint the entire doll with a thin coat of white poster paint. When dry, lightly sketch the design on with pencil and paint in the colors. As soon as the paint dries, add whatever beads or feathers you wish, and the individual touches that distinguish each kachina. For these details it is suggested that you consult a copy of the small, paper-bound booklet compiled and distributed by the Museum of Northern Arizona, Flagstaff, Arizona, titled *This Is a Hopi Kachina.* It was written by Barton Wright and Evelyn Roat, and the photographs are by Parker Hamilton. This authentically documented account of kachina dolls and their origins and meanings is invaluable for the dollmaker and also for visitors to the museum's annual Hopi Craftsman Exhibit of arts and crafts, scheduled to coincide with the All-Indian Pow Wow in Flagstaff during the July 4th weekend. Here, hundreds of kachina dolls are displayed, and the ritual dances are performed.

This chapter is a greatly simplified version of a complicated subject, but it is hoped that it will add to your interest in owning and particularly in making your own kachina doll. If you prefer, call it a kachinalike doll. Whatever the name, kachina dolls do push the lore of dollmaking way back into the unreckoned past.

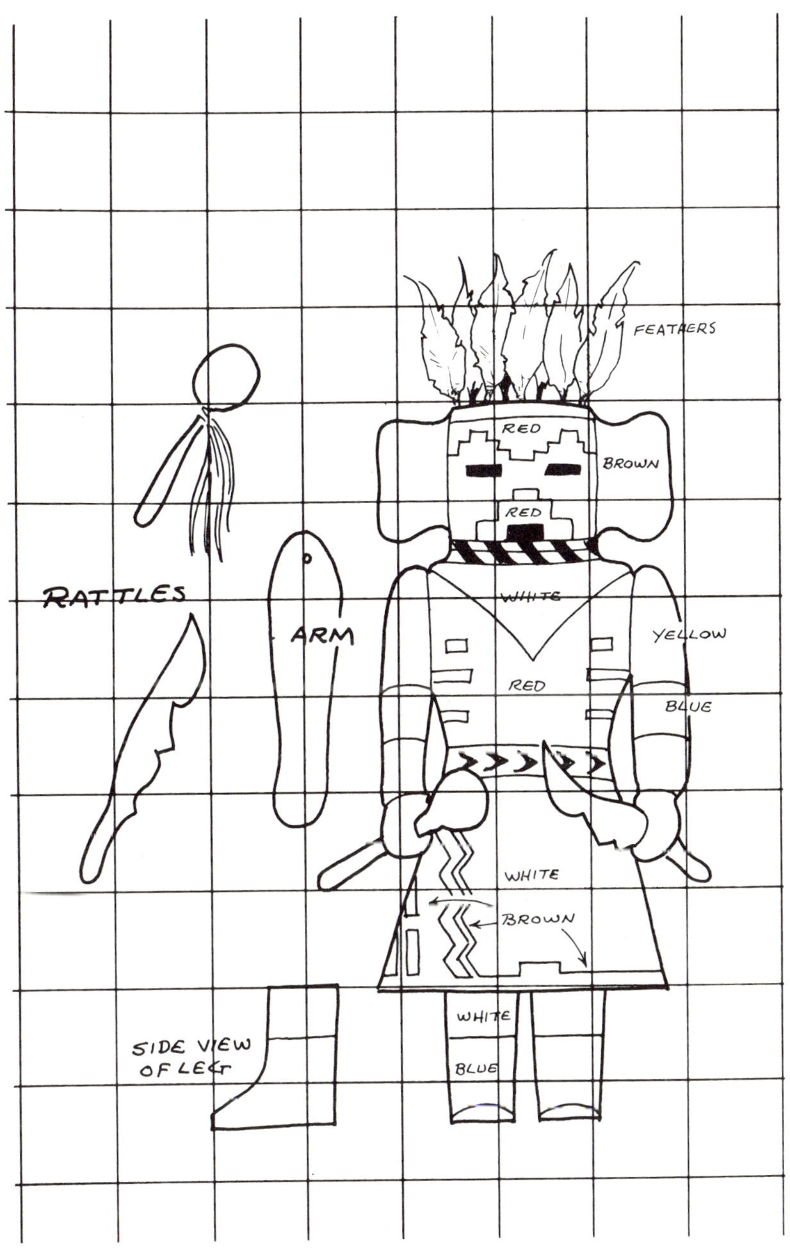


*Follow these patterns to make a kachina doll, using balsa wood. Paint in bright colors.*

# 16

# *Ways To Keep and Show Your Dolls*

Very few doll collectors wish to keep their treasures packed away in a trunk or box, so some method for displaying them and at the same time protecting them must be found.

From a purely functional standpoint, the glass showcases used in stores are the best, since they are made to both show and protect their contents. Not everyone cares to use space in this way, however, and there are more decorative solutions to the problem. Next, perhaps, we can mention the old-fashioned china cabinet, much sought after by collectors. The ones with curving glass fronts are especially attractive as well as practical.

One collector, building a new house, had an entire side of the dining room turned into a huge display case with shelves built behind sliding plate glass doors. This extravagance proved to be excellent for protecting her dolls, but discouraging for the housewife who had to keep polishing the glass, since visitors invariably left fingerprints on the doors.

Then there are the modern clear plastic domes and cases that are reminders of the old-time glass bells that once protected Great-grandmother's feather flowers and hair-wreaths. The latter are still on the market, at a price, but their plastic descendants are much less expensive and come in many shapes and sizes.

Another type of display case may be made of a glass aquarium if a piece of glass is cut to fit the open side, as a cover. Stand the aquarium either upright or on one side, depending on the size of the dolls. The original floor may be covered with a piece of cardboard cut to fit and then covered with satin, brocade, or small-patterned wall-paper or gift-wrap. The removable glass top allows for both seeing the dolls and also being able to remove them when desired.

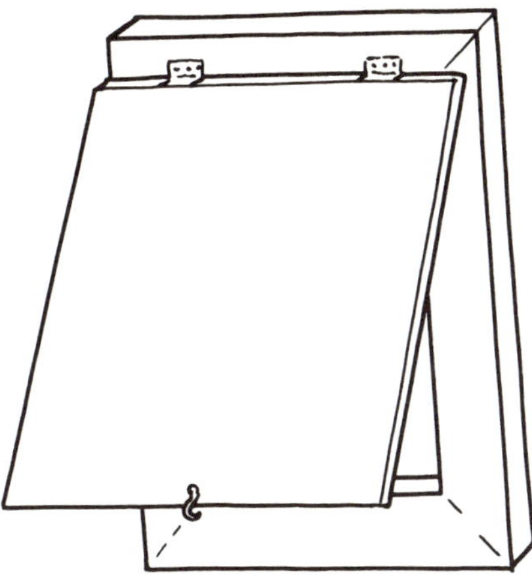

*Shallow shadow box made from a picture frame is ideal for displaying paper dolls and may be made deeper for other dolls.*

Still another variation in a doll case is to make the back of the case a mirror, so one may see both back and front at once.

A common and practical display device is a shadow box, making use of an old picture frame. The one shown here was a swap-meet frame, about two inches wide, with the glass held securely and invisibly by tiny brads. A shallow box the exact size of the opening was built of plywood by a home carpenter, and fastened to the back of the frame with small brass hinges. A simple brass catch fastened at the bottom held it shut. This particular box was shallow, designed to hold a paper doll, but could be much deeper for a larger doll. The new section was covered with a rough, gold-colored silk stretched smoothly over a piece of heavy cardboard and glued to it. In a deeper box, the sides should also be covered.

In much the same way, a pair of small bisque dolls, hard to display effectively, were closed into a shadow box made of an old wooden clock case whose works were gone. The only needed touch was a backing to conceal the holes in the back of the case.

Dollhouses are excellent ways to amuse both grownups and children and to show off your dolls. If you have made the miniatures shown in chapter 10, place them in either a single room or an entire house built of plywood. Furnishing it is a delightful matter that can go on for years, and it is a charming place to use the trophies from your travels.

There are good precedents for dolls and dollhouses, with many famous ones having been made by doll lovers from queens to movie stars, and they seem to have great nostalgic appeal.

Similar to shadow boxes are dioramas, which are most often made quite deep, and often with a curved back to give perspective to a scene in which dolls can easily be incorporated. They are favorites of collectors of military miniatures, who build up entire battle scenes, the figures fastened in position and placed in natural landscaped settings. The same method can be used for building replicas of famous paintings, using costume dolls as the subjects. For ideas, visit museums.

Whatever case or cabinet you select, you will also need a stand for your doll, and there are several factory-made types, one of the most popular being made of metal, with an adjustable upright piece ending in an open-ended circle to clamp around the doll's waist. These are light, durable, and inconspicuous.

The one in the drawing is another kind of stand—this one made

*Two simple doll stands will work effectively in showing dolls and you can make or buy them in a variety of sizes.*

at home and particularly suitable for ethnic dolls or where it is good to have a visible stand, rather than one concealed by the doll's clothing. To make it, buy a one-inch-thick cork panel, twelve by twenty-four inches in size. Building supply stores have them. The chunks of cork are pressed tightly together and are colored dark brown. Mark the panel into eighteen squares of four inches each. For the uprights, buy one-quarter-inch wooden doweling and stain or paint it to match the cork. Saw into ten-inch lengths. Dab white glue on one end of the dowels and push them into the cork squares at one side. These stands are used by pushing the dowel up under the doll's clothes, next to its body, so that the doll is standing securely upright. Or the doll may be fastened to the dowel with fine wire at waist and hips. Quite a large doll may be held up on this kind of stand, both the size of the base and the height of the dowel being increased in size as needed.

An inventive craftsman will be able to make doll stands from heavy wire by coiling it at the base, and at the other end bending it into a loop that will circle the doll's waist. The stand should be light, strong, and unobtrusive.

The cardboard cone shown in chapter 14 with the hoop-skirted doll may also be adapted to use with other kinds of dolls by making it of thin metal, plastic, or fiber that fits a particular doll. This is a more sophisticated stand than if the doll were stood up in a glass vase or bottle with its skirts covering the container.

You can make a pleasing three-dimensional picture by fastening a doll to a cardboard backing and placing inside a picture frame—even though the frame may not have a glass in front. A pair of small dolls from Guatemala, for example, were placed in an eight by ten-inch natural wood frame that set them off much better than if they had simply been displayed on a shelf.

It is to be hoped that you will use your imagination in displaying your dolls, and not always use conventional treatments. Change them occasionally, or do as the Japanese do and have a special spot in a room reserved for a changing display—ideal for dolls.

As in preceding chapters, the dollmaker is urged to use the patterns and suggestions given here only as starting points for his own creativity. There is always something new.

# 17

# *Make Your Own Patterns*

Dollmaking generally includes clothes-making as well, and up until now you have been using patterns made by someone else. But there is nothing to prevent you from designing and making your own clothes for dolls, thus broadening your skills as well as expanding your doll's wardrobe. By the time you have done this, you may perhaps decide to design your own dolls.

Only a few measurements are needed for making any basic pattern, and the diagrams here show where to take them, as indicated by the broken lines. For example, first measure the base of the doll's neck, then the distance from the neck to the top of the sleeve, the chest directly under the armpits. The bust measurement is taken over the fullest part of the bust to directly under the arms. The next measurement will be around the top of the arm, then around the wrist. Measure the back to the underarms to complete the bust line. Next comes the waistline, then the distance from the underarm to the waistline. Now take the measurement around the widest part of the hips, then the distance between the waistline and the length you wish the dress or pants to be.

Using your measurements and the diagram, proceed to make your pattern on a sheet of paper. The result will be a basic pattern that will exactly fit your doll.

You can do many things with this pattern. Try combining the straight sleeve pattern and the waist pattern at the arm-to-waistline point and make kimono sleeves. You can cut the sleeve pattern off at a chosen point and make short or three-quarter sleeves. You can add

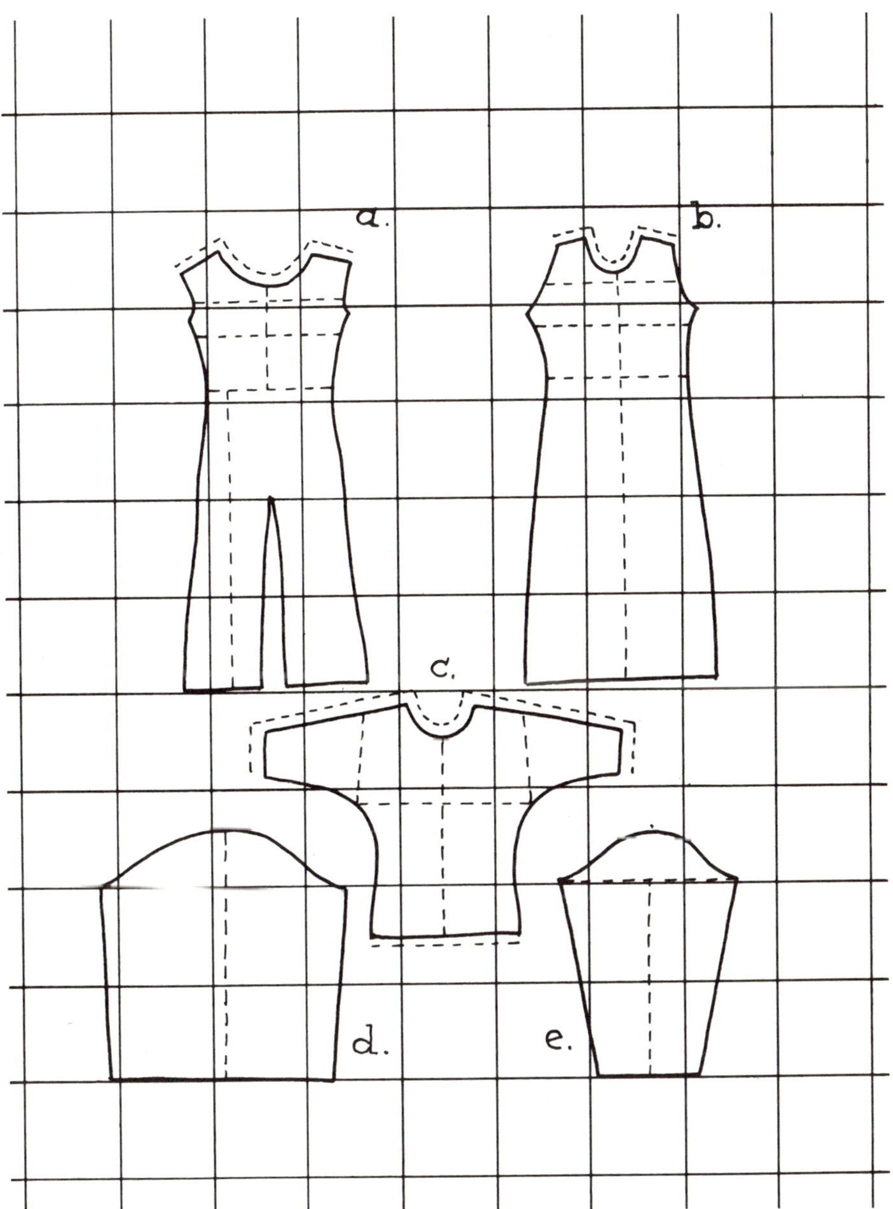


*Basic measurements to be used in making doll clothes patterns are indicated by the broken lines: a—pants suit, b—drcss, c—waist with kimono sleeves, d—gathered sleeve, e—tight sleeve.*

width to the entire sleeve and then gather both top and wrist, attaching the wrist edge to a tight cuff or allowing it to hang free, or cut it into a point at the side opposite the seam and have a medieval sleeve.

It is best to always make the top edge of a sleeve curved, as shown, to allow it to cup slightly at the shoulder. The extra width should be spread out over the top edge, and may be either worked in without noticeable gathers, or be quite full.

Much variety is possible also with the waist itself. By adding length to the lower edge of the top, and a little more width, you can make a blouse top. Close the waist at the front or at the back and the entire garment is changed. If you do this, be sure to add enough extra for a placket or closing. In the event you want to make a tuck-in blouse, cut the waist long enough to be held by the skirt waistband. If the blouse is to be worn outside the skirt, cut the desired length and add a narrow seam allowance at the bottom.

Tucks or gathers may also be added to the waist, and should be allowed for in the pattern.

While discussing the waist, many neck finishes are also possible. The edge may be bound with a bias binding, faced with self-material on the wrong side, or a collar may be used, and there are many types of collars, a few of which are shown in the illustration.

Collars are to be made double, sewed on the wrong side, then turned. This is another place to add seam allowances on all sides. To get the size for a collar pattern, spread open the patterns for the front and back of a waist, and hold them together temporarily while you draw around the neck opening and the garment as far over the shoulders as you wish the collar to be.

If you have cut your basic dress pattern into two sections, waist and skirt, you can now explore the kinds of skirts to be made. The most simple is a dirndl skirt, which is nothing more than a straight piece of material cut the length you wish, then gathered at the top edge and hemmed at the lower edge. Allow for these in the pattern. The skirt is wrapped once or twice around the waist, its waistbands then tied in a knot in front. No fastenings are needed. This skirt is of course of peasant origin, and because it is bulky, should be made of the softest material. It is a good idea to cut a skirt of this type on the lengthwise grain of the fabric, so that the gathers will fall into place without bunching.

Another skirt, almost as easy to make, is a straight, unflared one, with the top gathered to fit the waistline. A placket must be made for this type, and some sort of closing, depending on the size and type of doll. A play doll would preferably have a button and buttonhole closing, hooks and eyes, or a snap fastener. If the doll is not to be

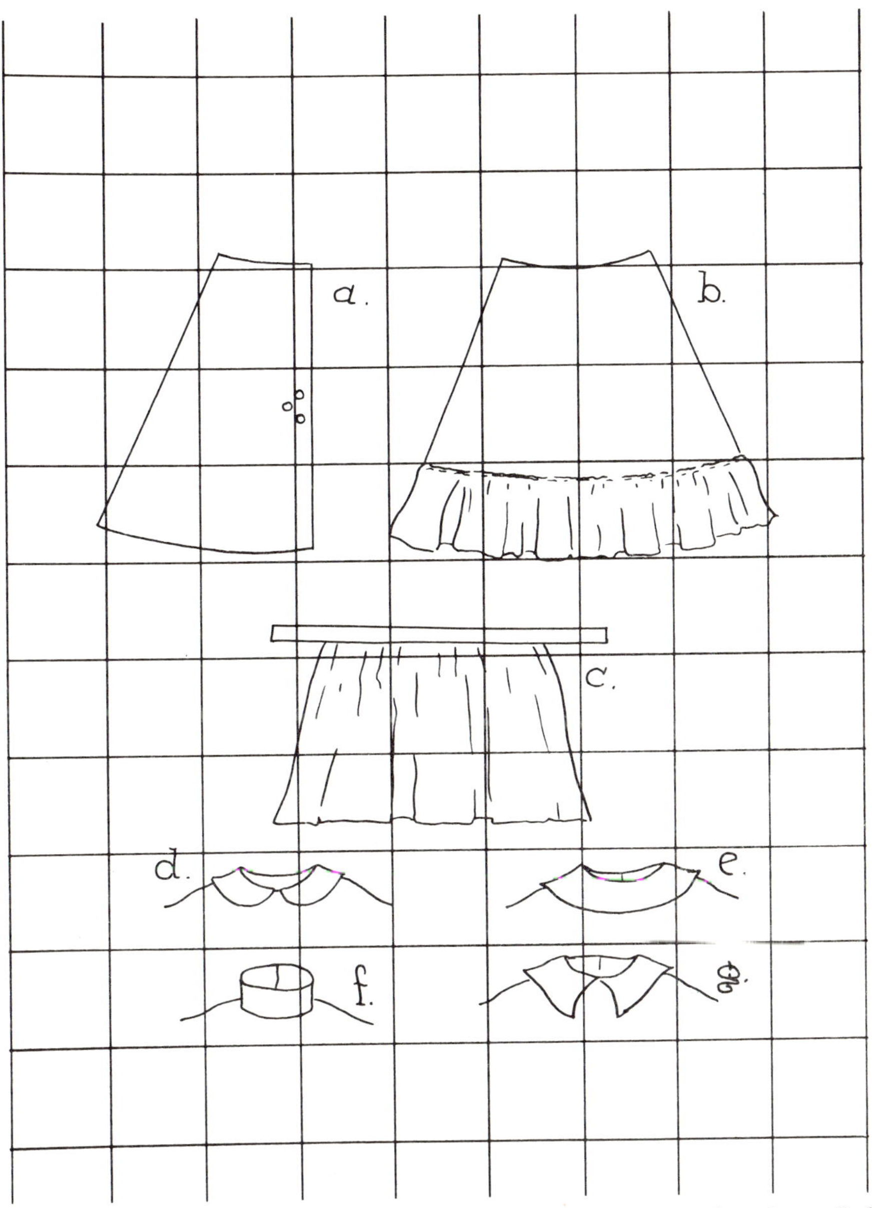


*Basic designs for cutting doll clothes patterns: a—slightly flared skirt, b—ruffled flared skirt, c—dirndl skirt, d—Peter Pan collar, e—cowl collar, f—standup collar, g—pointed collar.*

dressed and undressed, tack the skirt on the doll with a few hidden stitches.

The flaring skirts shown in the illustration are cut to fit the waistline, but also flare enough to give graceful fullness. They may be closed on the side or at the center back.

For a one-piece dress, where the top is cut separately, then joined to the skirt, make a separate belt to cover the joining or plan to use a sash to cover it. A placket, generally made in the center of the back on a dress of this kind, should be finished after the waist and skirt are joined, either with a narrow turned hem or a bound edge.

Closings on this placket, as on the separate skirt, vary with the size of the doll and the type it is. It would be easy to say, "Use a zipper," but zippers don't belong on costume dolls, for example, or those in foreign costumes. It is better to be on the authentic side or simply leave the matter unresolved and sew or pin the clothes on the doll.

Ruffles are most useful in making doll clothes, and the rules for making them are not complicated. It is the most important thing to cut them so the fullness comes on the length of the grain, as was mentioned in cutting a dirndl skirt. Briefly, cut ruffles either on the bias or by spreading the fabric out on the table and cutting strips across it from selvage to selvage. Narrowly hem one edge and gather the other.

For beginners, let me explain that a bias is made by taking a square piece of material and folding it through the center diagonally, then cutting on the fold. Measure from this cut edge and make chalk or pencil marks for the width you want the strip to be. No pattern is necessary for doing this but a straight edge of some sort is a help.

When your pattern is finished, place all the pieces in an envelope and mark it carefully as to size and the doll it was made to fit. Make a rough sketch of the garment on the envelope and file it away for the day when you'll be using it again.

There is another way to make doll garments, and it is well to experiment with it. Try the method French dressmakers use, and build the clothes right on the doll, bypassing entirely the making of a pattern. You can do this with the material itself, or with a paper towel or piece of facial tissue. Drape on the doll, then pin, snip, and fit it to get the effect you're after. If you use paper, this can then be used as a pattern. In making a pattern from this kind of dressmaking, be sure to add seam allowances when the garment itself is cut out. This system does away with the making of darts to arrive at a good fit, and is easier than making a pattern by measurement. Do try both ways, and decide for yourself which is best.

# 18

# *How To Sell Your Dolls*

Very seldom do dollmakers keep all the dolls they make. They are used more often as gifts, donations to bazaars and sales, and for children in homes and hospitals. Sooner or later, someone who admires your dolls will say, "Why don't you sell them? I saw some the other day that weren't half as interesting and they were priced way up."

This is an angle of dollmaking I have not mentioned earlier, but which might be of interest, since there are some people who enjoy making things, and others who would rather sell them. Very seldom do the two preferences meet in the same individual. In fact, a creative dollmaker often resents the time spent in selling. Ideally, selling dolls is a joint operation with the one who makes them. But before you even decide to do that, it is wise to consider several things about the selling end of dollmaking.

In the first place, do you want to make a few extra dollars, or start a business that will eventually be a full-time occupation and even call for the hiring of other people? These are two distinct questions with perhaps different answers.

Making dolls and doll clothes for sale can be an ideal project for the housebound mother of small children, or for a semiinvalid, or for a person who wants to earn a little money doing what is enjoyable. These are perhaps the first people to be reminded that they are not being paid for their time, which at best is not apt to be spent continuously in making dolls, but that whatever money they make is what their grandmothers called pin money. Their friends will be full of advice, shocked because dolls bought in stores sell for twice what the home worker asks, ignoring the fact that she has considerable leeway in the time spent in dollmaking. For example, she can run the washing machine, cook stew for dinner, keep an eye on her toddler, answer the telephone several times, and work on a doll—all at the same time. No piece worker could make a living at that kind of timing.

At the same time, dollmaking is a craft with no age limitations and no employer is going to quibble about your wrinkles and gray hair. You can be your own boss.

Presumably, the greatest number of beginning dollmakers have had no experience in selling a product, and must learn a few of the rules the professionals know. The first determination is the price to ask for your product, because until you know this you won't know whether or not to try to sell your dolls, or to give them away. In doing this, let's leave out the question of how much your time is worth entirely, for that obviously cannot be determined.

Visit toy shops, toy departments, specialty shops, and wherever dolls are on sale and note their prices and the type of merchandise they offer. If the price given is, for example, ten dollars, the chances are that the store paid only half that price for it, wholesale, since the theory of markup is to double the original price. You, as a wholesaler, must therefore be prepared to sell your dolls for half what the store's price will be. Are you willing to accept this?

On the other hand, you may decide to sell the dolls yourself, directly, and think that in that way you can boost your price up to equal that of the store. Perhaps, but don't be too hasty. Try something lower at first, since it is easier to raise than to lower a price, and your doll may not be as professional as your friends suggest.

If you are convinced that being your own salesman is your answer, check your costs with extreme care, and in order to do that you must keep careful records of every penny spent and how much each doll costs you in cash to make. While your business is small, these costs will be at retail prices, but the larger it becomes the more important it will be to buy at wholesale prices. Until that time, cut all the corners you can and eliminate every expense possible, all along the way from materials for the dolls and their clothes to wrapping and packaging them. Frills can come later. Better than buying materials is the art of salvaging them, begging scraps from your neighbors, never throwing away any of your own, and keeping your eyes open. A bright bird feather from your lovebird's cage, or short pieces of wood from a house-builder's trash pile are worth saving, and other things as trifling.

Even a home worker can learn from production line operations. Watch a short-order cook, for example, as he makes every motion count, with one swift motion buttering a slice of toast, or turning a hotcake on the griddle. He never pats and dabs. In the same way, make a motion study of your own work. Do all of the same kinds of things in succession instead of each one separately, as you do when canning fruit and fill up the jars you've lined up for filling, then filling each one in turn, with measured amounts of food, replacing the jar-tops in turn, screwing them on, in turn, and eventually labeling them, in turn. If each step were carried to completion individually on each jar, it would take longer to complete the project and consequently cost more, since time is money. It may seem tiresome to make dolls this way, but if you are lucky enough to receive an order for several dozen of the same kind of doll, time indeed is money.

After cautiously investigating the doll market and the probable profits you can expect, the next decision will be of the best way to sell the dolls. In reading the classified ads in a woman's magazine with a wide circulation among women in rural and small-town areas. I found a number offering patterns and doll clothes for sale. Apparently these were being run by homemakers wishing to make a few dollars but not able to operate a full-time business. Advertising is one obvious way, and these women have chosen an excellent medium, going straight to potential buyers. Prices listed were most realistic.

Another method of doing your own selling, particularly if you dislike the idea of making the rounds of buyers, is to find one good wholesaler and make an arrangement with him. This is what Catina Harvey did, a number of years ago. She had been making dolls in her spare time and decided she wanted to sell them, so made a few samples and called the buyer of a large department store for an appointment. She was told that it would be a waste of her time because the store did not buy from individuals. More determined than ever, Catina then wrote to the owners of a large mail-order doll business and offered to send samples of her dolls. The doll people responded with an immediate order, and thus began what turned out to be an association that lasted for years, each side dealing fairly and promptly with the other. Five or six years after the first order, as the result of publicity and the publication of magazine and book mentions of Catina's dolls, the department store that had once turned her down attempted to get the mail-order people to give them her address, saying they wanted to buy her dolls. Her wholesalers quite rightfully refused to comply, saying that they had been the ones to discover and promote her dolls at a time when the store refused to even look at them. You, also, may be so lucky.

Edith Flack Ackley wrote two books about the dolls she made and the shop she operated in her own home for selling them. Her example has inspired many dollmakers to follow suit, and if you live in a place where there is the right kind of foot-traffic, as in a summer resort, this idea may appeal to you. It would certainly have many attractive angles, such as getting near-top prices for work done at home. The hours of opening and closing could be posted, and if the workroom were visible from the sales room, that alone would attract customers, although Mrs. Ackley points out, it may also attract people who only want to talk.

Once you feel confident that sales warrant or require someone to help you, think about finding a person who really enjoys selling. Write out an agreement covering the commission to be paid. Write it—don't rely on a spoken understanding. It is customary to pay a ten percent commission for selling, and in that way you won't have to bother with it, but again, be cautious, for all human relationships are subject to disappointments and change.

Selling on commission is perhaps better than leaving dolls in a shop on consignment. This means that the dealer will sell them at a price determined beforehand, then deduct the percentage of his commission from the total price. Many antique shops do this all the time, and if everything goes well, it may be a good way to sell dolls. However, you must take the dealer's word that he is really going to display and attempt to sell your dolls, not put them under the counter and sell his own. There is also the possibility of having damage done to your dolls, and if carelessly displayed, they may become grimy and shopworn. It is just as well to know these things before building up false hopes and possible loss.

At some point, if your operations are successful, you find yourself with more orders than you can possibly fill. There is a definite point where orders and profits must balance with costs, and exceed them, before becoming an employer can even be thought of. In other words, volume must increase right along with added costs in order to pay for them. It is sometimes a temptation, then, to call in a friend. Once again, be careful, remembering that it is hardly ever a good idea to mix business with friendship. What happens if your friend's work is sloppy and impossible to put with your own? If you say so, you may lose a friend. People are touchy about being criticized.

In addition, if you have to hire someone to work for you, you step into an entirely different role than you intended to play in the beginning. You are now in business, and if you're not careful, you will have no time to make dolls, but instead discover that you are another office worker, occupied with tax forms, reports, audits, and insurance policies. You will also have to expand your bookkeeping methods considerably, because tax returns require verifiable receipts and sales records and the small notebook you began with may have to be augmented with journals and ledgers. So, all kinds of gloomy things may happen because of your lack of experience and good advice.

Professional business advisers customarily recommend that a new business venture be backed by enough cash or its equivalent to carry it for at least one year. The lack of savings or investment to fall back on while a business is becoming established accounts, they tell us, for most business failures.

Another suggestion experts make is to take out of earnings during the first year only enough cash to pay for necessities to be plowed back into the business, and to save all other earnings. When volume increases and you are definitely sure of your success, you may then think of spending some of the profits on yourself.

After facing these realistic words on professional dollmaking, you may decide that your enthusiasm for dolls won't carry you any farther than to make dolls for yourself and your friends. Since enthusiasm is one of the ingredients of any success, follow your strongest urge and do what you enjoy the most, because you have truly learned that dollmaking is for you. Doll selling may be for someone else.

# *Index*